THE SYLMAR TUNNEL DISASTER

THE SYLMAR TUNNEL DISASTER

by JANETTE ZAVATTERO

Everest House
Publishers   New York

Copyright © 1978 by Janette Zavattero
All Rights Reserved
ISBN: 0-89696-006-4
Library of Congress Catalog Card Number: 78-57409
Published simultaneously in Canada by
Beaverbooks, Pickering, Ontario
Printed in the United States of America
First Edition

DEDICATION

To Those Who Died

I.U.O.E. Local 12
John Drobot, Reg. No. 1324575
Gary A. Nichols, Reg. No. 1377157
Jose Carrasco, Reg. No. 1184876
William J. Snodgrass, Reg. No. 1344083
Alvin H. Spreen, Reg. No. 1247373
William I. Ashe, Reg. No. 717732
Robert W. Warner, Reg. No. 1028371
Russell Overstreet, Miner
Willie Carter, Miner
Danny Blaylock, Miner
Mike Gutierrez, Miner
J. V. Peters, Miner
R. E. Ballow, Miner
R. K. Stovers, Miner
Ronald Demo, Miner
Forrest Aldridge, Electrician
Louis Richardson, MWD Inspector

All the events and people in this story are real. They all figured in an astonishing drama of human concern.

Their actions and behavior are a matter of public record. But reality is both objective and subjective. This book is the subjective account of one man's experience, as well as an objective account of a series of events.

There have been many who have assisted me in the reconstruction of the story of the Sylmar tragedy. I am deeply indebted to them all. Most of all, of course, to my brother and his wife who so willingly shared their experiences with me.

Thanks also go to George Bane, Roosevelt Dorn, and Richard Helgeson who all took the time to talk to me, and opened their files to me, as did the Assembly investigators, Jack Johnson and Jerry McFettridge. To the many others who discussed the tragedy with me, especially Kenneth Gosting, thanks are also due.

A special word of personal thanks goes to Roberta Johnson and her "syndicate," Larry and Anne Kulchin, David Reith, and Roy Berg for their financial and moral support.

A very, very special word of thanks to Margaret Hamrock for her patient, thoughtful, and perceptive readings of the manuscript in progress.

PART ONE
PROSECUTION

"The Captain
he said
to John Henry
A man ain't nothin'
but a man,"

*(The Ballad of John Henry,
tunneler in the Big Bend tunnel on the
Chesapeake & Ohio Railroad
West Virginia, 1870)*

CHAPTER ONE

Sylmar is one of that string of small towns that seem to hang like bracelets on the outstretched arms of the San Fernando Valley freeways. On a hot June night in 1971 while driving a tunnel 175 feet beneath its sleeping surface, seventeen men were blown to bits.

The men were miners—anonymous tunnel stiffs who wander the nation looking for jobs working underground. The tunnel was being built by Lockheed Shipbuilding and Construction Company to bring water to the parched Los Angeles basin from the Feather River.

The tunnel was five miles long and nearly complete. It was a big operation, what miners call a highballing tunnel. That meant they worked three shifts, twenty-four hours a day, hammering at the unyielding earth. Every moment and every inch advanced meant money. Lots of money.

Especially to the Lockheed Shipbuilding and Construction Company, where it meant millions. It was, therefore, in Lockheed's accounting department that the tremblings were first felt with unabashed anguish.

True, everyone regretted the loss of the men, but not nearly so much as the lost time and money. After all, the men were all highballers. They knew the hazards of their work and if they chose to whistle at death, that was all part of the ball game.

To Lockheed the disaster was just that, part of the ball game, or, as it was more piously referred to, an "act of God."

That is, it was until the ball fell into the hands of an industrial safety engineer who caught it and sent it spinning on to the scales of blind justice, where it landed with a long, loud clatter.

To him no disaster was part of the ball game. His name was Wallace Zavattero, and he had been a safety engineer working in the tunnels and mines of California for seven years.

Neither his position in the division as a safety engineer nor his size was likely to be a cause of alarm to Lockheed.

He was no John Wayne in a hard hat, though sometimes he wished he were. He was a short, blunt man with a hard, compact body. Even his hands were blunt, with square fingers which he used with great eloquence to describe, punctuate, outline, or emphasize anything he felt had not been adequately conveyed by words.

He often used them to point out (with more vehemence than his superiors in the Division of Industrial Safety considered absolutely necessary) that "a man had a right to go to work in the morning and expect to come home at night."

It was his motto, and as far as he was concerned acts of God were rarities, like immaculate conceptions. He believed what he said, and that's the way he did his job.

The Lockheed tunnel at Sylmar was part of his job. The day before the explosion he had spent twelve long hours at the Sylmar site, searching out every possible hazard that might threaten the right of the men to come home.

He had come home satisfied with the day's work, and he looked forward to a good night's sleep. But, he didn't get it.

At 3 A.M. the shrill staccato of the night phone beside his bed woke him. It was June 24, 1971.

He was awake in an instant, and before his feet hit the floor he exploded "That damned tunnel blew up!"

The voice on the other end of the line sounded high,

hysterical, almost as if the speaker were crying, but struggling to sound calm, matter-of-fact. Official.

With a grunted "OK," Zavattero hung up and reached for his clothes which were hanging on the dressing table chair.

His wife, Mercy, stared at him sleepily. This was the second night he had been called.

As he stamped his feet into his boots, he punctuated each stamp with a muttered curse, "The damned lousy bastards!"

Mercy did not move. She had heard this before. When she had once chided him about his language, afraid their two daughters might hear him, he had replied tersely that at moments like these he was convinced that the entire world was populated with nothing but SOBs, regardless of age, sex, race, color, creed, religion, or place of national origin.

Her half smile vanished. His hands were shaking as he laced his boots. She couldn't tell if it was fear or rage. Wide awake now, she rose up on her elbow.

"Wally, was it? . . ."

"Yeah, Sylmar," he snapped.

"Was anyone . . ." again her voice trailed off.

He stood up.

"I don't know," he said, "but there were eighteen men in that damned tunnel. That was Balerczak. He didn't say where Savage was. Maybe in the tunnel. The damned fools!"

Mercy got up quickly to make some coffee.

Zavattero walked into the front room to make a quick telephone call to George Denton, a friend and the safety engineer who had been in charge of the tunnel before Zavattero took it over. Denton would get there fast.

He took the coffee cup from Mercy and went to stand in the doorway to wait for Denton. Slowly, he sipped his coffee, staring out into the dark, suburban street. It seemed so deathly quiet to him. It was just past 3 A.M., a strange hour, like a dark sponge which hung between midnight and dawn—black, silent, and shadowless. It calmed him.

But as the hot cup burned his lips, his mind began to race over what had happened and what could be happening now.

The day before, the tunnel had exploded with a small flash fire that injured four men, none too seriously. Loren Savage, Lockheed's project manager, had called him at 6 A.M. and he had spent the day at the tunnel going over every inch of it, testing for gas and hazards so threatening that there would be no alternative but to close the tunnel. The testing meters showed no gas, and he had no evidence of danger that would have allowed him to close the tunnel down. That it was potentially dangerous was the problem. He had written orders to Lockheed for them to follow to prevent what apparently had just happened.

He shook his head. When he had left the tunnel they were following those orders, and he was satisfied that they would go on following them.

What could have happened? He trusted Loren Savage. He had worked with him before and trusted him as much as he trusted any engineer from Lockheed, or from any other corporation for that matter.

Angrily he wrenched his mind away from what might have happened to Savage, whom he had grown to like as well as trust. Then his mind turned to the corporation, that immense, remote structure to which power and money meant everything, and life was some pitiful little gratuity allowed by the board of directors.

"That damned Lockheed! What were they? A bunch of maniacs? They never learned. You'd think they'd have learned something from the Angelus Tunnel, but no, all they'd done was go right on drilling like a bunch of half-crazed groundhogs!"

He stood there cursing Lockheed, God, the Metropolitan Water District, the Santa Susana fault, the pico formation, the bureaucrats in his own office, and anyone else he could think of until at last he started cursing Denton for being so slow.

It had been, in fact, fifteen minutes when Denton arrived.

Without a word to Mercy, Zavattero was in the car before it stopped.

"Where the hell ya been?"

"Ah, can it Wally. If you wanna get there so fast put on your Superman cape!" Denton, thirty-five years old, had four children and five TVs.

Chastened, Zavattero grinned.

Smoothly George maneuvered onto the Golden State Freeway heading for the Roxford turnoff.

"So what's comin' down?" George Denton also watched "Kojak."

"Hell, man, you know as much as I do. It wasn't Savage that phoned. It was Balerczak. He sounded like he was crying."

"Who was killed, did he say?"

"No. Maybe all of them. They can't get in the shaft, but if they've got those breathing units, maybe some of them can save themselves."

"Did they have them yesterday before you left?"

"Yeah, they had 'em." Zavattero snapped. "Hell, what are you, a lawyer—sure they had 'em, and they had the meters and trained men standing by—my orders—they had everything—everything—everything."

"OK, OK," Denton mollified him. "I just wanna know what's goin' on, that's all."

"Well, you know as much as I do and all I know is somebody sure screwed up."

"Somebody sure did," Denton said softly, and he was glad this one wasn't his baby.

They rode on in tense silence without speaking, their minds focused on what was facing them. Fear and anger crackled in the car like a disconnected wire.

At the Roxford Street turnoff they took the slight rise into the hills.

As they hurtled onto the off-ramp, they both gasped. Before them the whole sky was burning a flaming red.

"No!" Denton breathed. "They've blown up the whole damned mountain!"

Zavattero nodded, his mouth hanging open and his eyes bulging. "This time they got the whole damn city!"

They both stared in wordless horror at the searing red sky, and then suddenly Denton jammed on the brakes. He gripped the steering wheel and his body began to shake in great heaving waves of laughter. He was gasping helplessly.

Zavattero stared at him aghast. *He was laughing!*

Then he looked in the direction of the "fire" and he too began to laugh, a high, infectious bray that brought tears to his eyes.

There rising over the mountain, as sedately as the moon waiting to be heralded by Kate Smith, was a large, neon sign blazing forth its message: BENDIX. Neither one of them had ever noticed it before. Still laughing they drove on.

Relief and laughter had restored their comradeship. Nothing could be worse than what they had imagined.

They were wrong. In many ways it was worse. Much worse.

The residents of Sylmar, a tract so new it seemed still to smell faintly of wood shavings and varnish, knew little of the strange world 175 feet below them until they found themselves the subject of blazing headlines and the agitated pronouncements of TV newsmen.

Only the faint sound of thumping, as of some giant animal trapped in the earth, sometimes puzzled them.

If the thumping worried them, it was because a few months earlier the earth had given one of its terrible writhings, and an earthquake on the Santa Susana fault had wrenched the San Fernando Valley, destroying the new county hospital and making a skein of tangled yarn out of the freeway. Of the tunnel being built by Lockheed, they knew little or nothing.

This was not strange. The portal of an underground tunnel is not the type of bustling construction that invites the contemplation of the bored onlooker or the cogitations of the "sidewalk superintendent."

To the passing motorist there is little to indicate what is happening underneath. The earth is thrown up all around the portal as casually as the sand from a child's sandbox. The cranes and carts, the locomotives, the portable toilets, the change house, the trailer-housed offices seem all tumbled about like toys.

Inside the tunnel is another reality. Only the dark trip downward in the man cage is menacing. At the bottom lies a sort of fantasyland. The wide tube of the tunnel is lit every few feet by lights like fairy lanterns, its damp, concrete lining as luminous as the inside of a pearl. The ventilating fans and fan lines cling to the side like a benign serpent: an extended arm embracing the entire length of the tunnel.

The floor of the tunnel glistens with the narrow gauge rails that carry the diesel locomotives, the square, blunt carts, muck cars, and man trips, each bearing its load in and out of the busy underground thoroughfare.

At its end is the face, the flat disk of hard, unyielding earth that must be teased, coaxed, pushed, dug at, pickaxed, and scooped up by man or machine until it yields a few more feet.

Sometimes it moves easily and that's a good day for the company and the miners. The days are bad when the earth sullenly refuses to yield, and the time to be feared is the moment when the earth may crack open in defiance at man's violation and breath its secret store of flame and gas in a blast of fiery outrage. Then the whole fairy world of lanterns collapses, and in the incandescent light, the bodies of the miners are hurled about like bits of glass in a child's kaleidoscope.

To the men who worked there, though, this underground world had no fantasy quality. To them it was the hole, and it was hard, dirty work. Hard, dirty, and dangerous. They were miners, rough men, nomads come in from everywhere to sign on for tunnel jobs.

Fierce men, most of them liked highballing tunnels. The intense competitiveness—and sometimes bonuses—relieved the crushing monotony of working underground.

The men working at Sylmar were proud of it. They had driven twenty seven thousand feet through muck at the rate of sometimes as much as hundred feet a day. They would finish the job almost a year ahead of schedule.

They had not been deterred by the earthquake, and it mattered little to them that the excavation was now that much nearer to the seeping cracks of the Santa Susana fault.

All that mattered was the number of concrete sets that could be rammed through in a day.

They were proud of the job. To them speed was everything. It was up to management to be cautious.

And that was when the Sylmar tunnel exploded.

When Zavattero and Denton arrived at the site, there was no sensational sight lighting the sky like the Bendix sign. There was little aboveground to indicate the ravages of the underground world. The explosion had dug its volcanic blast into the earth.

In the trailer-office at the main portal, nearly five miles away from the blast, there was the concentrated, desperate flurrying of men phoning for help and rescue equipment, some grappling desperately with cumbersome breathing apparatus.

Standing in the center of the melee was Bob Ree, Lockheed's project engineer, his normally bland face creased and sweating with rivulets of anxiety. He was snapping orders, phone in hand, at the gathered men, trying to coordinate every rescue team. He hung up the phone, nodded at Zavattero, and raced for the door. The miners were threatening a fight with the fire department.

As Ree rushed by Zavattero grabbed his arm. "Where's Savage?"

Ree just shook his head and kept going.

Zavattero turned to Denton and shouted over the noise and confusion, "I'm taking a locy back to the Gate shaft—meet me there. Get on the phone, and get Signer—get anybody, but get all the damned equipment they've got. Tell them to get some testing stuff down here real quick. If that smoke isn't too bad, maybe we can get in—"

Denton nodded and pushed through the swarming men to grab the nearest phone.

As Zavattero arrived at the Gate shaft the scene was a strange contrast to the hectic activity at the portal office. No one seemed to be moving. It was a paralyzed tableau of rumbling fire engines surrounded by helmeted firemen standing perfectly still beside unhooked ladders and coiled hose.

Gathered in a clump, away from them and nearer the shaft, was a group of miners. They were in deep shadow, but the dawn was just beginning to break. It would be a hot day. He could not see who the men were. All he could see was their hats. The first rays of the sun danced off them. They shone in the dew-stricken light, and as the men's heads bobbed up and down, they looked like a circle of mirrors deep in conversation.

He headed for the fire chief who told him in a flat voice that his men were not going into the tunnel, and no further rescue efforts would be allowed.

Zavattero stared at him, "Damn you," he raised his hand menacingly, then shrugged and ran toward the gathered miners.

In the growing light he could see that they were gathered around one man who was sitting on the ground, gasping for breath.

The man, a miner, was encrusted with black muck, and he kept holding his hand up in front of his face. "You can't see your hand three inches in front of you—not three inches—" he repeated, staring disbelievingly at his hand as if it were the offender.

Zavattero did not know him. He knew few of the men.

He had only taken the job over from Denton a month ago.

But one of the men knew him and nodded "Hi, Wally," and instantly the circle of men converged on him, all screaming at once.... "We're goin' in! —tell that lousy fire department—you got the authority! Tell 'em we're goin' in."

Zavattero spread his blunt hands, waving for silence. "OK, I haven't got the authority—but you're going in anyway—calm down."

Into the split second of silence that followed his reassurance, he inserted a demand for information, "First, I gotta know what the hell's been goin' on in there. What's been happening? I gotta know," he suddenly pleaded.

He pointed to one man who seemed a little calmer and said, "You, you tell me."

Interspersed with angry muttering from the miners, the man told him what he knew.

Loren Savage, Lockheed's project manager, who had been in the tunnel through the second shift, was on his way out with Bill Livingston when they heard the explosion. They were about two thousand feet from the face, and the blast had blown Savage's hat off. Livingston had driven the loaded muck train out to clear the tracks.

Dutch Badgely (he waved his thumb in the direction of one of the men) kept going back in to try to save somebody, but the only one he could get was Renteria (he pointed at another man).

The narrator choked a moment and then said, "He could hear them screaming in there, but—" Calmly he went on. "Jim Hall even went in with a wet rag over his face." He shook his head. No way. Jim Hall was the man who had been sitting on the ground gasping.

"Breathing apparatus?—" Zavattero started.

The man shook his head impatiently. Bill Livingston finally got some breathing apparatus from somewhere and with Savage and Arvid Rasmussen and the fire chief, they'd made it into the tunnel. Something had derailed the man car—the narrator paused, "a body, I guess." He shrugged, took a deep breath, and went on. "The heat was frying their asses off and they had to get out as soon as they could get the car unhooked." The man stopped.

"So then what?" Zavattero prodded.

At that point all the men started talking at once, but they were all saying the same thing, only the expletives were different. They added up to the fact that the fire department had closed the whole thing down, and no one was to enter.

Zavattero looked at them all for a moment, and he knew what he saw. They were ready to fight. They were more like a lynch mob than a rescue unit.

Quietly he said, "Wait here a minute."

Then he went over to the fire chief. What he said was short and to the point. He was assuming control. He wanted some breathing apparatus and for them to stand by with whatever equipment they had. And he wanted them *now*.

The fire chief's threatened splutter of outrage was silenced as Zavattero continued, thrusting a blunt finger in the chief's face, "Otherwise those guys are gonna come over here and beat the hell out of your fireboys and then go in that tunnel with paper bags over their heads if they have to." One fight had already broken out.

The chief nodded, Zavattero grinned graciously and thanked him for lending them the breathing apparatus.

He returned to the miners. He knew one of them, Paul Dyer, was an experienced man, and so was Joe Bates.

He motioned to them. Both of them had taken off their hats in the morning sun. They were joined by Bill Livingston.

Zavattero observed them closely. Dyer, with his round face and startled crew cut, looked alert and rested, and so did Joe Bates, though his long, drooping nose and furrowed eyebrows always made him look like a thin, doleful Labrador. But it was big Bill Livingston who worried him. He had been on the last muck car with Savage when the explosion hit, and he'd been back in when the man car was derailed. His broad, cheerful face was black with smoke and looked drawn with fatigue. But he was one hell of a locy operator and knew how far back the derailed car was.

"You OK, Bill?" Zavattero asked.

"Great." Livingston straightened his burly body to prove he meant it.

"All right," Zavattero nodded. Then he began a precise outline of what was to be done. The breathing units he explained were good for only fifty minutes, no more, maybe less. They were to go into the tunnel, find out exactly what the scene was, clear the track of the derailed car, and they were not to exceed the time. They were to take twelve minutes to get in, work for thirty minutes, and then get the hell out. *There were to be no heroics.* They were to be out in fifty-one minutes.

The men nodded. They were calmer now. There was something to be done.

That was to be the longest fifty minutes of Zavattero's life. One whiff of the deadly gas meant instant death.

Far above the shaft where Dyer and the others had entered the tunnel, George Denton was having his own problems, trying to maintain peace and helping to train men to use the heavy, self-contained rescue breathing apparatus.

With the daylight growing, and the seven o'clock news breaking on TV screens, more and more people were gathering.

The miners, who didn't have to wait for the news—their news had come from their buddies—were growing in number, and as the dimensions of the tragedy grew, more firemen were added to the existing crew.

Though another fire chief had arrived whose influence was more calming, the frictions between the miners—ready, but hamstrung by the lines of authority, to risk anything to save their buddies—and the firemen were as near to exploding as was the tunnel.

Officials began arriving from everywhere. They were all good, competent men working with swift expertise, but working against a deadline they knew had already passed.

Above the face of the tunnel, men were digging frantically to put down an air shaft, even though they knew it was useless.

The most maddening part of it all was that everyone seemed to be tripping over everyone else's jurisdiction, as if jurisdiction held as many traps as it had syllables. The Bureau of Mines had to screen every man on the use of breathing apparatus before he could be allowed to go into the now-certain death tunnel. The fire department refused entrance to anyone, and chaos seemed to be rolling out of the tunnel as threatening as the smoke that was now beginning to belch ominously from the mouth of the Gate shaft.

Helicopters were beginning to swarm overhead, and the police arrived to cordon off the crowd beginning to swell below.

In this melee, Denton tried to keep order, hoping that someone from Lockheed, Ree or Savage, could pull together more rescue units and equipment. It was Ree, back at the portal, who was screaming over jammed telephone lines, loudly threatening men who were phoning all over the west coast for help.

Savage had disappeared. Ree's and Savage's wives had arrived at the site almost immediately. Ree had gone on working, but Savage had left with his wife. No one knew exactly when.

In contrast, everyone at the shaft with Zavattero was quiet. They all waited tensely, watching Zavettero, who would take his eyes off his watch just long enough to peer into the smoke-blackened tunnel, like a commuter tilted impatiently on the curb waiting for the bus.

"How long they got, Wally?" someone asked, but he got no answer.

One man leaned over to listen for a whine of sound along the iron tracks. It was the only way they could tell if Livingston was moving the locomotive out. "I can hear them," he said.

Suddenly a distant sound like a single blow on an enormous drum made them catch their breaths.

"They've gotta be on their way out," Zavattero murmured. "They gotta be, that's too far back. If it's blowing up again, it's back at the face—" He looked at his watch.

They'd been in there forty-nine minutes.

The men stared at the tunnel. The locomotive began slowly to emerge.

They could see Livingston and Dyer, and behind them Bates bent over what looked like a shapeless mound of muck.

As they ran toward the locomotive, Dyer shook his head. They had made it in exactly fifty-one minutes, but the man they brought out was dead. They themselves were so exhausted by the heat from the tunnel, they didn't even bother to lift the dead man out of the car but almost fell out of it onto the ground.

Other hands lifted the body out. Someone muttered, "It's Will Carter" and the body was shoved up against a pile of muck as everyone began to converge around the locomotive.

Zavattero looked at the body, oblivious to the shrill arguments ringing round his head. Will Carter lay there completely ignored by the arguing officials.

"Aren't you going to see if he's dead?" he asked. He knew the question was senseless, but he had to ask it anyway. He couldn't help it. He was shocked. He felt you just don't do that—someone ought to at least feel his pulse. As if such a gesture would be a sort of Extreme Unction, a last sacrament for the man. He started to lean down toward Carter, but stopped, feeling stupid.

"He's dead," a fireman said flatly.

Though no one touched it, the sight of Carter's body ran through the crowd like an electric current.

Surging forward, the miners, now eager for action, began scuffling among themselves. Standing behind the locy that had carried out Will Carter's body were John Wallace and John Rathbun, union men and brothers to the trapped miners. They had been given hasty training by Denton in the use of the cumbersome breathing appartus.

The fire department had demanded that the tunnel be closed and all the men declared dead. The young firemen began uncoiling rope. They now knew there was fire in the tunnel and were preparing to take over.

The miners stood around, mouths agape, as they watched the fire department pull up its hoses. What the hell were they doing? Were they planning to pull in nine thousand feet of hose to put out a flash fire? Water to put out fire caused by gas? The miners who knew the ways of gas and tunnels were dumbfounded.

They were in no mood for such ritualistic nonsense. The sight of Carter's body had not discouraged them, but seemed to fill them with a furious energy—a passion to get into the tunnel, to reach their friends, to save someone just to prove that the evidence of Carter's body meant nothing.

As Zavattero tried to calm the shouting and milling around the first locy, he heard shouts from the men at the other side of the shaft. Denton, standing by the other locomotive, was hollering angrily at the men there. No one could go in.

Suddenly Denton seemed to have been hit by something. He was hurled up against the muck car as if he'd been tackled. He hadn't been. It was Wallace and Rathbun. They were on their way into the tunnel. Denton could not stop them, and Zavattero didn't care whether he stopped them or not. The men had to do something. Standing still and waiting was not taught in any tunneling manual.

"Come back, you crazy bastards—no one's allowed— they're all dead—" Shouts and cries came from everyone, but Wallace and Rathbun kept right on going.

Suddenly everyone was quiet. The locomotive was beginning to move.

There was nothing anyone could do. They had started into the tunnel.

The two miners paid no attention to the cries from the

outside. They were going in. They had breathing apparatus and even though the Bureau of Mines training crew had said they were unfit, did not meet qualifications, and did not know enough about using the breathing apparatus, they were still on their way in.

Blinded by smoke and nearly knocked over by the wall of heat, they kept on going, inching their way back into the tunnel.

The concrete walls closed about them like raw earth ready to crush them. As the voices from the portal drifted away, they could hear the faint trickling of water, and a distant rumbling.

Dyer and his men had cleared the track, and as they passed that point, they slowed down, cautious and uncertain whether another body might derail the locy and plunge them all into the hot, humid muck.

Slowly they worked their way from the California Switch, the rail switch where cars passed each other going in and out of the tunnel. The switch was nearly fifteen hundred feet from the gantry of the huge excavating machine, its enormous iron body now twisted and scarred by the explosion. The huge air vents fanlines were crushed and twisted on the ends, as useless as party horns left over from a child's birthday party.

"No one could have survived in this."

The smoke was so dense they couldn't even see if any bodies had been blown this far back by the blast.

Weighed down by the heavy breathing units, they could hardly move. They would have to turn back.

Then they heard it. At first they thought it was just a trickling of water. It was a voice.

"Hey, aren't you guys gonna take me with you?" The voice was small and plaintive as a child's.

Clumsily they searched around, wondering if they'd really heard anything. At last they saw him. He lay crumpled up near the broken fanline with his face in the water. Feebly he was splashing water on his face.

With a triumphant whoop, that made their face masks

tingle against their mouths, they pulled him away from the precious air coming from the vent, threw a rag over his face, and then they pushed that locomotive out of there as if it were old '97 comin' down the line.

As they emerged from the tunnel, they cried out with the delight that only life snatched from death can give. Hands reached out for the body of the confused and mumbling miner, half lifting, half dragging him onto the waiting stretcher. His name was Ralph Brissette.

Jubilant now, the other miners, the firemen, everyone, began gearing up to make a rescue assault on the rolling earth. There was no question now of denying entrance.

Ralph Brissette had survived.

He was the only survivor.

It was seven hours since the tunnel had exploded and nearly as many since Zavattero had left the house. At home Mercy had called George's wife and while other women spoke of lunch and dinner, high prices at the supermarket and their neighbors' activities, Mercy and Laura inquired anxiously of death and waited for news.

Though they knew it would be futile, they went to join the throng at the portal but could see nothing in the cordoned-off crowd. (They hadn't expected to see their husbands, but it had been something to do.) So they returned home. It was simpler to watch it all on TV. "Not very reassuring, but simpler," Mercy said ruefully.

Their vigil was to go on for seventy-two hours, and the only sight of their husbands they'd have, except for what was on TV, would be to watch them fall woodenly into bed and get up again in a few hours to return to the doomed tunnel.

After three days of interminable delays and repeated efforts to clear the tunnel of smoke and gas, the recovery began.

From the moment the first bodies had been brought from the tunnel, as if in some solemn funeral cortege, everything that followed was something Zavattero could only recall in dreams.

He was not unfamiliar with death. He had been in Korea and had been wounded himself. These were unexpected, not like corpses on a battlefield where you expected to encounter death.

Later, he would recall other things. Mechanical things like the desperate efforts to tear fanlines open, hoping that someone had crawled into one. He would recall all the details, but what he saw now was the stuff of his nightmares, and they never changed.

Charred skin peeled back from a skull, bared teeth grinning with the gold glint of a filling—a precious metal for identifying what was left of someone. Who knew who it was?

An arm torn from its socket, the fingers curled in a gesture of beckoning. Who knew who that was?

The first, though, had been the worse. Working with Butterfield, a miner from the swing shift, nearly at the face of the tunnel, they had each found separately two halves of a man, entrails coiled and wet as unborn snakes. The stench made him retch.

He and Butterfield looked at each other and bent to their task placing the two halves of the body on the cart with dreamlike gentleness. Then as they started to move on, Butterfield paused. He stooped to pick up something purple-black and slippery. It was a liver. Symmetrical and intact. It was all that was left intact of the man. Even the brain had been blown out into the cup of his hard hat. The man had no face.

Zavattero looked up at Butterfield who was holding the object out toward him. Zavattero took it, looking at it helplessly.

It was so *whole!* Why hadn't it been cut in half too? He didn't know what to do with it. Retching again slightly, he wrapped it carefully in some plastic and dropped it into the muck cart.

What could that useless organ mean to anyone? It wasn't even good for identification. He didn't know what good it would do, but it was as if he and Butterfield had silently agreed that nothing that had ever been living bone or tissue should be left to be ground into the muck of the tunnel.

Butterfield started out of the tunnel, but Zavattero remained. He had hardly left since the recovery had begun. It was, he knew, pure cowardice. He did not want to see the stony, paralyzed grief on the faces of those waiting outside. Waiting, not just for the bodies, but for identification. Maybe if this one were not *him*, *he* might have managed to crawl into the fanline. They didn't know for sure yet. They were hoping where there was no hope. After all, Brissette had found a fanline.

Across the screen of his nightmares he would sometimes see the drifting figures of the others working to recover bodies—moving shadows with strange, loud voices.

There were firemen: union men like Bucky Micelli; Bates and Dyer had come back and Wallace and Rathbun were still fighting; Bob Ree, Lockheed's engineer; and Loren Savage, Lockheed's ill-starred project manager. He spoke to no one as they worked, not even to Savage.

He had not seen Savage when he had first arrived at the site. Someone had said that his wife picked him up as soon as the fire department arrived. She had taken him home, nerves shattered, on the point of freaking out. What black hours Savage spent that night when he left the tunnel Zavattero would never know. He would never ask him.

That would have demeaned the mystique, the macho of the lost highballing miners. They knew about that mystique and they respected it. It had more meaning to them than the endless jurisdictional disputes of the fire department, the Bureau of Mines, the Division of Industrial Safety, the Metropolitan Water District, and Lockheed. Later, like old soldiers at a convention, they might even recall the battle with laughter, booze, and mockery of the incomprehensible.

All that, though, would come later. It was for the daytime. What was happening now was the stuff of his nightmares.

Then at last it was all over. The last shard of bone that they could find was pulled from the tangled depths of the tunnel and they all plodded wearily out into the light.

There was nothing to do now but go home.

He crawled into the car beside Denton, and as they drove toward Granada Hills and home, neither man spoke. They were exhausted.

At last Zavattero said as quietly as if he were continuing a conversation they'd been having, "Tomorrow, we'll write a show cause order. This one Lockheed's gonna pay for. We're going to prosecute."

Denton nodded his head. "Yeah." Then added, "It could cost us our jobs. Lockheed's big! Remember the Angels tunnel."

Zavattero nodded. "It could. Does it matter?"

Denton shook his head. "Nope," he said almost cheerfully.

Zavattero grinned feebly and they fell into peaceful silence, but memory kept crowding him, nagging at the edge of his peace.

Then he remembered. They had brought the last bones out in a bucket, and they had just left them sitting there in the hot, evening air. Oh hell, he'd forgotten to call the coroner. Maybe he'd remember to call when he got home.

He thought back to his feelings—when they'd brought out that first body, Will Carter's, and set it aside so casually. How shocked he'd been. Now, he had just walked off and left the remnants of a man in a bucket! He leaned back, closed his eyes and tried not to think about it. They were only bones.

At home, Mercy waited for him. She had not seen him for so long. When he came in, she knew that it was over and that it had been awful.

His clothes hung on him sodden with soot and dank water. His face and hands were charred black, and his burning eyes looked like slits of flame from the tunnel.

As he walked heavily, wearily, into the bedroom, she noted wistfully that he was leaving a trail of grime on her lovely carpet.

She followed him into the bedroom. He undressed slowly, carefully letting the foul-smelling garments fall to the floor. Swiftly she crossed the room to face him. Silently she stood there, waiting. For a long moment they looked at each other.

Finally she reached out and touched him lightly on his bare, white shoulder, so white against the blackened face. Then slowly she stooped to gather up the ugly black pile of clothes.

She carried them away to burn them so that he would never have to touch them again. He watched her carry them away. He was grateful to her.

They smelled of death.

CHAPTER TWO

Whatever thoughts of prosecution held sway in Zavattero's mind that night, no such thoughts occupied even a small niche in the brains of the Lockheed powers, or, in fact, any of the other powers to become involved in the tragedy. The herd that was stampeding their brain cells was the press.

In the Division of Industrial Safety, Zavattero's own office, former Lockheed safety manager Jack F. Hatton—appointed to the lofty post of Director of Industrial Safety by Governor Reagan in 1967—had no thought of reprisal when he first heard the news.

In the city attorney's office, City Attorney Roger Arnebergh and deputies George Bane and Roosevelt Dorn caught the first word of the explosion on the A.M. news, but it intruded little on their preoccupations with their current chores.

In Sacramento, Governor Reagan also noted it briefly and considered the merits of a quick visit to the East Portal on McClay Street, where the gathering throng of the anxious, the curious, and the bored offered a promise of high visibility for a display of his energetic solicitude, so he jotted it down on his calendar.

Assemblymen Moretti, Keysor, Fenton and Russell may

have stirred uneasily, sniffing the political possibilities that might blow from the smoke of such a major calamity in their districts, and they also noted it on their memo pads.

Prosecution was not in Mayor Yorty's mind when he made his reassuring visit to the site, shortly after the befuddled and terrified Brissette was pulled from the tunnel.

In the offices of the Metropolitan Water District, only Lou Richardson, engineer, might have given the idea of prosecution some thought, but he had been one of those blown to bits in the holocaust.

Even after the early morning news when the magnitude of the disaster began to be felt, there was little concern with reprisal, but there was instead a rapidly growing concern with what tack the always noisy and unpredictably careening news media would take.

One tack was certain. The newsmen and women would arrive with the first emergency truck and stay until the last bit of meat had been scraped from the bones of the charred victims, ready to serve up this disaster for the evening news at mealtime, cheek by jowl with the standard fare from Vietnam, the robustness of the sportscasters, the solemnities of the Dow Jones, and the quaint eccentricities of weather reporters.

That much was certain. What was not certain was where they would go from there. To assist them in finding a direction, the public relations men began to fall out around the East Portal almost as fast as the press.

Not all of them were there to head off bad publicity at the pass. The most notable exception was the young man from the fire department. He was an eager young man, who, pencil and pad in hand, hovered near the fire chief, peering over his shoulder like a solicitous guardian angel.

When he urged the fire chief to climb into the man trip, at the bottom of the Gate shaft, and then stepped aside to survey the sight with motherly pride, it was the only moment that caused Zavattero to stop dead still, forgetting briefly his frantic efforts to keep the men moving.

"What the hell is he doing?" he asked Denton mildly.

"Having his picture taken, I guess." Denton too was gazing at the performance with wonder.

"I know what that horse's ass is doing," Zavattero snapped, "but what's that guy with the pencil doing—taking his lunch order?"

Denton shrugged, "That's his public relations man." Zavattero stared at him. "Damn!" he started to spit, but his mouth was so dry from the heat and smoke all he could manage was a feeble pouf. And these were the bastards who hadn't done anything but close the tunnel and wave nine thousand feet of useless hose around!

He wondered what the Fire Department PR man would have said if he'd heard John Wallace screaming that if he'd been in that tunnel, he'd have lived just for the pleasure of kicking those bastards in the ass.

Still shaking his head, Zavattero turned back to the milling men, brushing aside a reporter as he hurried toward them.

While the fire department was so cheerfully adding luster to its image, Lockheed's man was busy no commenting to every question.

To Lockheed, publicity about the explosion was the stuff of their nightmares, and not without reason.

The corporation's top brass were busy trying to conclude negotiations with the Nixon Administration for a $250 million loan guarantee. They had cause to worry. Without that loan, bankruptcy stood blinking its ten-digit eyes at them, hence they needed every bit of favorable publicity they could get.

The loan was no certainty. They recalled only too vividly the fate of Penn Central the previous year in spite of all the pressure that had been brought to bear, and now they were in the same boat and a strangely ill-assorted crew were protesting.

General Electric, which should have been stirred to loyalty by its contracts to build Lockheed's C-5As, was making loud, rude noises all around the House and Senate. And just three weeks before, Vice Admiral Rickover, of the nuclear reactor program, had risen to sublime and impassioned eloquence before the Congressional Joint Economic Committee, crying out, "... when men in Communist Russia fail in government or industry, they are summarily dismissed. We, on the other hand, protect those who fail and grasp them to the government's bosom. We let them privatize profits and socialize losses."

While the vice admiral's posture was lamentable, it was counter balanced by the fact that Nixon officials were busy calling sympathetic bankers and industrialists all over the country.

And in addition, the little people's hearts were being touched and letter writing campaigns were organized. So stirred, in fact, were the emotions of the Wisconsin PTAs that they had begun organizing a boycott of Wisconsin beer and cheese to put some pressure on Senator William Proxmire, to stop his outspoken opposition to Lockheed.

While the little people, not yet raised to the stature of the silent majority, occupied a somewhat lower position on the ladder of Lockheed's esteem, they still did occupy a place, and they were the most likely to be affected by so solemn a tragedy as the Sylmar tunnel deaths.

The house vote was still being debated, and it was only June 24. An awful lot of little people could do an awful lot of letter writing in that time. One could only hope that in some way it would be possible to cry out about acts of God and thereby add to Lockheed's image as being once again the victim of bad luck.

Of practically no interest to the little people, but of great interest to Lockheed and its Seattle subsidiary which was the builder of the tunnel, was the possibility that not only would Vice Admiral Rickover be spurred to new heights of rhetoric about the care and feeding of Lockheed in connection with the $250 million loan guarantee, but Transportation Secretary Volpe might join Rickover on the podium to put his finger in the dike to stem the rising tide of Lockheed's international proclivities.

That could mean a loss of $52 million for the new ice-breaking machine (being built in Seattle to grace the stems and sterns of ships plowing through northern waters to the Arctic Circle), plus a host of other pending contracts that would put Lockheed neck and neck with Boeing in Seattle's economy. And if that weren't enough, heavy sums had been needed since early 1970 to insure aircraft sales in Japan.

All these dire considerations for Lockheed and its subsidiary were riding the crest of the chaos at the Sylmar site when Lockheed's public relations director Everett Hayes arrived to bring to the media's attention to the fact, "that work had been resumed at Sylmar with the approval of the Division of Industrial Safety."

Unlike the cheery young man from the fire department, Hayes' purpose was not to praise the gallant effort of Lockheed's men to rescue their buddies, but to point the press's investigative noses in another direction—preferably in the direction of the Division Industrial Safety.

That, at the time, seemed the safest way to point it, this side of an act of God. Jack Hatton, head of the Divison of Industrial Safety, was a former Lockheed employee and could presumably be counted on to be discreet. With Jack Hatton at the helm, public investigation was unlikely, and prosecution was inconceivable.

None of these possible economic and legal gaucheries occupied any space in the consciousness of Wallace Zavattero or George Denton on that Sunday morning after the explosion. In fact, they paid little attention to the news coverage of the event. They hadn't had time for it.

"What did those damned maniacs at Lockheed think they were doing?" Zavattero would ask in earnest bewilderment. It was a question he was never really to find the answer to, but he would keep asking it over and over.

He would ask not only George Denton, but Loren Savage and Bob Ree, and even at one point Lockheed's treasurer R. N. Waters.* There was never any answer. He knew it was senseless to ask, but he couldn't stop asking it, as if some vast, cosmic riddle would be solved if he could find the answer.

The day before the disaster, an explosion had occurred and Zavattero had written seven orders to be fulfilled before work could be resumed in the tunnel.

It was the earlier explosion and the orders which he and Denton were discussing on that Sunday morning while preparing a report asking for prosecution of Lockheed for the disaster.

"See, right there it says 'before further work,'" he stabbed a finger at the words written on the order form. The form was a standard one issued by state safety engineers whenever there was a question of failure in safety practices.

"Yeah, I know, Wally, I know. You don't have to holler at *me* about it," George Denton tried to mollify the other engineer whose volatility sometimes puzzled him.

He himself went at things more methodically. It was not, he thought, that he was less dedicated than Zavattero, but just that their natures were different.

He was tenacious and methodical. Zavattero was volatile, an experienced tunnel man and aggressive. They both arrived at the same conclusions, but by different routes, and neither of them liked where they were arriving at the moment.

Moreover, he had not been at the tunnel the day after the

---

* R. N. Waters, along with A. M. Folden and M. Ingwersen were the responsible managing officers of the Lockheed contract. Waters was promoted to assistant treasurer of Lockheed at Burbank in October, 1971. On August 24, 1975, Waters shot himself at his Valencia home. His suicide occurred the day before the story on the Lockheed payoffs broke. When asked by Senator Proxmire if there were any connection between the assistant treasurer's apparent suicide and the payoff scandals, Daniel J. Haughton, Lockheed board chairman, stated only that Waters had "been under some pressure from work." The family made the same statement when they withheld Water's suicide note. Those who knew him said of him that he was a gentle, scholarly man and his suicide is perhaps as a poignant a tragedy as any of the deaths in the Sylmar tunnel.

first explosion when the orders had been written.

"Wally, can you cool off and tell me exactly what happened that day?"

Zavattero grinned, "OK. I think Mercy's temper rubs off on me sometimes. They'd better not ask her any questions, they'll think they tangled with Pancho Villa, right, Merc?" He glanced affectionately at his wife who put a couple of cans of beer on the table before them.

She nodded with a small tilt of the head. She'd seen him angry at his job before and had been angry with and for him, and her anger often had a fine Mexican heat to it.

The beer tasted cool in the hot afternoon sun, and he swallowed nearly half of it in one gulp.

"Savage called me on the twenty-third. It was about six, as usual. Nothing ever seems to blow up in the daytime."

Denton nodded, "Maybe we oughta get a government grant to investigate it. That would rattle Reagan's budget!"

The Division of Industrial Safety was feeling the pinch of budget cuts made by the governor in one of his most recent frenzies of thrift, and though both men were staunch Republicans, they shared the common wish that "belt-tightening" would begin with someone else's department.

They were also ticked off at the governor's attitude toward the disaster. When he was first in office, he seemed to feel called upon to hop into his helicopter and, like a moth with too many wings, fly to the site of every minor accident in the state, but unaccountably he had chosen to avoid this one, the most tragic accident in the history of tunnel construction in the west.

And an appearance at the Sylmar tunnel wouldn't have even required a helicopter! The governor was at the Biltmore addressing an American Legion Convention, and his comments to the *Los Angeles Times* were restricted to a terse no when he was asked whether he personally felt any guilt because of alleged cutbacks, for budgetary reasons, in the number of state safety engineers.

"He added that to his knowledge, there have been no

cutbacks involving safety engineers, although some consolidation of various department staffs is underway" said the *Times* story.

Then presumably the governor had departed to consolidate other staffs in other departments.

"Sure, we could ask for staff to study night blindness and insurance for pneumonia when we travel at night," Zavattero joined in.

The *Times* article though, had given them more serious things to think about than political posturings.

The front-page story had quoted one of the miners, and his statements had confirmed their own speculations as to what had happened during the swing shift.

The miner was Arvid Rasmussen, fifty-seven years old, a Norwegian, whose slight accent made him sometimes seem like a hard hat version of Mrs. Olson, but who was in fact a man of considerable education and experience.

His story had appeared on Saturday, June 26. It merited the accusatory headline "10 Gas Alert Levels Before Explosion Told," and had detailed Rasmussen's account of how they were compelled to halt work on at least two occasions because of increasing concentrations of methane gas. Zavattero suspected in fact that it had reached that level and even more dangerous levels several times during the critical swing shift.

Though the natural accusation should have followed, the statement somehow floated freely in what was obviously a round-up story of the disaster, and this worried the two engineers.

In the story, it was clear that Lockheed, through its corporate director of publicity, Everett A. Hayes, was trying to brush away any mention of the seven orders that Zavattero had given to Lockheed the day before the explosion.

They had been simple, explicit orders that, if followed, would certainly have prevented the disaster, Zavattero knew. With Rasmussen's statement latched onto so vigorously by the press, a follow-up seemed called for. There was none.

Hayes had simply denied that the work crew had

"encountered anything that would approach the minimum danger standards."

Not that the orders had been completely ignored, but the Lockheed publicity man had adroitly managed to eke out a note from them that would cast a virtuous glow over Lockheed's public image.

After piously mentioning the fact that Zavattero had required that the minimum safety reading for gas would be two percent by volume, he hastened to add that Lockheed had suggested that the danger level be changed from two percent to one percent.

This had, in fact, been the case, but the two engineers reading the story wondered how Lockheed hoped to get much mileage from it when they had obviously ignored the readings at any level.

It was a game, of course, a game to be played with the press and the public, but to Zavattero and Denton it was no game.

They knew what lay behind the fact that those orders had been kept from the press, and so airily dismissed by Lockheed's PR man as mere suggestions. He was doing more than preserving Lockheed's public image. He was subverting any possibility of prosecuting Lockheed for the disaster that caused the deaths of the seventeen men in the tunnel.

"Those sons of bitches are gonna bury those orders," Zavattero muttered.

Denton nodded. "Who's got copies?"

"I sent one to Crabtree with the request for investigation, and one to Bob Waters at Lockheed, and I've got the other. I'm a file freak. I keep a copy of everything for my personal file."

"Hang on to 'em. You may need 'em."

"Yep, but I'm sure as hell gonna find out from Crabtree where he's hiding them."

Neither man asked why. They both knew. There was to be no prosecution, and that probability worked on them like the methane in the tunnel. They were angry, frustrated men.

And they had a right to be. They had been in the division too long not to have experienced the repeated denials of requests for prosecution.

Zavattero still had his first memo requesting prosecution and he still stung from the blunt refusal of his office to prosecute. There had been other occasions—many of them—but none had so affected him. He had been suffering from the naive disillusionment of a newly appointed safety engineer, gung-ho and afire to save every man who ever went underground. He had been new and young and it had hurt.

Time had changed that. It no longer hurt. It made him mad.

It had made him mad too when Hatton, within a year after his appointment by Reagan, had made a change in the guidelines for prosecution. In a memo to all safety engineers. Subject: Prosecution; Dated 10/23/67, Hatton had changed previous instructions stating that prosecution should be considered when repeated violations of the safety codes occur, whether or not such violations involve serious injuries to employees, to read that prosecution should be considered only *if* a serious injury resulted from such violations.

So a man had to die before they should think about prosecuting anyone! That just made his job a real zinger. Many men had died, many had been maimed all in different parts of the state, and the reasons for their deaths had passed unnoticed and were rarely prosecuted.

But this time seventeen men had died in the worst disaster since 1922. Seventeen men dead because Lockheed had ignored the perfectly simple orders he had given them. Seventeen men and still no prosecution. He was damn well going to find out who was burying those orders. When he told Denton that he planned to go to Harold Crabtree, his superior in the division, and the one to whom he had given the orders, he got a skeptical look and a muttered "Good luck!" They were both too old at the game not to know how futile this effort would be.

And futile it was. Harold Crabtree's response to his question was a masterpiece of bureaucratese, complete with upward-pointing finger to indicate higher powers and a broad sweep of the hand outlining the dim and distant shores of some appropriate channels. The orders would be processed at the right time.

Then came silence. The silence was to last until July 19, almost a month after the explosion, when Zavattero and Denton submitted their formal memo urging prosecution of Lockheed for negligence.

Not that the press was silent. As the headlines continued to mount, the media silence about Zavattero's orders became more and more inexplicable. There was only one answer. In spite of Crabtree's comforting talk of an appropriate time, those orders were being deliberately buried.

As early as June 28, four days after the tragedy and even before the final count of bodies had been made, probes and investigations were being promised in the press, but with no mention of the fact that Lockheed had in its possession specific instructions it had ignored.

Even though the newly formed federal agency OSHA had already leveled charges of negligence against Lockheed, the gesture seemed an empty one, as if the infant federal agency were trying its wings.

It came as no great surprise to either Zavattero or Denton to read on July 1 that ". . . preliminary plans of a public hearing on the Sylmar tunnel disaster had been cancelled."

Jack F. Hatton, Division of Industrial Safety, and Warren H. Fuller, Western Regional Administrator of OSHA, said "no need" existed for a public inquiry: "The state official said, as part of the department's normal procedure, 'We don't usually conduct (public) hearings.'"

Like Tweedledum answering Tweedledee, Fuller echoed the "no need" on behalf of the federal agency.

Fuller's hearty agreement was hardly surprising. His boss was James D. Hodgesen, corporate vice-president of industrial relations at Lockheed until June 1970. At that time he had been appointed by Nixon to be Secretary of Labor.

The fourteenth body had been identified. Louis

Richardson. There were three more to go.

A flicker of hope that their own department was preparing to move for prosecution and had been holding Zavattero's orders as part of the prosecution case, came on July 11 when a young city news service reporter Kenneth Gosting wrote a story of a proposed grand jury investigation.

The statement was simple, but definite. "The reports, written by Zavattero contained a set of conditions which Lockheed was to fulfill before work could resume...."

Their hopes died quickly. The story did not come from their own office, but from Ray Pasillas, a labor union official, who added his voice to the bitter voices of the miners.

Hatton had responded that "he was undecided if the Division of Industrial Safety would release to the public its findings from the investigation."

Mercy had handed Zavattero the clipping the minute he'd walked in the door.

"Is this what all those mysterious midnight calls are about?" she inquired. She had grown tired and nervous from the constant jangling of the midnight phone.

Zavattero just shook his head. "I don't know."

As he read the article, he was already dialing Denton.

Denton's wife had also clipped the article and almost in a single voice they shouted at each other.

"What the hell's going on. Does Hatton think he's still working for Lockheed?"

Nothing made any sense to either of them. It was too much.

At last Zavattero wearily shook his head. Angrily he shouted at Denton, "I don't know what they think they're doing. But Lockheed can't get away with this!"

That was July 11 and they were getting away with it.

CHAPTER THREE

As if suddenly its insatiable thirst for knowledge had been quenched, the news media was silent. At least for six days it was silent.

The search for knowledge was, however, being taken up swiftly and secretly by other powers.

Among them was the Metropolitan Water District. Its Assistant General Manager, Evan Griffiths, had flown home from the east almost immediately. On the plane his mind had been obsessed by an ancient Welsh mining story of men who had refused to enter a gaseous tunnel when it smelled, not of gas, but of roses.

The psychic minded Welshmen had accepted without question the assertion of the tale that the smell of roses meant death. It had been the smell of roses that clung to the grave of his beloved mother. The smell of roses in the black dirt of the coal mines meant death. The miner had been right. The mine caved in, and the story became part of Welsh mining lore.

On the plane, flying back to the more prosaic world of the San Fernando Valley, Griffith wondered vaguely if someone in the tunnel had smelled roses. He even wished they had.

Somehow it would be so convenient if the whole bloody mess were an act of God, though one geologist, Slosson, was already protesting that "it was no act of God but an act of human stupidity." Somewhere, floating free in his mind, was the possibility that human stupidity might be an act of God—probably was, come to think of it, but in a courtroom and to the public this didn't seem like the best possible approach. In any event, the Metropolitan Water District investigation was definitely directed heavenward, with a wary eye on the more earthly geological reports following the February earthquake.

The Sylmar or San Fernando tunnel as they preferred to call it, was only part of the Metropolitan Water District's $11 billion project to bring water to the barren southern basin. The project was a big one, and the Metropolitan Water District a powerful organization. They owned the tunnel, and the Lockheed Shipbuilding and Construction Company in Seattle, the lowest bidders on the contract, were building it.

The MWD had cause for worry. Buried in their files were geological reports on the Santa Susana fault. It had caused the earthquake that had wrenched the San Fernando Valley only months before the Sylmar explosion. Also tucked away, were reports of the oily gravel formation through which the men were tunneling when the explosion occurred. All of this could be open to some uncomfortable questions by Lockheed. Possibly, even probably, some legal nastiness about breach of contract. That could run into millions.

The kind and variety of legal forces that could be set into play by the catastrophe at Sylmar were not likely to bring comfort to either the MWD or Lockheed.

However, none of these thoughts was in the mind of MWD executive Griffith as he returned. His were genuinely thoughts of regret and the smell of roses, with perhaps a few uneasy ponderings on the bonuses promised to Lockheed for pushing the tunnel through as fast as possible. If the news coming over the radio and TV were correct, and they had really highballed it, the MWD had better start an investigation of its own. Fast.

There was no doubt that Sylmar was a highballing operation. Expertly and efficiently run, the three shafts were push-

Part 1/Prosecution   35

ing back as much as one hundred feet a day. The tunnel was months ahead of schedule and everyone was cheerfully expecting bonuses, even the least important miners, who had been promised Accutron watches. "Man, these watches don't even tick—they hum" was the graphic assertion of the happy donor, the builders of the powerful new excavating machine.

In its own investigation, Lockheed was relying heavily on its previous record of a smooth and brilliant operation to extricate itself from any stain of culpability.

The miners themselves were the best witnesses to the speed of the operation. They were proud of the way the earth was being forced to give before the driving shield of the digging machine, Lockheed's prized drilling-excavating machine which was designed especially for the Sylmar operation. It was a metal monster that would have deflated John Henry before he could butter his hammers.*

The excavating machine, affectionately called the mole—the subject of a long and laudatory article in the *Los Angeles Times* during a lull in the breaking news about the disaster—was a testimony to modernity. It was a 225-ton tube, 140 feet long and more than 21 feet in diameter, with a round shield as big as the circumference of the tunnel. The shield supported the earth instead of the wood beams used in the past. Inside it was a digging claw called a ripper hook which clawed at the earth like a human hand. The clawed out muck passed on to a conveyor belt and dropped in waiting muck trains.

After it clawed its way four feet forward, it automatically set into place four seven-thousand-pound reinforced concrete slabs, each curved to fit the circle of the tunnel and to be welded together by the miners. That done, it moved on to the next four feet attended by its crew of about twenty men.

It even included a laser beam to keep it moving along the proper line and grade of the tunnel's surveyed path. Unfor-

---

* John Henry is said to have used butter to keep the shaft of his mighty hammers supple.

tunately, it did not have a device to detect the smell of roses or convert gas to air.

It was the men who drove this machine forward each shift, competing to see who could push it hardest, who were being asked to explain the inexplicable to all the investigating bodies. "What had gone wrong. Why had so efficient an operation, plunging ahead so far in advance of schedule, blown up?"

The real answer was buried with the seventeen men who were still being pulled out of the muck on men trips and muck trains. But the awful responsibility of what had happened in the dark depths of that tunnel, lit so suddenly with incandescent death, confronted only two men: Loren G. Savage, Lockheed's Project Manager, and Otha "Bob" Ree, Lockheed's Project Engineer.

Both men had been at the tunnel the night of the explosion. Ree was working above ground and Savage stayed with the miners underground into the fatal graveyard shift. Savage had nearly been killed himself. He had left the face of the tunnel and had ridden the man trip only three-thousand feet out when he heard the first blast of the explosion. He knew this was no minor explosion such as the flash fire of the previous night. This one shook the concrete walls of the tunnel with such an impact it had blown his hard hat twenty feet ahead of him into the suddenly totally dark tunnel. It was the most terrifying moment of Savage's life.

To Bob Ree above ground, the distant boom sounded ominous, but he had been in underground telephone contact with Savage since early afternoon. Savage had assured Ree the gas readings were minimal. But as the ominous boom grew to a repeated rumbling, he was worried. He picked up the phone, but before he could speak the line spluttered with a ghastly, eerie whisper. All Ree could make out was "California Switch" and the fading whisper "big explosion at the heading." Then the phone went dead and Bob Ree too was terrified.

Loren Savage, tall and blond with sideburns that accentuated his long jaw, had worked for Lockheed before. He had taken his engineering degree at the University of Utah, and had worked in tunnels before that. Perhaps because of his first-hand experience on mining in Butte, Montana, he identified with the fierce, independent miners and their highballing ways. He always referred to them as his "troops," with affection for their habits of hard drinking and brawling.

Of the three crews or troops under his command, he regarded the crew on graveyard that night as the best. They were good men. They liked him and he liked them. He knew that his presence in the tunnel was needed by them that night and so he had stayed urging them on, but telling them to be cautious, too. When he had left them he felt confident that they would keep pushing, and that was what was important—keep pushing, digging the ripper claws of that mole into the earth, inch by inch, cubic foot by cubic foot. It had to be done, and he knew that if there was any crew that could do it, this one was it. He was wrong. The violated earth was stronger, and it exploded in their faces.

When Savage had worked for Lockheed before it had not been as a project manager but as an engineer. It had been at the Angelus Tunnel with Lockheed as only one of the contractors.

It was there that he had first met Zavattero, and had liked him. He knew that Zavattero also liked him and that he was always glad to work with Savage rather than the other engineers on the job. It had never developed into a real friendship. They had not met again until Zavattero had been assigned to Sylmar. They both felt a mutual respect for the other's expertise. But the Angelus tunnel, too, had blown up. And now this.

He did not like to think about Zavattero. He did not want to phone him that night. He told Ree to get somebody else to phone Zavattero. The Metropolitan Water District representative had phoned three hours after the explosion.

He had not waited for Zavattero, but had gone home, his nerves screaming with the sounds of the men trapped in the tunnel. There was nothing he could do. Everyone was there, the fire department, rescue units, everyone.

Nor did he see much of Zavattero during the rescue operations that followed. Zavattero was underground most of the time, and there was no way of contacting him.

On June 25, Savage prepared a careful report titled "Notes on Discussions Reached in the Meeting Held on June 23, 1971." It was to be given to all investigators.

Zavattero suspected that it had been done under the watchful eye of Lockheed's attorneys. The document was almost chatty in its open and innocent discussion of the events leading to the orders written by Zavattero on the day following the flash fire. The general content of the orders themselves was not attached to it. That had disappeared.

When Zavattero and Savage finally met for lunch, Savage was surprised that Zavattero's attitude was more curious than accusatory. He had expected Zavattero to ask immediately about the orders, but he hadn't.

Instead Zavattero shook his head. "It must have been one hell of a bang to cause all that damage." The two of them finally had been able to get into the tunnel to see what damage had been done to the equipment, and it had been considerable. All the bodies had been recovered. All except one miner, Ron Demo. There still had been no identification. "Do you think Demo got out? There's lots of ways of getting in and out of that tunnel," Zavattero said.

Savage shook his head "Who knows?" He looked like he didn't want to talk about it.

That was understandable. They were both still shocked and bewildered by the magnitude of the disaster. But the job had to go on, so they talked about the ruined equipment, the digging machine, the requirements for reopening the tunnel, and the time necessary to clear it. They talked on and on. They did not mention the dead men again.

At last Zavattero said almost casually, "We're going to prosecute Lockheed for this one, you know."

Savage shook his head, "No way. They got such big guns they'll blow you out with a bang louder than the one in the tunnel."

Zavattero shrugged, "Maybe."

Savage did not believe that there would be any real attempt to prosecute. In spite of his slow, deliberate speech and manner, and his identification with the miners, Loren Savage also identified with his employer's arrogant belief in its own power. This made him a valuable employee to Lockheed, indeed.

Not so, Bob Ree, Lockheed's project engineer. Though he was a highly skilled engineer like Savage, he shared none of his calm self-control. Yet it had been Ree, not Savage, who had remained at Sylmar that night coordinating the rescue efforts. Ree had a reputation as a bit of a brawler and a hard drinker, but these were all part of the macho image of the highballing miner. And there was no doubt he was highly qualified as an engineer. But there were other things—nothing concrete— but indications of a certain instability that made him bear a bit of watching.

His feeling for the miners was a close and friendly one. He had cheerfully accepted the additional responsibility of safety engineer for the Lockheed job. He fulfilled it well, dreaming up ideas to impress on the men the many hazards of working underground.

Shards of glass and what they could do to a man's feet when they pierced even the heaviest boot always bothered him. To draw the men's attention to what could happen if they ignored the deadly glass he had nailed a shoe on the bulletin board. The shoe pierced with glass and gory with catsup was a garish reminder to the men to literally watch their step. That safety reminder they didn't forget. Admired though it was and appreciated by the men on the job, this tendency towards imaginativeness could prove dangerous to Lockheed unless it could be monitored by Lockheed's attorneys.

Perhaps, since work on the Sylmar job would have to be discontinued for many weeks, Ree could be more useful to Lockheed working in the Seattle office. In fact, there were more cogent reasons for transferring the high-strung Ree away from Los Angeles, preferably as quietly as possible.

On July 16, the same story that had so upset Zavattero and Denton had also caused some uneasy ripples at Lockheed. At 11 P.M., July 16, Ree, accompanied by Lockheed's most knowledgeable gas tester, Arvid Rasmussen, and Lieutenant Biro of the Los Angeles Foothill Division Police Department, went down into the strange, dark world of the tunnel and found the gas meter. Zavattero, Denton, and indeed other people had searched for this gas testing device since the early days of the investigation. The trio's astonishing discovery was turned over to Lockheed, and Otha Ree was transferred. It would be a while before anyone would know where.

Zavattero knew nothing of this and after the July 16 story he was beginning to believe that Savage was right. There would be no prosecution. The guns were big and they were powerful.

Nevertheless, he and Denton slogged through investigations and used every moment away from their jobs to find out what had happened.

Then on July 19, they wrote a brief, two-line memo to Harold Crabtree, their senior officer in the Division of Industrial Safety. Unwilling to face another trip through the tangled thickets of bureaucratese, they submitted the memo formally, through office routine.

Neither Zavattero nor George Denton expected an immediate reply. That would have required a miracle, and Zavattero was therefore surprised when he received a call from Marty Coren of the *L. A. Times*.

Had a miracle happened? Had the Divison of Industrial Safety finally disclosed his orders and decided to prosecute at last?

He had been silent until now, waiting for his department to act. Now he was through. Let Lockheed sue him, let the department fire him. Six years of this messy job was enough!

In an hour-long conversation with the surprised and excited Coren, he spelled out the orders that he had written and that Lockheed had failed to comply with. He concluded with the bald statement that "if they had followed my requirements the tunnel wouldn't have blown up."

Then he quietly hung up the receiver and took a deep breath. He had just accused Lockheed of gross negligence, and all hell was about to break loose.

The story covered the front page of the *Los Angeles Times*. That was on July 20, and apparently somebody else had been interested in what had happened to those orders. A photostatic copy of them had been sent to Kenneth Gosting at City News Service. They were printed verbatim.

When Zavattero arrived at Sylmar that day, he was so relieved at having taken some steps to insure prosecution that he didn't care whether or not he'd just blown his job.

He was not surprised when Loren Savage met him in the trailer waving a copy of the *Times*.

"Hey, Wally, did you see this?" he asked.

"Yeah, I saw it."

"Where the hell did they get it?" Savage asked indignantly.

"I gave it to them." Zavattero said flatly.

Savage paused with the outstretched paper in his hand. "Oh," he said and laid the paper on the desk. He sat down, and stared at Zavattero for a long moment.

Then he shrugged and said "Hell, it's only a misdemeanor."

That startled Zavattero. In the week following the explosion, the two of them and Bob Ree had been drawn into a sort of beleaguered comradeship. They were the professionals, the men who had been underground and were being constantly questioned by those who had never been underground in their lives—those who knew nothing of the narrow, dark world where the crushing monotony of the work could only be relieved by living on the high, keen edge of danger.

Though they had never talked about it much, he knew too that Savage had liked the miners of the graveyard shift and had been badly shaken by their deaths. It startled him to hear Savage dismiss the whole thing as if all that mattered was the legal status of the event. Savage knew better than that. They were both pros and they knew what those underground deaths were.

"What do you hear from Hix?" Zavattero asked. Hix was Savage's boss in the Seattle offices of Lockheed Shipbuilding and Construction Company.

Savage shook his head. "Nothing, he says it's just a misdemeanor, forget about it. All he wants is to get this damned tunnel moving again."

"Is that what he wanted that night?" Zavattero asked.

Again Savage stared at him and then said coldly, "Look, it's only a misdemeanor. The city attorney's office can't do anything." He stood up, "Come on, let's get in that crazy tunnel and then I'll buy lunch today." As he left for the Gate shaft, Zavattero watched him, his eyes puzzled. Well, maybe he'd talk at lunch.

Savage was right, of course, it was only a misdemeanor. Before 1963, when a negligent employer caused a worker's death, the employer could be charged with involuntary manslaughter, a felony punishable by term in the state prison. Through a series of complex maneuvers, the law had been changed in California, reducing the seriousness of such a crime from a felony to a misdemeanor. Previously, district attorneys could prosecute the offense as a felony—manslaughter—using the full investigative resources of their offices. The new bill had left the prosecution to city attorneys, who handle misdemeanors and are not equipped to prosecute complicated criminal cases. And this was threatening to become the most complicated and longest legal case to be tried in a municipal court in the nation's history.

At the Fin & Feathers, a place nearly as dark as a tunnel but humming with quite a different kind of life, Savage and Zavattero, leaning over martinis and some incidental food, wrangled amiably over what was necessary to get the tunnel reopened. Nothing more was said of felonies or misdemeanors or of evidence or death. In the subdued cheerfulness of the Fin & Feathers, you would have thought that no other problem except the reopening of the tunnel existed. To Lockheed Shipbuilding and Construction Company, probably none did. At that time.

It was twenty-four hours later on July 21 that Jack Hatton, Director of the Division of Industrial Safety, made his first statement to the *Times* placing the blame on Lockheed. According to the story, Hatton had said, "The facts are, had Lockheed been in full compliance with the safety division's written requirements, written requirements issued to them on the day previous to that tragic accident, it never would have occurred."

The story continued, "Lockheed stated Monday that 'operations were conducted in full conformity with safety regulations and instruction of the California Division of Industrial Safety.'

"Hatton said that he normally would not make any statement regarding an accident until the investigation was completed, but that Lockheed was using the English language in a rather loose manner.'"

This splutter of semantic disapproval from the chief of the division brought laughter from both Zavattero and Savage as they read the story which again Savage had in hand when Zavattero arrived at the tunnel.

"Tsk, tsk, take that," said Savage.

"And next time we'll wash your mouth out with diesel oil," said Zavattero.

The story continued, "Hatton's statement is the first time the state agency placed the blame on Lockheed. The *Times* reported Monday that Wally J. Zavattero, the state field inspector responsible for inspecting the tunnel, said Lockheed failed to follow the requirements."

Savage and Zavattero were still laughing at Hatton's bumbling when Savage said "The poor bastard, somebody's going get their ass fried for this one." He did not look at Zavattero.

"Yep," said Zavattero, "maybe Lockheed."

"No way. They'll get him first." But Savage's voice sounded faintly conciliatory for the first time, even though for the first time he was right.

CHAPTER FOUR

As the news broke, what Lockheed feared most began to happen. The little people began making noises like an aroused citizenry.

Letters had been arriving at the offices of Bob Moretti, Speaker of the House and Democrat from the San Fernando Valley.

To the letters were added outraged telephone calls, some of them anonymous. In one instance, the investigators believed that Zavattero had made the call.

This was not true. Not that Zavattero wasn't mad enough to have called the president at this point, but simply because he was indifferent and not particularly knowledgeable concerning the political underground, which seemed to him as long, dark, and dangerously lit as any tunnel he had ever worked in.

Moretti, who was genuinely appalled at the tragic dimensions of the disaster, also saw an opportunity to score points against Reagan and the Republicans, and he assigned two investigators to the tunnel. They were Jack Johnson and Jerry McFettridge.

In the first days of August, ten days after the release of Zavattero's story to the *Times*, Jack Johnson and Jerry McFettridge were given authorization by Moretti to do an intensive investigation of the Sylmar tunnel explosion.

McFettridge, slender, with a bramble of red hair, appeared very young, very vulnerable.

Johnson, who had been a newspaper reporter and had owned a small news service before going to work for the legislature, was short, almost fat, with a dark haphazard sort of beard. He periodically wheezed uneasily into an inhalator. Zavattero thought he must have asthma. Zavattero himself had suffered from asthma as a child and had been surrounded by asthmatics all his life—his mother, his grandmother, and assorted other relatives.

Neither Johnson nor McFettridge seemed particularly formidable to Lockheed's attorneys from the prestigious firm of O'Melvany & Meyers. That was their first mistake.

Surveying the young investigators and sniffing the winds of political interests in Sacramento, Lockheed's attorneys thought that in any event they would be able to divert attention away from their client to Zavattero. That was their second mistake.

And besides that, they had in their possession the only piece of credible evidence about the gas readings in the tunnel—the meter. That was their third and worst mistake.

Nevertheless, by that time Lockheed had its attorneys wrapped around Loren Savage and Bob Ree as snugly as grape leaves and dolmas. When Johnson and McFettridge arrived at the tunnel site hoping to start their investigation with statements from Savage, they found, standing beside the booted, dungareed, hard-hatted Savage, an immaculately groomed young attorney from O'Melvany & Meyers. He was David Finkle, young, dark, smooth, good looking, and very, very confident. Otherwise, when he wasn't busy being disdainful on behalf of Lockheed, he was a nice young man who liked to surf.

At the tunnel site Johnson and McFettridge were not at that point so interested in a verbal interrogation of Lockheed's project manager, as they were in actually getting into the tunnel to view the scene of the crime.

This was to prove no easy chore. The tunnel had been yellow-tagged by the Division of Industrial Safety. This meant that no unauthorized personnel—that is no one—was allowed in the tunnel. To enter without authorization was illegal. Seated with legs crossed, and adjusting the lapels of his immaculate suit, Finkle, Lockheed's man on the spot, made this point with admirable legal grace.

Undaunted, Johnson, with the pertinacity born of years of reporting and going places he shouldn't go, wheezed into his omnipresent inhalator. He gasped some ominous things about subpoena powers and legislative authorizations, none of which really included forcing the investigating team's way into the tunnel.

Having surmounted this legal hurdle, another immediately grew in its place. Neither he nor McFettridge had the proper clothing. The tunnel was running with mud and water, and was filled with the stench of gas. Savage assured them that it would be positively unsafe to enter the tunnel without proper protective clothing.

McFettridge, who had adopted the "nice guy" character in the investigating team, stepped in and politely asked what the required clothes were. He made a careful checklist as the items were read to him. Then with a cheerful nod, he agreed, and everyone left to meet later.

During the brief interval for lunch, Johnson and McFettridge headed for the nearest war surplus store. They wanted to see what was in that tunnel! They brought heavy-duty farm overalls, boots, and whatever protective-type gear was necessary. Then they returned to East Portal at the Sylmar site.

Wrapped up in their new gear, the two approached the office trailer where Finkle, Savage and Ree sat having what seemed to be an amiable chat.

When they appeared Finkle looked at them and for the first time his cool slipped. "Hell! What's that?"

Johnson said that they were now ready to go into the tunnel. For a while the trailer office shook with the vibrations of shouts of legal authorizations, subpoenas, legislature, conspiracy and anything else anyone could think of to throw into the can of objections.

Johnson and McFettridge emerged the victors. Savage, who had actually been watching all this with some amusement, stood up.

He shrugged, "OK, come on let's go," he said as he headed for the Gate shaft where they would be lowered 175 feet into the tunnel.

As they started toward the door, Finkle stood up. There was no alternative. Savage was to talk to no one without an attorney. Certainly not legislative investigators. Those were his orders.

"I'm going with you." It was not a question.

Though the thought of what was going to happen to those fancy clothes crossed Johnson's mind, even made him tuck a smile away somewhere behind his beard, he said nothing. The rules were obviously less stringent for Lockheed.

During the slow descent, with the man lift creaking and brushing against the grime, the mud and stench of the burned-out tunnel filling their nostrils, nothing was said. Finkle stood as far away from the edge of the man lift as possible. His clothes would need a long, long cleaning but Johnson and McFettridge would learn nothing from Savage without his OK. Fleetingly, he thought perhaps O'Melvany & Meyers had underestimated the two young investigators from the legislator's office.

Johnson and McFettridge, indeed learned nothing, but they did see the carnage. The once-clean, concrete tube to carry water to San Fernando Valley was a mangling of twisted metal, muck, and stinking, gaseous filth. McFettridge and Johnson were appalled at what they saw, but they had scored an important point. They would investigate, no matter how powerful the offices that would try to stop them. They had scored a point, but it was the last they would score for some time.

Activity in the political arena was not viewed with delight by any of the corporate entities involved in the Sylmar tunnel, even though Jack Hatton had loftily waved his hand, and promised the utmost cooperation from the Division of Industrial Safety. Part of the promised cooperation was the assignment of both George Denton and Zavattero to the investigation. They were to investigate events prior to the first flash fire on June 23, and the meetings held on June 24, when Zavattero had issued his seven requirements. They were to try to determine what had happened during the swing shift just before the doomed graveyard shift took the man trip into the tunnel at midnight.

Much of their interrogation of the miners on the swing shift had to be done at night, after their working day was supposed to be ended. In spite of Hatton's promises, the two engineers were not released from their jobs for daytime investigation. It was time-consuming, hard, wearying work, and both men's wives wondered if it was all really worth it.

Denton had been assigned to the investigation because the tunnel had been his responsibility until the month before the explosion, and he was familiar not only with the operation, but also with the geological findings made before the tunnel went underground.

He had originally taken over the tunnel from Zavattero as a result of the shifting of boundary lines, and he had welcomed the assignment. This was his first really highballing tunnel, and he had enjoyed it. He was sorry when the boundaries were again shifted and the tunnel was returned to Zavattero. That was just a month before the explosion. Now, he admitted reluctantly, he was downright glad that he didn't have to hassle this one.

Newer to the Tunnels and Mines Division than Zavattero, he was just as conscientious and now he was determined to pull the truth out of the tangled mess of departmental red tape.

That the Division of Industrial Safety had been in a mess, even before the Lockheed holocaust, both Johnson and McFettridge, were vaguely aware of. The inequities in the department were, in fact, grist for the political mill.

Johnson and McFettridge talked first to Denton and then to Zavattero. Both men simply opened up their files and with that, a Pandora's box. After listening to the two safety engineers and others who were beginning to step forward, the legislative investigators were at first disbelieving, then elated. If what they were finding out was true, this would mean a full-scale assembly hearing, and Moretti would indeed have Reagan right by his budget cuts. There was nothing vicious about it. It was just politics.

Nor was there anything vicious about it when they allowed their attention to be diverted from investigations of Lockheed's project manager Savage and project engineer Ree to start an investigation of Zavattero. That investigation turned out to be a mistake. It revealed nothing. It was simply an ordinary potpourri of information:

Born February 2, 1931, Berkeley, California, shortly after the divorce of his parents; raised by his grandparents, a grandfather whom he deeply loved, a former chief petty officer in the navy. His other relatives seemed to wander around in his life in a somewhat disorderly manner. None of them was remarkable enough to investigate.

He had attended Petaluma High School which he left to join the army. He had been wounded in Korea, had received a Purple Heart, and returned home.

In 1950 he had married a young Mexican girl who worked in the record industry, Mercedes Sierra. He then picked up the threads of his education, took the equivalency test, passed it easily, and went to Los Angeles City College to study engineering.

He had received the usual A.A. degree and, following the birth of his first child, had applied for a job at the Division of Highways.

His tests showed him to be of better than average ability, and he progressed rather rapidly through the civil service testing system. He was assigned to the Tunnels and Mines Division as a safety engineer after seven years as a construction safety engineer.

He had bought a home in Granada Hills, complete with swimming pool for his two daughters. Neither he nor his wife were avid swimmers themselves.

In the division he was liked and disliked in the normal degree. His superiors in the division took exception to his occasional indignant protest, when the division appeared to be adopting a more than easy attitude toward prosecuting offenders, but other than this there appeared to be nothing. True, he drank, but no more than anyone else in a hard drinking profession, probably less than most legislators.

There were no fluctuations of income or expenditures that were not typical of a man who loved his wife and children and was reasonably content with his work.

He did seem to have a suspiciously easy relationship with the Lockheed managers, but nothing that wasn't normally required to maintain comfortable relations between the division and the construction industry.

In a word, the investigation of Zavattero was a washout. Not only was he not an engineer on the take, but he was probably the most vocal of the safety engineers in the state about the laxness of the division.

On the day of the explosion, the orders he had written were strong, clear, and unequivocal. However, he had not red tagged the tunnel. In view of the stringency of the orders that seemed a slim thing to object to. It wasn't much, but it was enough for their purposes.

Zavattero was not aware that he was under suspicion. He wouldn't have cared if he had known. He and Denton were not interested in the political ramifications of their disclosures. Their minds were on the prosecution.

By August, when the legislative investigators arrived on the scene Zavattero and Denton were working full-time on the investigation. It was the worst possible time. It was always hot. Zavattero sometimes thought that he could understand why they were called dog days. He couldn't remember where he had learned that they were called dog days, or why, but in Los

Angeles the heat and smog lay panting over the city like a yellow, dusty dog.

Not even at Sylmar was there respite. So far from downtown, there should be air, cool and clean. You would think people would refuse to live where there was no respite from the city's blight, but no, there they were, docilely, patiently choking to death on the rim of the city. Zavattero and Denton were on their way to interview one of the swing shift miners. They had hoped it would be cool, and there would be refreshing, icy beer to relieve the painful memory of what had happened that night. These men had all known each other and had been friends. Somehow, beyond the tunnel they deserved fresh air. There was none.

Zavattero and Denton had to interview the miners, had to force their every recollection of what had happened on the swing shift, because a prosecution depended on their statements.

The evidence that might have made such intensive interviewing unnecessary—the gas testing meter—could not be found. Its disappearance cast a strange element of mystery over the entire investigation, almost as much as the disappearance of the body of Ron Demo, one of the miners on the graveyard shift.

It was the question of Demo's body that Zavattero and Denton were discussing.

"Do you think he could have just walked out?" Zavattero asked.

Denton nodded. "Could be. After all, Romeo refused to go in. Why couldn't Demo have decided to walk out?"

"Yeah, but then where the hell did he go?" Both of them were thinking back to the night of the explosion when Mercy had received a telephone call a few minutes after Zavattero and Denton had left Sylmar.

The caller did not identify himself, but in a tense, rapid whisper asked to talk to Zavattero. He said he knew what had happened in the tunnel and wanted to talk to Zavattero. He refused to give his name, or where he could be reached, and he hung up hastily as if frightened, and indeed, he must have been.

It was frustrating to the two investigating engineers to think that somewhere in the city there might be someone who could tell them exactly what had happened. Just one person. Everyone else had died in the tunnel, except Brissette. They had talked to Brissette in the hospital, but the only survivor was in such a state of shock he had been little help.

"Could Demo have had your number?" Denton asked for the millionth time.

Zavattero shook his head. It did not seem likely, but it was possible. The big question of course remained: If he had gotten out of the tunnel where did he go?

"Maybe somebody paid him off and he went back to Canada." Denton suggested.

Zavattero shook his head, a quick, irritated shake. All speculation was fruitless now. After days of frantic searching, the hunt for Demo's body had become desultory, and it was generally agreed at a meeting on July 9 that further searching would be useless. What searching was done after that would be more to bring some comfort to Demo's distraught widow than in the hopes of really finding the body.

But not the search for the equally mysteriously missing gas testing meter. George Denton especially was dogged in his efforts to find the all-important meter.

In their first trips into the tunnel, Denton and Zavattero had found the gas reading logs. They had carefully wrapped them and sent them to the police department for photostating, and Zavattero had kept the originals.

Unfortunately, the logs showed nothing. Whoever had been assigned to record the readings in the log had either just forgotten to do so, or things in the tunnel had become so chaotic that there was no chance to record them. The grimy, burnt logs were meaningless, but only Zavattero and Denton knew that.

The meaninglessness of the logs made the loss of the

meter more exasperating to the two Division of Industrial Safety investigators. No amount of probing through the muck produced even the slightest shard of metal from the meter. Bob Warner, the miner who had been in charge of testing, had been nearly cremated, his body reduced to forty pounds of charred bones.

The meter must have simply blown to bits. Still, it did not seem reasonable that there was not even a splinter of it left.

"Let's face it. It's just not there," Denton said as they emerged from the moist, oppressive heat of the tunnel into the blast furnace of smog and July heat above ground. He said it but he did not sound like he meant it. As Zavattero headed for the office trailer, Denton stood staring down into the Gate shaft as if he were waiting for the capricious earth to give up its secret.

He followed Zavattero to the office still shaking his head. "I don't know," Zavattero muttered. Then laughing suddenly he said, "I know, maybe McNary came and took it. He said that Mine and Safety and Appliances would probably give a million for that meter. Maybe he stole it and sold it to them."

He was referring to a conversation that he had with Tom McNary, purchasing agent and a sometime protector of Lockheed's interests at the tunnel. Denton laughed too. "Not McNary, he'd probably have run to Lockheed with it in his teeth, waiting for a pat on the head." McNary did not stand high on Zavattero and Denton's list of Lockheed's personnel.

At the office, Ree and Savage were bent over some tunnel specifications estimating the costs of repairs to the equipment. The hazards of the tunnel were the Division of Industrial Safety's worry, not theirs. They were there to get the tunnel open, to push through that last twenty-five hundred feet.

They glanced up as the safety engineers entered. "Smell anything this trip?" Savage asked.

"Nope," said Zavattero, "didn't find anything either. That damned meter is just not there."

"Yeah," said Savage, marking figures on the diagrams.

He sounded disinterested.

"It must have blown up. That's the only answer."

"Yeah," again Savage sounded disinterested.

"Yeah," Ree said, but he didn't sound disinterested. He didn't look at them but still bent over the paper.

"Have a cup of coffee." Then he straightened up and said with a quick, nervous laugh. "In fact, I'll join you."

Zavattero pushed his hard hat back and there was a white line across his forehead where the sweat and grime from the tunnel ended. The heat both inside and outside the tunnel was deadly. It had been a long, dirty, frustrating day. Zavattero shook his head. "No thanks, I'm going for something long and cool, like a triple martini. If you find the meter, call me."

That had been in July. Now it was late in August. The assembly investigators Johnson and McFettridge were fishing in every stream to supply facts for the assembly investigation. There still had been no word from Zavattero's own office about a prosecution of Lockheed. There were rumors, hints, meetings, meetings, and more meetings. What all the meetings were about, no one could say for sure, but Zavattero was certain that no one was mounting any white chargers in the direction of Lockheed, either in Seattle or Burbank.

He had been brought into the office by Crabtree, the Division of Industrial Safety Senior Engineer, who for once seemed to have found his way through the maze of bureaucratic speculation. He asked point-blank if Zavattero still insisted on prosecution as per his earlier memo, and was Denton with him.

The answer had been equally point-blank: "Yes."

Then on August 24, the affair of the missing meter took a surprising turn.

On that day, Zavattero had gone with Jim Westfield to survey the tunnel and its damage.

Westfield was a mining engineer consultant, personal representative of the Director of the Bureau of Mines. On June 24, he had been called immediately to the scene of the disaster to check with the Bureau of Mines men about what was going on. It was no routine assignment. It looked as if Sylmar was going to be the worst tunnel disaster in the history of the state. His advice as an expert in first aid in mine rescue and prevention was needed. In the chaos of the rescue attempts, there had been little time for advice and certainly none for investigation. It had been impossible to go underground, and he had returned to Washington, D. C. The Bureau of Mines would definitely investigate.

That seemed to end his job as a consultant, but on July 8, Loren Savage called him at his home in Provo, Utah. This surprised him. In the confusion he had not met or talked to Savage. After the conversation he packed for his second trip to the San Fernando Valley, this time at the expense of Lockheed. He was obviously the most highly qualified consultant to provide advice on reopening the tunnel.

On August 19, Westfield was hired by O'Melvany & Meyers, Lockheed's attorneys, to investigate the causes of the explosion, presumably without thought of possible litigation.

Little was said of testing devices. Conversations with Lockheed were terse and to the point. Get the tunnel reopened or get out from under the contract with Metropolitan Water District.

Every step had to provide guarantees of safety, and those guarantees were the main preoccupation of Zavattero as he and Westfield worked back into the tunnel on August 24. Mud, oil, and dripping water clung to the tunnel, and the two men felt covered with it as they came to the base of the Gate shaft. There they sat down, as much to rest from the weight of their heavy, underground gear as to chat.

But chat they did. The fanlines could be made reversible. Rescue units could be made easily accessible, and testing should be constant and done with the best avilable equipment. At the first whiff of gas the men should be pulled out of the tunnel until the Division of Industrial Safety could check out the causes. They should be the ones to evaluate the dangers inherent in trying to tunnel through what was almost a shallow oil field, shaken by the earthquake, and seeping from every crevice with deadly gases of the hydrocarbon chain. Testing should not be just for methane, but for any one of the noxious gases.

As they gathered up their equipment, ready to ascend the gate shaft, Westfield remarked casually that he would like to talk more about the safety questions, especially testing devices. Would Zavattero like to meet him later at his motel, where they could talk in a more relaxed way?

Zavattero thought for a moment. Westfield no longer was acting as a representative for the Bureau of Mines, who had a real vested interest in safety, but for Lockheed and their attorneys, from O'Melvany & Meyers, who had quite other vested interests. He wondered vaguely if this relaxed talk would include any of those other interests. He nodded. He hoped it wouldn't take too long. He'd promised Mercy that he would stay home that night. There was so much for them to talk about. Nothing that had to do with the tunnel, but their two daughters, one of whom, Paula, had reached the age when romance was no longer a teenage fantasy, but a tangle of confused desires beyond either his or Mercy's control.

In the car going home he seemed to be pushed along the freeway by smoldering heat. It was the kind of heat that comes from smog, driving its way through the valley like a soldering iron smelling of metal and sweat. If only the heat would let up, maybe he could think straight.

There were so many questions. Uppermost in his mind were Bucky Micelli's questions about the search for Ron Demo's body.

Had someone, as Micelli claimed, gone into the tunnel to search once again for the missing body. Mrs. Demo had called Micelli to ask it they found the body, and the union representative had immediately asked Savage and Ree if they had gone in to search for Demo's body.

It was a simple enough question. So why had both Savage and Ree been so evasive about it? Had they gone in after the state safety division had yellow tagged it?

Then there was also the missing meter. When had Ree

and Savage started being so evasive about that, and more important, why?

Why hadn't they told him or Denton that someone was going in to look for Demo's body? True, it was a violation of the yellow tag, yet simple compassion for Demo's wife could have made them do something foolish. That was not very sensible, but it was, at least, understandable. But there was nothing understandable about why they had not called him or George Denton. What the hell, George had a wife and four kids. He would have OKd it, would have even gone with them. Hell, the poor woman must be half-crazy with grief and worry. He understood that, and he knew they sure as hell would, so why hadn't they called either of them, or Bucky for that matter?

And what was Westfield so anxious to talk about? Did he know that they'd been asking Savage about the meter, or did he just feel like a chat about the safety laws and the upcoming assembly hearings?

And as far as the city attorney's office, they didn't seem any nearer a prosecution than they'd ever been.

Somehow, it didn't add up; it just didn't add up. And what did add up, he didn't like. Not at all.

As he got out of the car and slammed the door behind him, he shook his head, "Bunch of maniacs, that's all. A bunch of maniacs," he muttered to himself.

When he entered the house, it was blessedly cool. From outside he could hear splashing, loud music, and sounds of wild disorder. Hearing them, he smiled for the first time that day. He had heard once of the lost generation, and this generation he decided must surely be the deaf generation, either because they were born that way or dedicated themselves to getting that way. Still, it pleased him. He liked music—all music—and had tape recording equipment of his own. He had even built an additional room on the house, just for the recording equipment. His greatest pleasure and relief from a difficult job had been sitting down in the early morning, before the screaming world woke, to listen to music—

Beethoven, Tchaikovsky, or sweet melodic records by the singers of intimate revelations. Large headphones shut out everything, the whole cacophony of a dismaying over-populated world, and left him with a sense of peace and solitude.

His hopes for that quiet evening were short-lived. Mercy kissed him briefly and pushed him away gently as he moved closer.

"You just got a call from some man. He didn't leave a name but he wants you to meet him at the Mission Hills Inn"—she paused— "tonight." She said it as if she wished she could say tomorrow at dawn or any other time. It was two months to the day since that wretched tunnel had exploded and she had not known a single moment's peace. Wally was gone almost every night, and when he wasn't gone, he might as well have been. All he seemed to do was brood over the Sylmar disaster. She was worried about him. He had lost weight, his eyes hardly ever seemed to laugh any more, and he was drinking way too much.

Nevertheless, she offered him a drink before he showered. Anything to take the edge off.

"That's Westfield. Why didn't he leave his name?"

Mercy kissed him lightly on the cheek. "Who knows? So go take a shower."

But when he was ready to leave, she looked at him and said in a low voice, "Wally, please come home early. It seems like you're never here anymore. We have to talk about Paula. I'm worried about her."

"I know, I know," he hugged her, enjoying the scent of her hair. "Don't worry. It will soon be over. It can't go on forever." She smiled. As far as she was concerned it had already been forever.

When he arrived at the Mission Hills Inn, Westfield was lying on the bed in his shorts sipping whiskey from a half-filled water tumbler. It did not surprise Zavattero that he didn't move. He looked tired and hot even though the air-conditioner was doing its industrious best to live up to its claims of arctic-cool air.

The scene had a strange quality to it, like something he'd seen in a late-night movie. Burt Lancaster in *The Killers* maybe. Zavattero wondered for a moment if the room were bugged.

But Westfield was no Burt Lancaster, and Zavattero's uneasiness disappeared when he said casually, "Pour yourself a drink," and sat up.

He was not a young man. He had first signed up with the Bureau of Mines in 1928.

"This damned heat," he said apologizing for his clothes. "I'll be glad to get back to Provo."

Zavattero nodded sympathetically.

"I've got almost all the information I need. I can go back to Provo once I find the logbook. I need that info—" He waited, looking curiously at Zavattero.

Zavattero nodded. So that's what they're worried about, he thought.

"You're interested in the logbook?" he asked noncommittally.

Westfield nodded.

"I have the book."

Westfield grinned, "Good, good," he said heartily.

As he watched Westfield, it hit Zavattero. If all Westfield needed were those log books, then that meant Lockheed had the meter and it explained the mysterious trip into the tunnel. It had not been for Demo's body.

"And I'm interested in that MCA-2 meter."

"Oh," Westfield said, not so heartily. Then after a long pause, "They've got it."

"Who's they?" (So he'd been right.)

"Lockheed."

"Where?"

"Burbank."

"Who's got it, and why the hell did they keep it?" Zavattero's voice was genuinely puzzled. It had been such a stupid thing to do.

Westfield shrugged.

Exasperated, Zavattero went on, "Why didn't they give it

to us? We've been asking for it."

Again Westfield shrugged. "I don't know."

Zavattero snorted, "Bull! You don't know. You're not working for the Bureau of Mines now, you're working for Lockheed."

"So?" Westfield poured himself another drink.

"So if Lockheed wants those logs, they'd better damn well give us that meter."

Zavattero could think of no other way to force Lockheed to surrender the meter except to dangle the gas logs over their heads. There was nothing on those logs, but Lockheed didn't know that. They could have tampered with the meter, but they couldn't erase what might be in those logs, unless they had them. They needed those logs. Bad.

Westfield stared into his whiskey glass for a long moment and then, with an imperceptible shrug, pursed his lips, "OK, so what do we do?"

"You have Lockheed bring that meter to the tunnel tomorrow so I can check it over. Then you wrap it, seal it, and send it to the Bureau of Mines."

Westfield sighed, "All right. Early?"

Zavattero nodded, set his drink down, and walked to the door, breathing a sigh of relief as he closed it behind him.

Inside Westfield stared after him, took a long drink, and muttered, "Well, you can't win 'em all."

When Zavattero returned to the house, it was still early, but the house seemed ominously quiet. It was just a little after nine, and the kids were usually still splashing around the pool. It was nice on a summer's night.

He felt uneasy, the same kind of uneasiness he'd felt at the Mission Hills Inn. There had been so many harrassing telephone calls lately that both he and George had had to have their telephone numbers changed. The calls had not been threats of violence exactly—just harrassing, and the meeting with Westfield had been far from reassuring.

When he opened the door, his daughters Gina and Paula and their friends were standing in the center of the room in their wet bathing clothes. They were clustered together and dripping like a forest of small trees caught in a summer storm. They looked frightened.

"What's up?" he asked Gina.

They all started talking at once. Mercy had been trying to chase their old dog away from the pool. Mercy had fallen and they were afraid her leg was broken. They didn't know whether to call an ambulance or not.

He calmed them down and turned to Mercy. She was lying on the couch, her arm thrown over her eyes, and he saw that her leg was badly twisted.

For a moment he felt a wave of irritation. He was supposed to be a safety engineer, and he couldn't even enforce a safety rule in his own house!

When he sat down beside Mercy and pulled her arm away from her eyes, he felt ashamed of his flash of irritation. Her dark eyes were wet and wide with pain and fear.

He took her hand and tried to reassure her. The young people, calmer now, offered to carry Mercy to the car so that he could take her to the hospital.

The trip to the hospital had been a short one. Mercy winced with pain when they moved her from the car, then near tears but smiling slightly, she almost wailed, "Oh, Wally, the one night you're home early, and this has to happen!" He kissed and grinned, "Don't worry, I'm going to prosecute the dog just as soon as I can find out which part of the safety code she violated."

Mercy's knee had been broken and her leg would be in a cast from hip to ankle for a long time. She was to remain in the hospital that night and possibly the next day. It looked as if they never would have that evening alone.

It was two A.M. before Zavattero left the hospital. On his way home, he wondered wearily if the day would never end. Tomorrow he had to try to get that meter out of Lockheed, if he had to blow up the Burbank plant to do it. If Westfield backed out of his agreement, he just might have to.

More than that he was worried. When he'd seen Mercy

lying there, he'd been scared. This whole thing was getting to him. He was beginning to be afraid of his own shadow.

About six hours later he was at the East Portal office. The tunnel was completely quiet. Without the movement of the muck trains, the locomotives and the bo-gangs working, the tunnel mouth gaped uselessly. Who knew when it would be working again?

In the trailer office he was glad to see that Savage was alone. There weren't too many times these days when Savage wasn't accompanied by Finkle. This often made him and Savage laugh. They couldn't talk to each other without an attorney. He didn't suppose it mattered much. Today's talk wouldn't be very pleasant.

Savage offered him a cup of black, gritty coffee which tasted surprisingly good in the early summer air. At least it wasn't mixed with smog.

Savage handed him the coffee and said amiably, "You look like hell."

Zavattero nodded. His eyes felt like something left over from the La Brea tar pits. He started to tell him about Mercy, but thought better of it. Savage was probably having enough trouble with Gwen and his own kids.

"Want a drink?" Savage asked. "There's some whiskey down at the change house."

Zavattero shook his head. "Just coffee. Where's Bob, by the way? I hear he quit Lockheed."

"He was going to, but they just transferred him. Bob Waters talked to him about it."

"Since when?"

"August 18. What do you care?"

"He's the one who took that damned meter, wasn't he?" Zavattero said, setting his coffee cup down as if the formalities were over.

Savage also set his cup down. "Look, Wally, I don't know any more than you do. They entered the tunnel without my knowledge. That's all I know, and I'm giving you a memo on that right now." As Savage sat down to write the memo,

Zavattero said "You'd better, because if you did know about it, you could be as guilty as they are for going over that yellow tag."

"All I know," Savage said, "is that Bob and Arvie and some cop went in and found the meter. That's all I know, and that's all you're going to find out from me!" Savage wasn't angry, just very, very sure of himself. "Well, it doesn't matter now. They're supposed to bring the meter over here today, and Westfield's going to send it to the Bureau of Mines."

"I heard something to that effect."

Abruptly Zavattero changed the subject, "How's Demo's wife?"

"Alright, I guess. I think she talked to Bucky." The union man had been the one most diligent in trying to bring some help and comfort to the wife of the still-undiscovered man.

At that moment, Finkle and another Lockheed executive, George Tomer, arrived.

With them they carried, as if it were some sacred chalice, the disputed meter wrapped in cloth and carried in a box.

It was a simple device, but in a tunnel probably more important than any piece of equipment except the fanlines that brought air into the hot and steaming underground. Its needle pointed the moment when the air in the tunnel had reached an explosive gas level.

Tomer set the meter down on the work-table and stepped back. Zavattero walked over to it and unwrapped it. He gaped at it for a moment astonished.

"What are you guys trying to pull? This isn't the same meter. It looks practically new."

Rapidly he checked over the meter. The serial number was right, but he had not recorded the machine number itself, and he cursed himself for it. This couldn't be the same meter!

He asked if any of them had touched the meter or handled it in any way. No one had. Tomer even pointed to a small rock encrusted with dirt that perched precariously on top of the meter as evidence that it had not been tampered with.

Zavattero laughed to himself. What did they think they were doing with that stupid pebble?

Still without the meter number, he was boxed. All he could do was make sure that the meter went to the Bureau of Mines and not to Lockheed's Truesdale lab. He knew Lockheed was hoping to keep the meter to send it to their own lab.

They weren't going to get it. He had promised them the logs in exchange for the meter and they weren't going to get them until he saw Westfield wrap and seal that meter to be sent to the Bureau of Mines.

As the four of them stood there watching Westfield wrap the meter, Zavattero wondered why they had taken it in the first place. He was certain that this was not the meter in the tunnel, but there was no way he could prove it.

Lockheed had kept the meter for a month, and had deliberately said nothing about it even though they knew everyone but the coroner was looking for the damned thing.

The Occupational Safety and Health Administration people had been asking for it since they first started investigating. Komar's speculation that it might have been the meter itself that set off the explosion made sense.

Whatever they had in mind, as far as Zavattero could tell, the meter, so long held in the vault at Burbank, no longer had any credibility no matter what Lockheed had hoped to prove by it. All Lockheed was likely to get out of it was a charge against them for concealing evidence. It would in fact, be tampering with evidence if the Division of Industrial Safety could prove it wasn't even the same meter.

Zavattero and Savage had agreed to meet for lunch that day and Zavattero hoped he could get him to talk after a few martinis. They'd all been drinking a lot lately, especially Ree.

Ree, he knew, wanted out. He was becoming a nervous wreck. There had always been a certain amount of tension between Ree and Savage, but now the hostility between them was hotly open. That, he suspected, was why Ree had tried to quit Lockheed, but agreed to a transfer instead.

In any event, he was pretty sure Lockheed didn't want

Ree running around shooting his mouth off. But what did he have to shoot his mouth off about? He was outside the tunnel when the explosion occurred, and had to take Savage's word for the gas readings. He wondered what was really bothering Ree, and also if Ree had been solely responsible for the phony finding of the meter. He had no doubt there was something phony about it, and about Lt. Lewis Biro's accidental presence.

It was true they'd all been pretty shaken by the deaths of the men in the tunnel, but Ree seemed to be taking it harder than anyone else.

Savage should be the one who was really sweating it out, but he seemed remarkably unperturbed. After the first night, when he had gone home almost physically shattered by the events, he only rarely mentioned the men whom he had liked and known so well.

His attitude sometimes puzzled Zavattero. Savage seemed almost to relish the complicated investigations and maneuverings going on over his head. The fussed and anxious faces of the top brass investigating the tunnel seemed to make him want to laugh.

Zavattero shook his head. Well, they'd talk later.

As Westfield finished wrapping and sealing the meter, Zavattero handed the logs to Finkle. There was nothing in them that would do their case a bit of good. In fact, there was nothing in them, period, but let them find that out for themselves.

As they left the hot and cluttered trailer, Finkle motioned to Zavattero to walk with him to his car.

Zavattero shook his head irritably, but then changed his mind and agreed to accompany the attorney.

He was getting awfully sick of Lockheed and its host of important people, ranging from attorneys to purchasing agents and experts like Westfield, brought in from distant places.

Savage and Ree, he understood. They were only half Lockheed men. First they were engineers, tunnel men.

But Finkle? What was he? He'd never been inside a

tunnel before he'd gone in with Johnson and McFettridge. Besides, he knew what Finkle wanted. He wanted to send that meter to the Truesdale lab. Well, he wasn't going to.

With Finkle at this point, it was all easy chatting and reassurances that Lockheed was anxious to do everything possible to discover the cause of the explosion. They felt that the meter would help them to determine the real cause. The Truesdale lab could do the job quicker, more efficiently than the federal agency. If Lockheed could send it to them, the taxpayers would be saved money, and Lockheed could do some really important work on testing devices and discover the real reason for the tragedy. He almost said tragedy in quotes as if he were about to wring the hearts of some distant jury with the depths of his emotion.

As he and Zavattero got into the car he added, "Besides, the whole thing is only a misdemeanor anyway."

Zavattero had started to light a cigarette, and for a moment he stared at the flame as it burned towards his fingertips. His hand began to tremble slightly and he shook the match. When Zavattero spoke his voice was tight as a wire.

"Misdemeanor! Misdemeanor! Loren's been giving me that garbage. Sure it's just a misdemeanor. You've all seen to that. There isn't a corporation or contractor that hasn't worked us over. Safety doesn't mean a damned thing. You just got a few careless employees. Never a negligent employer, and if he is, so what? It's only a misdemeanor!

"Well, I've seen enough misdemeanors in this state. All you bastards can talk about is misdemeanors. You sound like a bunch of cats who crap on the carpet and are only squalling because you might have your noses rubbed in it. It doesn't hurt, you just don't want to smell bad.

"Believe me, you can't bury this one. There were seventeen men killed in that tunnel. I helped pull them out piece by burnt piece. They were men, not mouthpieces.

"I've worked in tunnel and mine safety for seven years and I've seen men maimed, crushed, scraped to the bone by lousy equipment, electrocuted, and just plain killed. And you know why?" Zavattero jabbed a blunt finger at the Lockheed attorney. "Because some smart lawyer figured out how to spread a few bucks around and turn manslaughter into misdemeanor.

"What happened in that tunnel wasn't even manslaughter. It was murder. OK, legally it's a misdemeanor. Well—that misdemeanor somebody is going to pay for up to the bloody hilt, and I'm going to see to it because I wrote those orders.

"And you can tell that to Hix or Waters or anybody else in Seattle or Burbank or wherever they're holding these meetings to figure out ways to sweep this under the carpet."

Zavattero let out a long breath. He felt relieved.

Finkle stared at the clock on the dashboard as if time held an answer. "OK, Wally, calm down. I don't make the laws, you know."

Then a hard edge crept into Finkle's usually smooth voice. "Besides, I don't know what good you think it's going to do you. You're the only one who's so gung-ho about prosecution and all you've got is a few minor violations of the labor code. The city attorney's office doesn't seem very interested in any of it."

"Yeah," Zavattero said with disgust as he got out of the car.

As he walked back to his own car Zavattero felt completely deflated and just a little annoyed with himself. For weeks he'd been complaining about everyone acting like a bunch of maniacs, and now he was acting like one himself.

Besides, Finkle was right. It was now August 27 and no notice of prosecution had gone to the city attorney's office, and the assembly hearings were to start on September 2.

And to top it all off, Mercy was in the hospital with a broken leg.

He felt depressed as hell.

CHAPTER FIVE

In the city attorney's office, Roger Arnebergh, who had been city attorney for twenty years, was thinking about lunch at the club where he could chat amiably with some of the city's most important lights. Not the least of those lights were Lockheed's attorneys from O'Melvany & Meyers. He was trying not to think about the Lockheed tunnel disaster, and the formal request for prosecution by the Division of Industrial Safety.

He supposed that they'd have to follow through on the prosecution for concealing evidence. There was, after all, going to be a full-scale assembly hearing, and Assemblyman Jack Fenton, was known to be a harsh and sarcastic interrogator. Most of that harshness and sarcasm would hopefully be directed at the Division of Industrial Safety rather than Lockheed, but still, too much foot lagging from the city attorney's office could hardly go unnoticed. It was responsible for prosecuting safety violations.

So thought Roger Arnebergh. He was a thin, precise man, who had always managed to keep out of the public eye.

He was, in fact, Lockheed's kind of man. He kept a low profile. He was a man Lockheed could understand. He had no chivalric desire to rake through the muck of that doomed tunnel. His was more an appreciation for the fruits of the earth—like real estate in which he had been making considerable money. Lockheed could appreciate that. They themselves had just reported a $3 million profit in real estate. Not a large sum for Lockheed, but tidy enough.

Arnebergh's office specialized in civil cases, lawsuits against the city for damages, and the like. The criminal section of his office handled such misdemeanor cases as the tunnel disaster, but that section was deemed by most deputies to be unimportant at best and ineffectual at worst. There were few funds for investigation in the event of prosecution.

Arnebergh had taken to heart one of the most important lessons of politics—to make his office sound unimportant. He played it low-keyed and quiet. He had been pleased to observe to his influential friends that he was never involved in controversy, and had been returned to office for nearly twenty years without a contest. Lockheed had little reason to fear that Arnebaugh's office would prosecute the Sylmar disaster.

Arnebergh was annoyed at the stupidity of the meter theft. He would have to go through the motions of prosecution of Lockheed for concealing evidence. That was certain. However, the statute of limitations on any misdemeanor was only a year. Perhaps, the whole thing could bog down in technical details until the year had past. In the law, stalling around for a year was really no problem at all.

Nevertheless, he would have to assign someone to the case. He thought of George Bane. George was young, not too long out of law school, and a good Republican with a feel for business. It figured: George Bane it would be.

That was a decision he was going to regret. It would cost him his office after all those sweet, soft, uncontroversial years.

After his blowup at Finkle, Zavattero continued to feel depressed. He had reported back to his own office, and there Crabtree had again asked him if he insisted on the prosecution. He looked as if he were about to start on a speech about educating contractors instead of prosecuting them. It was Hatton's party line and Crabtree had recited it often.

"We prosecute," said Zavattero flatly. As Crabtree started to speak, Zavattero waved him down. Between clenched teeth he said, "Do not tell me about how cooperative employers are when they understand and are given the opportunity to discipline themselves in the matters of safety. I've heard it all. I don't need to hear it again." Zavattero paused. He was not going to start another tirade about misdemeanors like the one at the tunnel with Finkle. His voice was calmer as he went on. "Whatever happens, you can bet it won't cost Lockheed much!" He turned on his heel and stalked toward the door. There would be no tirade, but he sure as hell was going to slam the door on his way out. He did.

He felt a little better when he joined Savage and Ree for lunch. In spite of the tense feelings over the demand for the meter, everyone seemed almost cheerful.

All the talk was about assembly hearings which were to start in five days. Loren Savage, Zavattero, George Denton, Bucky Micelli, and who knows who else had gotten subpoenas.

They had all talked several times with Johnson and McFettridge, but the two legislative investigators either didn't know much more than they did, or, if they did, were not talking.

Zavattero wondered if the whole hearing wasn't really just a fishing expedition.

Savage agreed that it probably was and said, "They don't know what they're going to catch, but you can bet we're going to read about it in the newspapers."

"And see it on TV," said Ree, who seemed surprisingly cheerful considering his part in the meter incident.

"And Keysor will write about it in his newsletter to us constituents," Zavattero added. Keysor was the chairman of the committee and assemblyman in Zavattero's own district in Granada Hills.

Suddenly Zavattero said, "Why the hell did you guys take that meter? Whatever credibility the instrument had is gone now. Look, why don't you tell me. It doesn't matter, I'm just curious."

For a moment Ree looked abashed, "Oh, come on Wally. Forget it."

"What the hell did you say to Finkle this morning. He didn't like it." Savage asked.

Zavattero shrugged, "Nothing much. I just told him what I thought." Then he added, "I like Dave Finkle. He's OK, but I wish he'd quit acting like he was working for God. Lockheed's only driving a tunnel, not creating the world in six days."

They all laughed and signaled for another drink. When the pretty, harried waitress brushed right past them into the dark vastness of the Fin & Feathers, Ree stood up. "I'll get 'em." he said.

As Ree left, Zavattero carefully buttered a piece of French bread. He did not look at Savage. He was worried about the assembly hearings. Nobody really knew what their plans were, or what questions they would be asking. Johnson and McFettridge had been reassuring but vague.

Zavattero wondered if they would ask the one question that kept burning in his mind. "Loren, why the hell did you do it? Did you get orders from Seattle? Did Hix tell you to get your ass back in that tunnel or what?" Zavattero believed that this must have happened. Hix was Savage's boss in Seattle and there was little love between the two men.

Loren Savage shook his head impatiently.

Exasperated, Zavattero said, "Come off it Loren. You're too good an engineer not to know what was happening. You know all about gas buildup when the ventilation is on a blow system. Why'd you take those men back in and damn near get yourself killed, too. All I want to know is why, why?"

Suddenly, as if making a decision, Savage said, "Look, Wally, I can't tell you now. Someday maybe, but not now."

Ree had caught the end of Savage's remark as he brought drinks to the table, spilling them with a splash that made a small puddle in front of each of the three men.

"I could tell you plenty—" Ree started.

"Oh shut up, Bob. You don't know anything," Savage interrupted harshly.

Ree's eyes widened in surprise. "I thought . . ." he blurted, but his voice trailed off.

The three men finished their drinks in silence.

September 2 dawned hot, as if the city had held its heat all night, and, at the first sign of the sun, expelled it over the city.

Zavattero and his wife and daughter did not talk much during breakfast of eggs with tortillas. They had to be just the right texture and thinness or the Zavatteros would return them to whomever was misguided enough to try to palm second-rate tortillas off on them.

Mercy, in spite of her broken leg in its cumbersome cast, was determined to attend the first day of the assembly hearings, and nothing could have kept fourteen-year-old Gina from going. Mercy's friend would drive them, and Bucky Micelli would take them in charge at the hearings. A kindly man, he had offered to protect them from too much questioning.

It was strangely exciting to them all, as if it were all some sort of performance—which in many ways it was.

It was no prosecution, much to Zavattero's increasing despair. He had not told Mercy, but he had frankly given up any hope that the division would move to prosecute. Ever since the day he had forced Lockheed to give up the meter, Zavattero had been increasingly depressed.

He drove slowly to the San Fernando Valley City Hall where the meetings were to be held. He didn't much care what they asked him. He'd tell them that he thought the whole division, plus Lockheed, plus the Metropolitan Water District, stunk.

At least the parking was easy enough, though there seemed to be quite a few cars already there when he arrived.

As he got out of the car, a young man, rather short and very well dressed, came towards him. Who now? he thought. This man was neither a tunnel stiff nor did he look like a newspaper or media man, though there were enough of them floating around.

The young man was carefully coiffed, well groomed, and

wore a vest even though it was such a hot day. The vest gave him the look of a fighting cock surveying the terrain as he moved toward Zavattero.

He thrust out his hand and his eyes were smiling, a nice smile, unaffectedly warm. "Hi, I'm George Bane," he said. Zavattero nodded and wondered again who the hell this one was. "I'm from the city attorney's office," Bane said.

Zavattero's eyes widened. "Oh?" he said curiously. Then looking at the scene around him he added. "Come to see the festivities?"

As cars began to arrive, along with TV trucks and assorted other official-looking vehicles, there was a certain carnival air about it all. Zavattero wondered if someone had the hot dog concession and who was going to be the barker. Not that there was any need to pull them in off the streets. It looked as if everyone who had ever been near the tunnel was showing up.

Zavattero found to his surprise that he did not feel particularly nervous. After all, he had appeared in a number of court cases concerning the industrial safety code. Anyway, he'd been too discouraged lately to feel anything.

"No, I'm here to see that you don't say anything prejudicial to the prosecution."

Zavattero gaped at him. "They're going to prosecute? Since when? Nobody told us anything about it."

"Since August 30," Bane told him. "Can we talk?"

Zavattero nodded. He wasn't scheduled to appear immediately, and whatever happened he'd hear it on the tapes being made by his friend, Bill Ross, another safety engineer. Now he wanted to know what the prosecution was going to be, and when.

The talk they had that day was a long one. They needed to talk. Bane knew far better than Zavattero the grueling, time-consuming effort that this first prosecution would take. Further suits were being prepared, but this first one was all-important.

Bane explained that this prosecution would be aimed primarily at convicting Lockheed for concealing the MSA

Explosive meter.

"What about the wrongful death violations?" Zavattero asked.

Bane nodded again. "Most of them will be dealt with in another prosecution. This time we prosecute Otha G. Ree and Lockheed Shipbuilding and Construction Company only."

For a moment Zavattero looked as if he were going to protest, but shrugged, "OK."

As they walked toward the courthouse Bane explained to him that the city attorney's office could do only a limited investigation. It would be up to Zavattero and George Denton to do the investigating, and they would be the ones to sign the complaint when the time came. Would Zavattero be willing to do it?

Zavattero gave a snort of laughter. "You'd better believe!" As they walked on, he felt good, or at least not so dejected. He'd felt for weeks like he'd been trying to drive a tunnel with a toothpick. At least Don Quixote had an honest-to-God spear to tilt at his windmills. He felt better. He wondered if Mercy would be relieved.

At last there would actually be a prosecution against Lockheed. It puzzled him that it had all moved so sluggishly, and now when the confrontation came, it was the result of Ree's bizarre performance with the meter—an action undeniably criminal under the penal code. Yet it really didn't mean too much, the concealing evidence case, compared to what had happened the night Sylmar blew up.

He shook his head. The ways of the law, he concluded, were wondrous indeed.

The San Fernando City Hall was a one-story building as monotonous and uninspired as most of the rest of the San Fernando Valley terrain.

The assembly hearings were to be held in one of the larger hearing rooms. It was assumed that there would be a large audience. The assumption was right.

There was a large crowd murmuring intense whispers,

most of them carrying newspapers. The benediction of the air-conditioner whirred over their heads. At least it would be cool. Whatever sweating would be done would not be caused by heat, but what would come from that strange conglomerate of organs and glands that generates in everyone the smell of fear, the anxious dread of the unknown.

As Zavattero and Bane walked in, Zavattero looked around for Mercy and Gina. He could not find them. Bane nodded to him curtly and took a seat back in the crowd. He was not there to take any legal stance—yet. He was there simply to assess the strengths of proposed prosecution and its witnesses. His note taking was constant but unobtrusive.

Zavattero found a seat near the front and sat down. He nodded to Loren Savage who was seated directly behind him, staring down at his shoes, motionless except for the arc of his hand as he smoked one cigarette after another.

Zavattero wondered why Ree was not sitting with Savage. Ree was in the far back, seated a little aside from the crowd. He looked like he was sweating. His hands hung down between his knees and occasionally he would wipe his face nervously, pressing his hands to his eyes as if to seal them shut.

From a short distance away Jack Johnson was watching Ree thoughtfully, and, Zavattero realized, so was Jerry McFettridge, who was seated at the dais along with members of the committee. He wondered what was up. Somewhere a train whistle blew.

Along with McFettridge at the front were the members of the committee. They were shuffling papers around, chatting and making the usual preliminary small talk. Someone made a joke and it flew like a fly from mouth to mouth causing each mouth to open briefly like a fish taking bait. The laughter subsided and the chairman, Jim Keyser, picked up the gavel.

When the gavel fell, everyone was silent, as if a motor had been turned off. Everyone except the attorneys seated in front. McNary and Finkle were exchanging notes in rapid whispers. Beside them was the man from the attorney general's office. Zavattero assumed he was there to protect the interests of the

Division of Industrial Safety. There appeared to be no one there to provide assistance for Ree, unless there was someone lost in the crowd like Bane.

As Keysor's light, pleasant voice began making the introduction, Dave Finkle turned to look back at Ree. Then he whispered uneasily to McNary and the two of them rose, stooping a little politely, as one does when leaving a theater. McNary sat down beside Ree and Finkle remained standing. They did not appear to be trying to calm the obviously agitated Ree down, but seemed to be urging him to do something.

Nearby, Jack Johnson watched them carefully. In his notebook he jotted a brief note to be given to McFettridge. Ree was saying, "I hope they put me on the stand. I'll tell them what really happened." His whispering was an angry, barely audible hiss. When someone turned to stare at him with annoyance, he stopped and again wiped his face, pressing his eyes closed.

Johnson made a mental note to talk to Ree himself, as soon as the hearing was over. He did not want to talk to him with his attorneys present. He felt remiss that he and McFettridge had not paid more attention to Ree, who was acting like the weak link in some overlooked chain of events.

Johnson never had the chance. The next day, the second day of the hearings, Ree disappeared.

Keysor's voice blended with the whir of the air-conditioners as he concluded his statement of the committee's intent to "examine safety orders, the labor code as it applies to tunnels, and general safety requirements for protection of persons engaged in hazardous work."

He assured everyone that the intent was not to name responsible parties, but that subpoenas issued were for appearance before the committee only, without any promise of immunity from criminal prosecution.

Zavattero wondered if the committee knew why Bane from the city attorney's office was there. Apparently not.

In spite of the simple statement of intent, there was

actually a mixed bag of motives for the assembly investigation.

There was, no doubt, genuine concern for the men who had died in the Lockheed tunnel. But for at least two members of the committee there were sound political reasons. Reagan had been cutting budgets with the exuberance of a farm boy wielding a scythe in a field of new corn. Some of those budget cuts had been in the Division of Industrial Safety, and the holocaust at Sylmar might curb some of the governor's exuberance. And in addition, there had been considerable heat generated by their constituencies, who expressed an honest desire to know what was happening in the Division of Industrial Safety.

If they had asked Zavattero, he would have told them. He and nearly everyone else in the field knew that the Division of Industrial Safety had been in a sloppy state for some time and had been growing sloppier since Reagan had appointed Jack Hatton, ex-safety director for Lockheed, as head of the division.

Zavattero had no reservations about the investigation. He hoped it would lead to a more effective safety law. Though he felt some mistrust of the political motives of the Democrat-dominated committee—he himself was a Republican—he still had hopes.

The committee, composed of two Democrats and one Republican, would be dominated by one man, Jack Fenton, assemblyman from Montebello.

Jim Keysor was the chairman, but with his amiable, boyish face and rather thin, searching voice, he had little force. Newton Russell, the only Republican, was a necessarily somewhat subdued minority, but seemed genuinely earnest in his questioning. Or so Zavattero thought, but then Zavattero was also a Republican.

Jack Fenton was something else. Fenton was tall and angular. He wore high-heeled boots with easy indifference, as if to prove he didn't mind being tall. His hair was bushy black and his voice was even blacker, a strong, compelling voice that took over the proceedings within minutes. And he did have flair.

The interrogation was to begin with the politically powerful Metropolitan Water District, owner of the tunnel. The Metropolitan Water District had been formed in the 1930s to bring water from the Colorado River to Los Angeles, San Diego, Ventura and Orange Counties, and to parts of San Bernardino and Riverside. Five pumping plants, each with nine pumps powerful enough to push 91,500 gallons of water a minute, forced the water across the Mojave Desert and over the mountains from Parker Dam on the Colorado River. Pasadena, the Rose Bowl city and a member of the Metropolitan Water District, received the first water on June 17, 1941, just before a spell of dry years.

Since then the agency had grown in power, run by a board of directors, politically appointed and not answerable to the public at election time.

On March 11, 1969, the Board of Directors of the Metropolitan Water District had awarded Lockheed the contract for the building of the Sylmar tunnel which was to bring water from the Feather River instead of the Colorado. The bidding had been competitive and when the contract with Lockheed was signed, the company was promised bonuses by the Metropolitan Water District as an incentive to early completion of the project. The job progressed well but the line between speed and reckless disregard of men's lives was a fine one. On that hot June night, someone had stepped over it.

The Metropolitan Water District was as vulnerable as any of the other corporate entities involved, to charges of having been a party to stepping over that line.

There had been the promised bonuses for early completion. Lockheed had everything to gain from haste. Then, too, the geological reports were open to question. They had rather optimistically assumed that, though there was a possibility of encountering oil and gas, it was not significant. The Sylmar disaster had proved them more than mistaken. At least Lockheed had considered it so and was making the point in a $10 million breach of contract suit. It accused the district of failing to warn the company of possible damage from the February 9, 1971 earthquake, or of the real danger of the gas and oil. In addition, one of Metropolitan Water District's own men had been killed in the tunnel, and that made them, as well as Lockheed, open to prosecution.

The MWD was indeed vulnerable, and when its representatives were subpoenaed to appear before the committee, there was some fear that the MWD might be hit with all the force of the ninety-odd thousand gallons of water being pumped each minute through its $11 billion water project.

Burdened with the weight of the MWD's responsibility was Garland Grey, their resident engineer in the San Fernando Valley. With him, Fenton was to step in and show his special virtuosity. Fenton was a lawyer as well as an expert politician and he knew all the tricks. He was completely in accord with the avowed purposes of the hearings, to discover the cause of the explosion, examine the effectiveness of the safety codes, and not assign responsibility. He also sensed quite accurately that guilt was spilling over the hearing room like a runnel of mud seeping from the shafts and portals of the tunnel.

Besides, the TV cameras were at the ready. (However, while such background material as they had acquired was necessary it was hardly the stuff of drama.)

The present line of questioning showed more promise. Newton Russell was questioning Garland Grey concerning the extent of awareness in the district that a serious hazard existed following the flash fire on the night of June 22.

Russell was prodding Grey gently: "So at the time of the—between the first fire and the final, disastrous one, when the men went back into this tunnel, you at that time, or whoever was in charge at that time, did not deem it necessary or particularly dangerous to absent themselves from that particular area, is that correct?"

Grey replied to the tangled question as if he knew what he was being asked. "That man is not with us," he said, seeming verbally to cast his eyes heavenward.

Russell only faltered for a moment, then, with a slight blink said "Well, OK. Then he was one of the seventeen."

Grey nodded, still solemn, "Right."

Russell continued his gentle prodding to determine how much the Metropolitan Water District knew of the dangers and whether there had been suggestions that their men be removed from the tunnel. None of the answers was very enlightening and Grey faded off into mumblings about "an area of extreme caution."

As Russell concluded and Grey started to get up with an almost audible sigh, he was stopped by the chairman who indicated that Assemblyman Fenton had a question.

Fenton, who had been leaning back, watching carefully and occasionally jotting a note, suddenly leaned forward toward the man at the witness table. He was about to take over. His approach would be quite, quite different. His voice matched the thrust of his body. His questions would be short and harshly probing, vastly different from Russell's quiet prodding.

He eyed the Metropolitan Water District's engineer coolly for a moment and asked quietly, "Mr. Grey, you're the tunnel engineer for this project?"

Grey, still a little lost in the low-key, humble image of himself projected during the encounter with Russell, replied "Just an engineer for the Metropolitan Water District."

There was nothing politely subdued about Fenton's statement regarding the "man who is not with us." He said, "The gentleman who was one of the seventeen that got killed, he was under you?"

Grey nodded, "Correct."

Fenton's voice was touched with reproach in his next question, "He went down but you didn't. Correct?"

"On that ship, yes." Grey said, rising to the occasion. His manner suggested that he spent most of his working day preparing himself to go down with the water tunnels of the Metropolitan Water District.

Fenton made a brief note asking "Well, did you ever go down subsequent to the flash fire?"

"No." Grey shook his head. He looked embarrassed. Fenton had obviously not shared his own view of himself as the humble custodian of a foundering vessel.

"Why?" Fenton persisted. "I had a blood clot in my leg and I couldn't climb the shaft." This time Grey looked abashed as though he'd been caught malingering.

Fenton glanced at him, and then, as if he had established a point and set the scene, his questioning became direct and matter-of-fact.

FENTON: Did you ever go down previous to this?
GREY: Correct. I did.
FENTON: Were you aware of the conditions that division put on after the flash fire?
GREY: I was not informed.
FENTON: Was anyone in your department informed?
GREY: No.
GREY: Well, let me ask you, in your experience when there is a flash fire with the indication the gas is there, don't you then subsequently, at least as far as your personnel are concerned, concern yourself with the problems that involve subsequent thereto and prior thereto as to the safety to your personnel?
GREY: Correctly, I do.
FENTON: Then you didn't contact the Division of Safety afterwards to find out what measures they then recommended subsequent to the flash fire that you say would affect the workers?
GREY: I did not contact them nor did they contact me.
FENTON: Well, then how do you become aware of the hazardous conditions and how hazardous it is?
GREY: The state does not contact us directly.
FENTON: No, no, I understand that but you had a flash fire. Isn't that correct? And that alerted you to the fact that

Part 1/Prosecution   *83*

some hazardous condition was there. You had personnel connected with your water district such as the gentleman who is now deceased, who went down in the tunnel, who was subjected to the possible dangers therein, so subsequent thereto, your department, your engineering department, took no steps to find out from the Division of Safety what measures they recommended should be taken, and whether these measure were taken. You let your personnel still go down in the tunnel. Is that correct?

GREY: That's correct.

When he turned the inquiry back over to Chairman Keysor, Fenton had established the fact that his interrogation would differ markedly from that of the other two members of the panel. Though the panel's avowed intent was not to place responsibility but determine causes, his queries would definitely range somewhere between nudging reproach and outright accusation. That, he figured, was what he owed his constitutents. Keysor did not know it, but he had lost dominance of the committee of which he was chairman, though he would do a creditable job. As the proceedings continued Keysor would be so overpowered by Fenton that the chairman would even take on some of the other man's locutions.

Zavattero watched all this with considerable interest. What he had heard about Fenton was true. He was tough and sarcastic. Though he had no particular regard for Garland Grey, Zavattero couldn't help but feel a little sorry for him. But most of all he wondered where Fenton was heading.

Apparently no place with the Metropolitan Water District as far as Zavattero could discern. The next person called up was Dick Balerczak. Balerczak was the one who had phoned him the night of the explosion. How he'd sounded scared! Zavattero waited to see what would happen to him before the committee.

Little did happen. Balerczak's questioning was mostly technical and he answered the questions with what seemed to be relieved precision. Next up would be the Division of Industrial Safety.

With the spotlight switched to the Division of Industrial Safety, the panel found the first tangible object to gnaw on, and gnaw on it they did.

It was no vague contractual agreement, no lofty statement of purposes, no fuzzy references to areas of responsibility, no dimly perceived commitment to the working man and management, no spongy hinterland of geological research and pico formations.

It was quite tangible. It was a red tag, and it's existence was to provide Fenton with his most dramatic triumph, and Zavattero with his bleakest hour.

Not that its uses weren't as murky as any alluvial substratum of geology (this soon became apparent under the scrutiny of the committee), but most important, it was tangible. It could be held in the hand and described.

The description of the red tag was given by Jack Hatton, first to be called as a witness for the Division of Industrial Safety. Hatton was the head of the division. Many of the men called him "Fat Jack." An amiable leader, former Lockheed safety engineer spending his time in a sinecure—a nest feathered by the largesse of Ronald Reagon—disturbed almost never except by the sigh of air escaping from the naughahide cushion of his swivel chair. He had come confidently to the committee without bothering with a prepared statement such as the one Metropolitan Water District had presented. When asked about the red tag he was marvelously precise:

"The red tag is a square tag about 4 inches by 4 inches, and it states on there that a member of the Safety Division has been through it, and it is put on the people at that particular place that such conditions have been observed. It does not have the legal significance of the yellow tag which is a special order, and this yellow tag legally can shut the job down where the red tag cannot."

That was about the last clear statement made on the subject. This time Fenton moved in and took over so positively that Keysor wouldn't be able to drown him out again, no matter how loud he hollered in what he boyishly referred to in his "Sacramento Reports" column as his "loudest bleacher voice."

Keysor may have been the chairman, but Fenton was the star. Just by his manner he had lifted the dull recital of technical data to the height of drama. The news media relished it, and one newspaper gave an almost verbatim account of Fenton's encounters with the Division of Industrial Safety's witnesses.

The story read:

The Industrial Safety Division it was learned has a system whereby it uses a red or yellow tag to indicate a hazard to workers.

After lengthy questioning and several contradictory statements as to what the red and yellow tags indicate, Fenton exclaimed, "This is ridiculous."

Hatton explained that a red tag indicates a hazard which should be corrected but that work still may continue. A yellow tag, he continued, indicates a hazard serious enough to warrant shutting down the project until the hazard is eliminated.

"If I'm on a job and you know something which would make it hazardous for me to work," Fenton demanded, "how can you allow me to continue working?"

Harold Crabtree, Senior Safety Engineer of the Division of Industrial Safety construction section, explained the tagging system differently.

"A yellow tag is issued after a red tag if there is non-compliance with the first order," he said, adding that the inspector must show cause to issue a yellow tag.

"Do you mean to tell me an inspector cannot shut down a project on the spot if there is a hazard so serious as to make it dangerous to continue?" Fenton asked.

"Yes," Crabtree replied, "the field inspector has the authority to shut the job down."

"Then what are the tags for?" Fenton asked.

"That's just our procedure," Crabtree responded.

Fenton said after the meeting, "I still don't know what red and yellow tags are for or what the difference is between them."

The news story had made no reference to a brief encounter Fenton had with Zavattero about the red tag, but instead went on to conclude with an account of Fenton's freewheeling tactics with Lockheed.

The assemblyman has asked Zavattero if it were true that he had not red tagged the tunnel because it had already been closed down by Savage, and he'd said yes. Fenton had then asked "Wouldn't it be more logical as a procedural matter to red tag it to make sure that the men don't go back in on the job until you make an investigation, make your recommendations?"

Zavattero had answered, "I agree."

The story concluded:

Also at the hearing, controversy flared up over whether or not newsmen should be admitted on the inspection tour of the tunnel.

David Finkle told the subcommittee and the roomful of reporters and cameramen that only one newsman—and no camera equipment—would be allowed.

Keysor severely criticized the decision, saying, "It is important that this committee let the public see this tunnel."

Finkle said Lockheed did not want to risk any pretrial publicity referring to a pending federal hearing over Department of Labor charges of "willful negligence."

"This can't be a subsidiary of the same Lockheed which utilized the news media so extensively to gain a government loan," Fenton declared sarcastically. This brought a laugh from the audience.

In regard to pretrial publicity, Fenton stated, "Let's

not kid ourselves, Mr. Finkle. I'm an attorney too. You know as well as I do that if you get any unfavorable publicity you'll ask to have the charges dropped on grounds of prejudicial pretrial publicity."

Zavattero said he felt that newsmen and their equipment would not create a hazard.

That had been true. Zavattero, in fact, had been watching the interchange between Fenton and Finkle with some amusement.

With Zavattero's blessing, the assemblymen and newsmen had been allowed to enter the sealed tunnel.

There had been nothing really newsworthy about the trip except a picture of Fenton and Keysor preparing to descend in the heavy, wire cage of the man lift, but it had been nevertheless an awesome experience.

At the East Portal on McClay Street where the locomotives and muck cars entered the tunnel there was the comfort of light being filtered into the tunnel from the mouth of the tunnel. But from the Gate shaft, far beyond the portal, the men were dropped in the heavy cage straight down into the earth. There was no chain of lights now to lighten the tunnel and the long, silent core of earth was frightening. Not with the reasonable fear of a cave in, or even an explosion, but unreasoning, primitive fear. Mud shifted like gargoyle shadows and the distant sound of running water was like the River Styx waiting to carry them all through the dark tomb of the tunnel to the eternal underworld form which there was no return.

The men who worked underground were at least accustomed to all this, but to those who had gathered there to view, as they thought, the scene of the disaster, it was unnerving. When they finally emerged from the Gate shaft, the jollity and camaraderie of the picture taking with the press was gone. No one seemed to feel particularly loquacious, not even the reporters.

The descent had not particularly affected Zavattero. He

had slogged through the muck and silt so many times since the night of the explosion that he almost felt that he knew every grimace on the face of the gargoyle shadows. Yet it was never an easy trip. He was glad when he got home.

He was anxious to tell Mercy about his meeting with Bane, and the first flickering of hope that there would indeed be a prosecution. His spirits lifted with every mile away from Sylmar. At home everything seemed cheerfully normal. Mercy lay on the couch glaring angrily at the cast on her leg and giving equally angry orders to her daughters about preparing dinner. This chore they were performing cheerfully, with little regard to the instructions being called out by their frustrated mother. The dinner might not be a classic, Zavattero thought, but it would sure taste good after all the heat of the hearing room and the dank gloom of the tunnel.

As he sat down beside Mercy and took her hands, he was surprised at how icy cold they were even though the day was so hot. He was a little worried about her. Lately she had seemed so miserably on edge, as if anger were the only way to fight back an avalanche of tears.

Still he was surprised when she asked him irritably and without preamble why he had agreed with Fenton about putting a red tag on the tunnel.

For a moment he was completely bewildered. He had been so engrossed in the rest of the hearings that he had not given a thought to the brief interchange between him and Fenton.

His agreeing to Fenton's question wouldn't have changed anything, but it would have been protection for him. Suddenly looking at it from her point of view, he realized his agreement could look like self-condemnation. He wondered uneasily what Fenton had in mind, but at the moment he wasn't worried about Fenton.

Still holding both her hands in his trying to warm them, he said soothingly, "Look honey, there is nothing to worry about. After the way Crabtree and Hatton fumbled around over those damn tags, they must know how meaningless that red tag can be. It's true I should have red tagged the tunnel. It would have saved my skin because the division would have been the ones to pull it off. And they would have the minute Lockheed got to Hatton. They did it before, remember?"

Mercy nodded, allowing herself to be reassured, "Yeah, but still—" she faltered, "I just don't trust that Fenton."

"I know," he said, "Now come on. Let's have dinner and forget the whole thing for tonight," and as he said that he meant it. He *was* going to forget the whole thing for tonight. He decided he would not tell Mercy about his talk with Bane. He didn't have the heart to tell her that there was more to come. With the hearings, it had only just begun. Tonight they would enjoy themselves and at least tomorrow the damned assembly hearings would be over.

That's what he thought.

CHAPTER SIX

The next day when he walked into the hearing room, it was as if the whole scene had been held over-night by a stop action camera. Everyone had taken the same places. Savage was behind him still smoking one cigarette after another. McNary and Finkle were seated in front, and the miners he had recognized the day before were all seated in the same places. The committee seemed to be shuffling the same papers and repeating the same conversation.

However, the exchange of jokes was different. It was no longer a private matter between the legislators, but one that could now be shared with the audience.

And for once Keysor was able to one-up Fenton. As they prepared for the first witness—a senior safety engineer, John Jepson—Fenton spoke laughingly, "Mr. Chairman, while he is coming up, could I ask you, was I red tagged here today? There is a little note here that this microphone mustn't be used in an unfriendly manner. I don't understand what a red tag does anyhow. Was this from the chairman?"

Keyser's reply was also a laughing one, "No it wasn't from me. But if you think it was bad for you, you were only red tagged. I was yellow tagged." Laughter rippled through the hearing room and Keyser's faint smile was almost a smirk of triumph. Fenton was hard to handle.

That was the last note of jocularity struck that day. The trip into the tunnel and the visible evidence of burned and twisted machinery had given the legislators a sense of urgency about discovering what could have caused such havoc.

Though the committee intended to continue its policy of determining the cause of the explosion, there remained still a faint echo of accusation. The cause might emerge if only they could ferret out one guilty party. Lockheed's representatives still hoped that eventually God would emerge as the culprit. All others were divided on the subject.

Zavattero knew Jepson as a capable engineer with twenty-two years experience, primarily in the construction section, and leaned forward, interested in how Jepson would fare with the red tag-yellow tag imbroglio.

He seemed to fare better than the others. His explanation was at least free of the evasive fuzziness of Hatton and Crabtree. His statement regarding the power of the red tag was straightforward, and Zavattero thought, helpful.

ASSEMBLYMAN NEWTON R. RUSSELL: By *tag* you mean a yellow tag?

JEPSON: No, the red tag, of which I have a copy here, is just a warning tag.

RUSSELL: They have to show cause before they do that?

JEPSON: No, sir. These are the preliminary warning tags. If the job is unsafe, we post that. But the power behind this tag is the fact organized labor has recognized and cooperated with the division over the years so when it's tagged or a job's tagged or portion of a job, they no longer work there until the employer has corrected the condition that our field engineer has given them to correct.

The testimony that followed rather surprised Zavattero.

He had not been aware that Jepson had offered his assistance in the situation. There was rarely any communication in the sections though they were under the same supervision. However, as he thought of it he realized how important it must have seemed to Jepson who knew that there had been seventeen outstanding requirements by the electrical section. These requirements had not been complied with at the time of the explosion. Zavattero had not known of these requirements, nor had Savage or anyone else informed him of them.

FENTON: When did you first hear of the explosion of the Sylmar tunnel—the first explosion—the fire on the 23?

JEPSON: The morning of June the 23 on radio, on my way into the office that morning.

RUSSELL: Did you confer with many of your supervisors that day relative to action that should be initiated?

JEPSON: Yes sir, I did, and the reason being that there was a situation that existed in our construction section, Los Angeles office, that I was concerned with. As a regular senior engineer, Mr. Zavattero's immediate supervisor was gone on a training period for that week and there was a young engineer sitting in there, field engineer, acting in his place who had a little or no tunnel experience to my knowledge. I then went to our assistant chief's office, Mr. Signer.

Jepson went on stating that he had explained to the assistant chief that the preliminary flash fire had been a warning and more serious things would follow. He then offered his services, but Signer had informed him that he was in touch with Mr. Zavattero "and that Wally was on top of it as far as he was concerned" and declined Jepson's offer of assistance.

At the conclusion of that statement Zavattero smiled slightly. Not only had he not been aware of Jepson's offer, but he had also been unaware of Signer's confidence in him, and doubted that it was all that great. But it sounded good and explained why it had taken Signer so long to get to the tunnel even after the fatal explosion.

It bothered Zavattero that the committee seemed to be so hung up on the red tag. They seemed to be unaware of the fact that the orders he had written had more legal significance than the red tag, which could be removed even if the contractor had not complied with the orders. In fact, they seemed to know nothing of the orders or what was in them. Well, maybe they were waiting to have them explained.

They did not seem to understand the difference in the legal significance even after Jepson explained that the red tag could be removed by somebody above. Fenton's statement about it, however, had seemed clear enough.

FENTON: So administrative-procedure-wise, the red tag is put on at the start by the field man but can be removed by an order from somebody up above, without the conditions being corrected and at that time, of course, then the job theoretically could proceed with the same unsafe conditions having prevailed before. Is that correct?

Jepson answered that it did happen and had, in fact, once happened to him on a demolition contracting job.

Then he stepped down and Keysor called Zavattero's name.

As he walked toward the table in front of the committee Zavattero thought he detected a faint rustling among the reporters and TV camera crews at the right of the hearing room. It made him curious. What were they expecting? He himself expected nothing dramatic or even very interesting. What he had done was all very technical and couldn't possibly interest anyone but another safety engineer, or—his gaze went up to the men seated above him—an assembly committee. It was anybody's guess what they would make of it. He grinned to himself then nodded with a quick dip of the head to McFettridge, who seemed to be staring at him. So did Fenton.

At the usual admonitions that there would be no immunity granted because of his testimony, he was glad. The one thing he didn't want was for someone to start handing out immunity to anyone. Immunity would have meant the end of his hopes to bring about a prosecution, and that would have been crushing to him now that prosecution was so close. He wondered how much today's hearing would affect the decision of the city attorney's office.

He ran swiftly through the history of the tunnel from the time it had first gone underground fifteen months before when it had been part of his area. He explained the change to Denton's area and its present status. His recital was flat, almost mechanical, and he noticed the reporters and cameramen were beginning to look intensely bored.

Not that his job hadn't been tough, but it was not tough in any way that would interest the public, or so he thought.

His account of the day between the first flash fire and the final explosion sounded smooth and mechanical, almost rehearsed even to himself, but in fact, it had not been. He hadn't really known what the committee was going to ask, and at moments he suspected they didn't know what they were going to ask themselves. They were not even sure who had been there nor whom they represented.

They needed the cast of characters sorted out for them. He did this. They were Loren G. Savage, Project Manager, Lockheed Shipbuilding and Construction Company; Otha Ree, Project Engineer, same company; Bucky Micelli, Business Representative Local 300, and himself.

He had no difficulty in recalling the events of that day. He had relived it so many times in his own mind, searching for a clue about what had gone wrong on the doomed graveyard shift.

Savage had phoned him at six that morning. Normally he was up at five-thirty because he liked a leisurely preparation for the day ahead, but not that morning. He was startled out of his sleep by Savage's call.

He had not been particularly alarmed at Savage's report of the flash fire. As he repeatedly assured the committee, the tunnel had been advancing well, the contractor was cooperative and mindful of safety.

Nevertheless, he wanted an environmental expert there to help assess the gas potential in the tunnel. He had phoned the environmental expert, Jerry Eisen, and asked him to pick up gas testing devices in Los Angeles and meet him at the tunnel project. Eisen had refused and though Zavattero's testimony was confined to the mild statement that "Mr. Eisen was unable to come to the project at that time," the exchange between him and the environmental man had actually been an angry one.

Zavattero felt that Eisen's expertise was needed and the situation demanded that Eisen give it some priority. Eisen had practically told him to go to hell, he had other things to do. Like what, Zavattero wondered, but he had no alternative but to accept the environmental man's references to other commitments and situations as if flash fires were burning all over Los Angeles county.

Zavattero banged down the receiver and headed for the tunnel feeling short-tempered and irritable. In fact, as he recalled, a lot of tempers seemed to be short that day.

When he arrived at the site, the first and most obvious thing to do after finding out how badly the four men had been hurt, was to get into the hole and find out what was going on.

That turned out not to be quite so simple. Savage had OKd the trip in with Rasmussen, Ree, himself, and Bucky Micelli, but Ree had taken exception to having Bucky go in with them.

Now when miners have any small matter to negotiate, that negotiation almost always starts with a few broken skulls and missing teeth. An appropriate climate for peaceful discussion having thus been established, an agreement can usually be reached.

When Ree shoved Micelli back away from the locomotive, Micelli grabbed Ree by the shirt front. Whatever the two men were snarling at each other about surfaced only between grunts, most of it having to do with the less savory aspects of the other's personality.

Zavattero recognized the symptoms at once and so did Rasmussen, a long-time tunnel man himself. They both stepped in to separate the quarreling men. The quarrel was quickly over but both Ree and Micelli sat in angry silence as the locomotive moved into the black hole of the now-darkened tunnel.

Zavattero wondered at Ree's objection to Micelli's presence. He, himself, felt that having Micelli along would be a good thing. Micelli, who had been a miner all over the country since the thirties, had learned firsthand almost all there was to know about the underworld of mines and tunnels. He was a good union representative and would protect his men, Zavattero knew. If Micelli saw anything in the tunnel that bothered him he would refuse to let them go in. Maybe that's why Ree had not wanted him along, though that didn't seem too likely to Zavattero. Anyway, Micelli might be the solution to Zavattero's very ticklish problem. How to keep that tunnel closed until they were absolutely sure it was safe to start excavating again.

That problem was complicated by the absence of any trace of gas in the tunnel. Rasmussen had carried the gas testing device into every crevice of the tunnel, probing into the muck. He moved the tester slowly over the gantry up against the crown of the excavation, and up against a dark seam which looked like decomposed granite that made a scar in the earth near the face of the tunnel. There was no gas, no methane—a lighter-than-air gas—nor any of the heavy gases. There was no flammable gas—period. There was only a welding lead burning with a flickering blue flame which they extinguished as they continued sniffing for gas. Zavattero half hoped they would find gas. He knew it was there potentially but without evidence he could not officially close the tunnel. He couldn't even red tag it without inviting a reprimand from his own office. He did not have the authority to yellow tag it which is what it really needed.

He sighed as they all emerged from the tunnel. Savage was waiting back at the office trailer. He was leaning against the door with a cup of coffee in his hand. His hard hat was pushed back and a trickle of sweat crept from under his long sideburns. He looked more uncomfortable than hot though it was almost noon and a hot day. Zavattero wondered if he had been talking to R. E. Hix in the Seattle offices of Lockheed. The engineer knew Hix would drive Savage to keep the tunnel open.

Zavattero's problem was how to keep it closed until it was safe. Savage had been joined by four other men. They were all seated inside the trailer talking, each spinning the wheel of his own concerns. There was a representative from the insurance company, another man employed by the tunnel laborers; also in attendance were Richard Balerczak and Garland Gray, of the Metropolitan Water District. The MWD was just as anxious as Lockheed was to see the Sylmar link in the $11 billion web of water tunnels completed.

The only wheel they all seemed to spin at the same time was remedial measures. In spite of the present lack of gas in the tunnel, Zavattero knew that the gas was potentially there. That and only that was to be considered in allowing the excavation to be resumed.

As the condition of the tunnel was discussed, the whole question hinged on continuous testing for gas.

Even as he was trying to give the committee the requested narrative of that day before the explosion, Zavattero wondered if they had understood the significance.

On the previous day of the hearings, a meter expert, R. Bart, who had given the committee the sort of long-winded and detailed description of the testing devices that only a man could give who not only saw himself as the repository of grave and weighty information, but had also mounted his hobby-horse. To Bart, if God had been provided with a properly calibrated meter, equipped with the right bulbs to squeeze and the right probes to thrust into the fiery chaos of the swirling universe, He could have managed the Creation in a matter of hours.

Following Bart's testimony it seemed to Zavattero that the committee looked a little dazed. He wondered if they realized that all that Bart had really told them was that there were devices that could be used for continuous testing and others that had to be manually squeezed and were not continuously testing.

The need for such testing had been one point of total agreement when the five men had met in the hot trailer office at the McClay Street portal. That and the matter-of-fact acceptance of the reality of potential gas.

All the rest of the orders Zavattero had given Lockheed rested on that. The remaining protective measures, the breathing apparatus that he had insisted they pick up from another tunnel, and the men trained to use them, were not so important as the continuous testing.

As he had finished going over his special safety orders with Savage and the others at the meeting, Zavattero had been sure that the tunnel was secure. The requirements had been met, and he was sure that Savage would comply with them.

The assortment of concerns which he recalled from that day were not the considerations of the committee. They were more interested in the question of red tagging the tunnel.

As Zavattero took the witness stand, Keysor turned immediately to the safety orders, seeking details on them, demanding chapter and text. Zavattero read them aloud in a monotone:

Attention; Mr. R.N. Waters, Responsible Managing Officer, Tunnel Construction at San Fernando Tunnel Site—Unsafe conditions by W.J. Zavattero, issued to L.G. Savage, project manager. *General Conditions:* Tunnel under excavation approximately 22 feet excavated diameter. Unsafe conditions—flammable gas has been encountered at approximately 1:00 A.M. 6/23/71 resulting in an explosion. Requirements: Dangerous or poisonous gases. 1) Provide and require continuous testing at the tunnel face for flammable gases with acceptable test equipment. Tunnel Safety Order 8425-A. 2) If the air in the tunnel atmosphere reaches concentrations of one percent by volume, work therein shall conducted with extreme care. Steps shall be taken to improve the ventilation system. The Division of Industrial Safety shall be notified of this condition. #8425-A. 3) When two percent or more of explosive gases are encountered, all productive work in the tunnel shall be discontinued. The Division of Industrial Safety shall be notified of conditions. 4) Test Procedures: Test procedures shall be the following: a) continuous testing for flammable gases while the excavating machine is being advanced. #8425—8410. b) Work areas in back of base shall be tested for flammable gases during the shift. NOTE: c) If 'a' and 'b' reveals flammable gases, more extensive testing will be required. The ventilation shall be improved. General Safety Precautions: 5) Prior to starting excavation of the face and/or advance of the excavating machine, drill a test hole ahead of the face in order to test for flammable gas #8410—8406. NOTE: Test the hole for flammable gases and the excavated material from the hole. 6) Oxygen breathing apparatus—Provide and maintain five self-contained breathing apparatus at this job site. #8422 7) Workmen using oxygen breathing apparatus shall be available on call and have training equal to U.S. Bureau of Mines training. #8422. These requirements are signed H.A. Crabtree, Senior Safety Engineer.

He doubted if the committee really understood what each of the requirements meant, but they had undoubtedly done their homework, and were ready with a host of technical questions.

Only Fenton seemed anxious to skip them and get on with the drama. He stepped quickly into the first break.

FENTON: Why don't you just get him to tell us?—

KEYSOR: I agree. As Mr. Fenton said, let him tell us what happened. You wrote up the requirements. What time was that, and what happened from that time until the explosion the following morning?

ZAVATTERO: All right. Mr. Savage and Mr. Ree, I told them I would not allow them to return to work until my requirements were satisfied. They took care of the test instrument and bought the new continuous pumps. At that time as far as item five is concerned, the excavation hole in the face that I required them to drill: he had an existing hole which was approximately seventy feet, an existing hole that they had put in for prewatering purposes. Mr. Savage requested that he monitor that hole and not drill another hole because he still had seventy feet of hole left in front of the face advance. I stated at that time to Mr. Savage that this would be satisfactory under the condition that if any measurable amounts of gas were encountered he would stop and redrill another hole. The oxygen breathing apparatus: this was a difficult item to comply with. Partly because of delivery space and this sort of thing. Fortunately, three years ago, I had required Shea-Kaiser-Lockheed-Neely—Los Angeles Tunnel Contractors—to buy some, and he obtained five units from that contractor and had them delivered to the job. I then requested him to search his roles for qualified and trained men in order to use the breathing apparatus—and he had them following all of his employees, and he did obtain five men that had had prior training. He then set up a Bureau of Mines training class, I believe, for July 15. At that time he wanted to start back to work. I told him that if any gas were encountered, he was to stop and call me. I left the project about 5:30 P.M.

During his account of the events of that day, Zavattero had not been nervous and he felt that he had been concise and clear.

It surprised him therefore that the committee's questioning did not turn to the legal significance of his orders, their purpose and why they had been deliberately withheld from the press. Instead their questioning swung like a needle hitting true north to the red tag.

He tensed slightly when Fenton began to take over the questioning, but then a slight smile flickered in his eyes. Fenton kept referring to him as Mr. Zavaterry. This did not bother Zavattero. He was used to a lot more startling pronunciations of a not really so difficult name, but the fact that Fenton seemed always so intensely positive about everything made his mispronunciation amusing. If Fenton was going to be so damn positive about everything he might at least get his name right.

However Fenton chose to pronounce his name, it was soon apparent that he was out to get Zavattero. The assemblyman's questions were hammered at him hard and fast. He knew he would have no chance to counter with his own questions or explanations.

With his first question Fenton proved that Mercy's fears about the red tag were well founded.

FENTON: Maybe I don't understand you, Zavattery. Yesterday when you and I had a little discussion and I asked you if you should have red tagged the tunnel, you said you should have.

ZAVATTERO: No, I said I agree with you.

FENTON: That's what I said. I said you should have red tagged it and you agreed with me. Now you're saying something different.

ZAVATTERO: No.

FENTON: Isn't it your job—Do you consider a position where four men have been burned, two seriously, unsafe enough to close the job down?

ZAVATTERO: Yes sir, I do. But the job was closed down when I got there.

Zavattero still wondered where Fenton was going. Mercy had been right. Fenton was reading his agreement as self-condemnation. He had agreed with Fenton that it would have been better procedurally, that was all. In fact, if they ever bothered to ask him, he could tell them that the division should get rid of the red tag altogether and give the division engineers the power to slap a yellow tag on a dangerous job right on the spot. The yellow tag carried legal weight. The red tag did not. Only the unions acknowledged it, and many nonunion employers worked right over the red tag.

Fenton's questioning indicated that he knew this.

FENTON: Your job, when you red tag it, you in effect are closing the job down because Mr. Micelli then for sure couldn't let his men go through. Isn't that true?

ZAVATTERO: That's true.

FENTON: All right. So you could have red tagged it anyhow, couldn't you?

ZAVATTERO: I could have.

FENTON: All right. Now, after you gave these seven conditions, and I was listening with very big ears to how you said that Mr. Savage complied with all these conditions, which you're only speaking from hearsay because you don't know if somebody was monitoring. Did you go down afterwards and watch the operation at all?

ZAVATTERO: No sir.

FENTON: Why?

ZAVATTERO: Because I thought it was the contractor's responsibility to maintain his place of employment safe, and Mr. Savage indicated to me a willingness to comply with the orders.

FENTON: What is your function, Mr. Zavattery, as a member of the Division of Safety and a field man?

ZAVATTERO: To enforce the safety orders.

FENTON: All right. You gave seven orders, didn't you?

ZAVATTERO: Yes, sir.

FENTON: And you gave them to Mr. Savage and he being an honorable man that you thought that he was, you went home. You didn't even go down in the tunnel to retest the gas to see if there was any before you left and before the men went on to work. You tested it around what, eleven o'clock. Was that it?

This had been Fenton's second sarcastic reference to Savage's willingness to comply. Again, Zavattero was puzzled, and the dismal thought that he was being set up as an engineer on the take working with Savage crossed his mind. But that was quickly followed by the thought that Fenton too might be working for Lockheed, and was hoping through his castigation of Zavattero and the Division of Industrial Safety to to remove the threat of prosecution to the corporation. He dismissed the thought. Whatever game Fenton was playing, he was no Reagan man. He was a fire-eating Democrat.

Fenton's questioning after that began to skim around over questions of gas testing, Zavattero's expertise and experience in gaseous tunnels. After a bit of skimming, he returned again to Zavattero's relations with the contractors.

FENTON: So you anticipated they might encounter more gas?

ZAVATTERO: I anticipated, but as far as my test results I could not verify it.

FENTON: So you weren't sure whether it was an unsafe or safe condition and so forth?

ZAVATTERO: As far as my review of the tunnel project, it was not an unsafe condition. But I had to put over the point to the contractor that there was a potential unsafe condition.

FENTON: Right. All right, let me ask you further. If you give seven conditions under which you are to go to work, and you give it to the employer, your function being to protect the employee, that's the function of the division, we're all agreed to that, how do you know that these seven conditions were undertaken so that he could go back on the job, unless you go back in and see that the seven conditions are being undertaken?

ZAVATTERO: I had planned a reinspection the next day, sir.

FENTON: It was a little late, wasn't it?

ZAVATTERO: I would believe so.

FENTON: You further allowed the men to go on the job. I repeat, you didn't at that time make sure that the seven conditions were being complied with?

ZAVATTERO: Well, I felt reasonably sure that the contractor would comply with them.

FENTON: Well you've got seventeen people that feel a little different. What I'm saying is, so that we understand, you thought it was unsafe, you set up seven conditions, you allowed the man to put these people back on work, without being assured other than you felt he was a nice man and he was going to do so. So that you sitting there can't tell me whether these seven conditions were actually undertaken, and even when the first men went back on the job, when you went home at five-thirty—I don't know when the men went back on the job, but you—did they go back at five-thirty?

ZAVATTERO: They went on to swingshift, yes.

FENTON: Swing shift?

ZAVATTERO: Yes.

FENTON: They went on at five-thirty. You can't even tell us at that time whether the testing showed whether there was any gas at all present, can you?

ZAVATTERO: Mr. Savage advanced—

FENTON: No, you, you cannot.

ZAVATTERO: No, I—

FENTON: You. I'm not interested in Mr. Savage. He represents the employer. You represent the employees. I mean I'm interested in you. You were protecting the men.

ZAVATTERO: That's right.

FENTON: So what you had planned to do was wait another day and then go in to see if everything was running all right.

ZAVATTERO: Yes, sir.

As he spoke, Zavattero's voice was cold and flat. He'd had about enough of Fenton, especially with his sarcastic referral to Savage as a nice man.

Fenton's scathing observations, however, were gleefully picked up by the press and referred to as acid.

And to Zavattero it was indeed acid, but the real acidity came with Fenton's sneering statement that he had allowed the men to go back to work simply because he "felt that Savage was a nice man and was going to cooperate."

He stared coldly at Fenton as Fenton waved an admonitory finger in his face, and the press began snapping pictures of the theatrically outraged Fenton. The picture would appear that afternoon on the front page of the *Herald Examiner*.

As everyone seemed to pause for the picture, Zavattero thought, what did this bastard know of their feelings? Him and his sneering "nice man" statement. They didn't need this loudmouthed, self-serving politician to remind them of death. They had lived with the smell and sight of it. Fenton hadn't even seen it or a tunnel until yesterday. But he'd read about it in the newspaper, and he knew a political advantage when he saw one.

At that moment the engineer hated the politician with a cold, flat hatred that showed in the hard set of his face, and though the politician did not know it, at that same moment the heat of his attack had forged a strange alliance between Zavattero and Savage that would last almost to the very end.

What could Fenton know of the feelings they never spoke of even to each other? For Zavattero and Savage had never spoken of their feelings of responsibility for what had happened at Sylmar. Even when Zavattero had asked Savage why he had done it, it was not the same thing. It was almost impersonal as if they were discussing a technical problem as they did nearly every day now in preparing for the reopening of the tunnel.

Even working in the wreckage, they never asked each other questions such as "What if I? . . ." or "What if you? . . ." or "What if they? . . ." The questions may have been humming through their brains like the whine of the special, self-encased light they were forced to use now, but they never asked them. The light they had to carry with them was the only light allowed in the graveyard of the doomed tunnel. As the light began to glow, the battery would echo with a high, shrill whine in the black depths. Sometimes it became so shrill that they would douse the light, just as they would have liked to still the questions in their minds. The men were simply gone. They had died on the job a tunneler's death. Lockheed was highballing a tunnel and the men knew the risks. Still, in the darkness the two men would often stand quietly, almost expecting to hear the voices of the miners asking about the next shift.

Yes, what did this bastard with his sarcasm know about death and the men who died underground. Zavattero hated him.

Fenton, however, had only been warming up, and he went driving on as the TV cameras, the photographers, and reporters kept moving around for a better view of the action.

Fenton kept hammering away at the question of the red tag, even though by now no one really knew what the red tag was supposed to accomplish.

Did Zavattero call his supervisor that day about red tagging the tunnel? Yes. What did he say?

Zavattero had read the requirements he'd written for Lockheed, and his office had said OK. But no talk of red tagging.

At this point the chairman, Keysor, stepped in to pour some oil on troubled waters.

KEYSOR: May I ask a question. We will have testimony that will show that the procedure was really a fantastic operation, because they had some days up around two hundred feet per day, which is really a tremendous rate of tunneling. Do you think that the enthusiasm of the crew possibly could have overlapped a little bit with yourself? In other words, everything had gone along so well and so fast, and they were setting so many records. Was there a possibility that people, including yourself, might be adverse to shutting down an operation such as this?

ZAVATTERO: I can only give you an opinion, sir. As far as my opinion is concerned, the job was a successful one. And a safe one. The problems that I have had with other tunnel contractors in this area did not occur on this contract. This contractor was willing to try and make his job safe.

FENTON: Wait a minute, wait a minute. What are—he was willing to make it safe. Hell with whether he's willing or not. I don't understand what's going on here? Who do you represent, the contractor?

ZAVATTERO: No, sir.

At that Zavattero wanted to laugh and tell the blustering politician that he wished he had been working for Lockheed. If they paid him the salary and bonuses they paid Savage, he'd have sat in that tunnel for twelve hours a day. And when he wasn't sitting in it, he'd have strung so many red and yellow tags on the lousy tunnel, it would have looked like Porter Junior High on sock hop night. He continued to stare coldly at Fenton as the politician kept on pounding away at him.

FENTON: Well, what do you mean he was willing? In the first place we have testimony here that you can red tag without calling anybody. Mr. Hatton said so and Mr. Jepson said so.

ZAVATTERO: That's right.

FENTON: You can red tag the job. You don't have to have the employer willing to do anything. You can close that damn job down until he does what you think he should, otherwise he doesn't operate. So what's this crap about willing? I mean we have seventeen men dead here, or eighteen. And you're talking about the employer being willing to do something to make the conditions safe—really, seriously Zavattero, I'm surprised.

ZAVATTERO: Well, let me clarify that sir.

FENTON: I wish you would.

ZAVATTERO: There are some employers that are not willing to run—

FENTON: I don't care whether they're employers or not—you have enough under the code section that you can close a job down and you make him either comply, and I'm not speaking of Lockheed, and I don't know whether they did or didn't, I'm speaking of you. You can stop the job. That's your function. You can red tag it, that's one way; labor won't go over it, and you can go through a speedy procedure as Mr. Jepson calls it, and you can yellow tag the job, and even if he doesn't want to comply with conditions his job doesn't go on, isn't that right?

ZAVATTERO: That's right.

FENTON: So let's not talk about his being cooperative. He doesn't have to be cooperative as far as you're concerned. He either does it or he closes down. And that's the purpose of our code section, that's the function of your job.

When Fenton finally wound down, he seemed to feel he may have gone too far. He made a sort of peace offering stating that he may have been a little unfair to Zavattero and asked if Zavattero had ever redtagged a job without calling in.

If it were a peace offering, Zavattero refused to accept it. Fenton had used him and he could soothe his conscience some other way. Fenton was no fool. He knew that red tag meant nothing. Zavattero turned down the proffered opening and told the committee that he had red tagged a job about a month ago without calling in. It had been a minor thing but he did not tell Fenton that.

And he had no closing statement to make either. He said simply, "I have no more today."

When Zavattero left the witness table he was borne up

more by tense anger than concern about the outcome of today's hearings. All he knew was that he had been clobbered and he didn't like it. Not at all. But he couldn't understand why. If he had kept his mouth shut about his orders when the *Times* reporter had phoned him, the investigation would have died right there. There probably wouldn't have been an assembly hearing.

Both Hatton and Fuller of the federal office of Occupational Safety and Health had close ties to Lockheed. They were not about to release any more information about the disaster than they absolutely had to. On the witness stand Hatton had remained securely undisturbed by the committee's questioning. He hadn't even prepared an opening statement, he'd been so secure.

The committee hadn't bothered to ask why his orders had been buried. They must have known it. Johnson and McFettridge surely knew that those orders had been so effectively kept from the press that someone had to send them secretly to the city news service.

It didn't make sense. Instead of asking him about what had happened, Fenton had simply clobbered him. Why? Why? It didn't make sense.

There was really nothing mysterious about it. It was just politics. There was no political advantage to be gained by going after a prosecution of Lockheed, but there was a great deal of political advantage to exposing the defections of the Division of Industrial Safety.

CHAPTER SEVEN

After he sat down, Zavattero began to feel calmer, and he wondered what would happen when Savage took the stand. He watched Savage as he approached the committee, but before Savage could reach the witness table, Tom McNary, now personal attorney for Savage, was on his feet.

For a brief moment Zavattero wondered if plans to prosecute Lockheed had progressed so far that McNary was going to insist on immunity or refuse to let Savage testify. But no, McNary was only making lawyer noises about the right to make objections while Finkle sat quietly by.

McNary, an attorney for forty years, as he pointed out to the committee, and now purchasing agent for Lockheed, was given to wearing natty, bright sports coats. This fact was duly noted by Fenton in a jocular moment when he asked McNary where he had stolen his jacket. McNary's reply was equally jovial; he'd bought it at Hollywood Park.

It was all so cozy. The little jokes, the knowledgeable asides. As if all that was involved was a few days lost pay for some unfortunate miners. It had nothing to do with the fact that they had lost their lives—the whole, total sum of their existence had been blown up at Sylmar. As Zavattero observed the chummy interchange, he wondered if McNary was one of the "big guns" Lockheed was going to use to shoot him down. He doubted it.

Finkle looked more likely to be the big gun, but at this point he just sat quietly by, not even taking notes. He didn't have to. He had brought a court reporter with him. Bane, in the back, had to take his own notes. Zavattero didn't like to think of what Bane's reaction to Fenton's attack had been, he guessed he'd find out soon enough.

Zavattero's attention turned to Savage, seated before the committee. His long face was stolid and impassive. Like Zavattero he wore a plain, business suit which made him seem almost a stranger. The two men almost never saw each other except in their working clothes, wearing the ubiquitous hard hats.

In the time that Zavattero had known Savage, he had always admired the project manager's slow, ponderous manner of speaking. Zavattero knew that Savage's slow and ponderous manner of speech was only partly natural. He had cultivated it for the same reason some men smoke pipes. To stall for time.

As Savage went through the preliminaries of his testimony Zavattero realized that Savage was going to take it very slow. Very, very slow.

Before the hearings Savage had announced to Zavattero that he intended to throw so much bull around that no one would be able to see the sun for all the flak coming down.

After the preliminaries Zavattero sat back to watch when Savage encountered Fenton. He did not know how thoroughly Finkle and McNary had briefed Savage, but it soon became apparent that in Savage, Fenton had met his match.

Fenton started his inquiry with the most important and disputed question, the gas readings in the tunnel just before the catastrophe. And Savage began stirring the bull around.

FENTON: Weren't you told by Mr. Zavattero that when it

reached one percent you were immediately to notify the Division of Safety? Did you hear Mr. Zavattero say that was one of the conditions?

SAVAGE: You misunderstand my statement. We were holding the most concentrated location at less than one percent.

FENTON: He said between one and two. He said he mentioned two too.

KEYSOR: Let's proceed.

FENTON: Now, wait a minute now. Just a minute I want to—It never hit one percent at all? Did your readings ever hit one percent?

SAVAGE: Mr. Fenton—

FENTON: It only takes a yes or a no. You can ask your attorney, either the reading read—In the concentrated areas did it ever read one percent or more?

SAVAGE: In the most concentrated location it would have been gas without air.

This totally irrelevant pronouncement from Savage made Fenton pause for a moment. When he resumed, he spoke with a sort of baffled patience.

FENTON: Listen to my question. In the most concen—In any kind that you ever took any testing with, in the most concentrated area or otherwise did it ever read one percent or more? That's the only question I'm asking.

MR. DAVE FINKLE: Mr. Fenton, the problem with the question I think is that it assumes two types of where you're measuring. Perhaps, Mr. Savage can explain what—

FENTON: Mr. Finkle, I don't care where he measured it because one of the conditions that he read—Mr. Zavattero read, and he didn't say where it was to be one percent. He said if it reads one percent—I think he said "I don't know"—you are to stop and notify us immediately.

FINKLE: That's not correct, Mr. Fenton.

Fenton paused again. Now Finkle had stepped in to muddy up the waters further with a statement about two places for taking gas measurements. Everybody seemed bent on answering questions he hadn't asked. There had to be some way to get a straight answer out of somebody—Savage, Finkle, McNary—anybody! He watched Savage warily as his testimony continued.

Zavattero watched all this with no little relish. Savage was really shoving it around and Fenton's sun was getting dimmer and dimmer. It would soon disappear at this rate.

With calm patience Savage provided the committee with the information that gas would not explode without oxygen and a source of ignition.

This not particularly startling revelation had caused the members of the committee to nod, as if it were indeed an interesting possibility.

Savage then explained that there were many sources of ignition, fifty to hundred pieces of nonexplosion-proof electrical equipment as well as twenty-five to thirty lights burning. "Temperature alone may have caused the explosion," Savage told the committee.

At that point Fenton stepped into the fray again with a simple question about smoking. At least the answer was equally simple but it proved a shocker to the committee.

SAVAGE: My instructions were no smoking up in the immediate face area but smoking was allowed back amidst other equipment that was not explosion proof. And once you have many sources of ignition one more don't make that much difference.

FENTON: All right, let me ask you this. You're working with the potential of gas that you had, and you have many sources of ignition. Eliminating some of them doesn't minimize the possibility of an explosion. Is that what you're saying? As long as you've got ten you might as well have fifteen? You don't really mean that I'm sure?

SAVAGE: Well, to ignite a flammable gas it only requires one point of ignition. It burns just as fast with one as with two.

Though the statement had seemed shocking to the committee, it was not to Zavattero. What Savage had said was perfectly true, and it was the truth that made the orders he had given to Lockheed—to constantly test for gas—the really critical issue. If they had followed those orders to test constantly, it would have made no difference if a circus full of fire-eaters did their act on top of the gantry. If the atmosphere had tested clear, the fire-eaters could have swallowed the Chicago Fire and the tunnel might have burned, but it would *not* have exploded.

Fenton then began cross-examining Savage on gas testing procedures. Savage was calm still, but his hunched shoulders made Zavattero think that he was probably sweating rivulets beneath his neat business suit. Or maybe he was laughing. He knew what he was doing.

This time Fenton approached Savage with the caution of a bee-stung bear.

FENTON: Mr. Savage, you stayed the whole swing shift, did you? You stayed on the job the whole swing shift.

SAVAGE: Yes.

FENTON: Normally, do you stay on the job that length of time?

SAVAGE: There have been other times when we had particular problems when I stayed.

That seemed simple enough but Fenton's next question landed him back in trouble again with the team of Savage,

McNary, and Finkle. He wanted to know how many men were to do the gas testing and who had made that decision.

FENTON: Now you decided on the number of people that should be testing, he didn't tell you how many to have testing, did he? It wasn't in the conditions that I saw.

SAVAGE: One man doing constant monitoring.

FENTON: He didn't tell you how many, you decided yourself how many to have testing?

SAVAGE: We discussed it.

FENTON: Why did you only have one?

SAVAGE: One was considered adequate.

FENTON: By whom?

SAVAGE: By me for one.

FENTON: By who for two? What I am trying to find is who made the decision to have only one person testing?

SAVAGE: I know, I have no objection regarding the number of men testing.

FENTON: I am not interested in your objection at all, I am interested in anything in question. Was it your decision to have one man test? As opposed to two, three, or four, that's my question.

SAVAGE: I knew of no one who objected of having only one.

FENTON: My question to you is did you make the decision that there only be one?

SAVAGE: I participated in that decision.

FENTON: Who made the decision? Did Mr. Zavattero tell you that one was OK?

SAVAGE: He was aware of the fact that we were having—

FENTON: That isn't my question, I asked you did he tell you that it was OK? Not whether he was aware there was only one. The seven conditions didn't tell you how many people should test, all he said was that when you get one percent—somewhere we will get to that in a little while, or to certain things that will prevail—but he didn't tell you how many people would do the testing, right? In the seven conditions? Nobody told you how many people were to test, so you made your determination there could be one person testing. Is that true? And you had him testing most of the evening?

MR. McNARY: Now just a minute, I don't think the witness answered the question completely.

FENTON: How do you know?

McNARY: Let's ask it again.

FENTON: We are not in a court of law, you want him to read it back, or would you like this reporter to read it back. Read him back the question, we will play courtroom here.

RECORDER: You made the determination that there would be one person testing?

SAVAGE: I participated in that decision.

FENTON: Would you read him the question again because his counsel said I didn't give him an opportunity to answer the question. He isn't availing himself of the opportunity.

FINKLE: Maybe if you rephrase the question.

FENTON: Mr. Finkle, you operate for Lockheed and I'll stand up here. I am not rephrasing the question, it's very simple. Somebody made a decision to give one tester, I didn't and you didn't. He was on the job, he got seven conditions from Mr. Zavattero. Mr Zavattero didn't tell him how many testers to have. All I am asking him is whether he made the decision to get one. He said before he got the one, and all I am asking is who made the decision? I can't rephrase that any differently, Mr. Finkle, seriously. Did you go get the one guy? Do it in lay talk, it doesn't matter to me, anyway you want. You want to answer the question?

SAVAGE: Well, I don't understand why your question hasn't been answered.

FENTON: I don't understand it myself. My question—we will go backwards. One man, at your instruction, after Mr. Zavattero gave you seven conditions, one of which was to test for gas, right? We are OK so far, you got one man to do it, right?

SAVAGE: Right.

FENTON: You didn't get two and you didn't get three. You went out and you called to find a man to do it?

SAVAGE: No. We reassigned the people on the job with us, calling on—

FENTON: I don't care how you did it, you got—You did—Why didn't you reassign two to do it?

SAVAGE: Because one met the requirements and seemed adequate.

FENTON: To you?

SAVAGE: And was adequate.

FENTON: To you. You made that decision that's what I'm asking you.

SAVAGE: OK.

Having wrung that OK out of Savage, the assemblyman sighed, and turned to querying the slow-speaking project manager about the state of the tunnel.

FENTON: Was your understanding with Mr. Zavattero that the point one of the one percent you are talking about—if it was found in a concentrated area, weren't you supposed to notify him? Was that your understanding?

SAVAGE: The order reads.

FENTON: I understand that. Did you have any understanding with Mr. Zavattero that if read one percent anywhere you were to notify him?

SAVAGE: I did not have that understanding—

As Savage said that Zavattero almost started from his seat to protest. He stopped himself, and leaned back, a puzzled frown creasing his forehead. He couldn't figure what the hell Savage was trying to pull. Up till now he had only been evasive, but this, a point-blank lie. . . .

He wondered whether Savage was looking at Fenton when he answered. It didn't seem like it. His head was bent looking at some papers in front of him.

Zavattero wished he were facing Savage.

What he was saying was a damned lie. They had gone over and over it that day. Savage would call. The orders read that he was to call. If he had called, Zavattero could have closed the tunnel, and he would have. Moreover, he would have protected Savage from repercussions from Hix or Waters or whomever else was calling the tune in the Seattle office.

That was the one thing that there had been no question about. There had been questions about making the fans reversible, about drilling an additional hole in the face, but there had been *no* question about continuous testing and notifying him if they detected any gas. Listening to Savage, Zavattero could not believe what he'd heard.

The guy was hanging himself. It was there in the written orders!

Then Zavattero's gaze shifted to McNary and Finkle, and he thought he understood. Lockheed *was* afraid of prosecution. Up until now they'd been so sure, but now they were not, if Savage's statement meant what he thought it meant.

No wonder Lockheed had been so anxious to keep his orders buried. They were going to substitute the minutes written after the meeting on June 23 for his orders.

When Zavattero had first read the minutes he hadn't read them very critically. He had noted a few minor mistakes. The minutes read that Savage had gone into the tunnel with him, and Bucky Micelli and Ree had not. Otherwise they seemed unexceptional, but the most significant part of the orders, that there should be continuous testing, had been reduced to something like an afterthought: "A suggestion was made that a continuous explosive gas testing device be procured and used at the face rather than the mechanical one presently being used."

This, of course, would all appear quite innocuous to anyone, but it would be a treacherous betrayal of the content of the division's orders. That was no suggestion. It was an order!

Whatever the story was, Lockheed was being very careful of Savage's testimony, as Fenton had just learned.

During most of the questioning Zavattero felt that the assemblymen were circling everyone. They were looking for something and their questions went in circles. He hoped that some good would come of it all.

But as Savage got up wearily from his place at the witness table to leave the hearing room with McNary, it seemed to Zavattero that all the investigation had accomplished so far was to stir things around. It reminded him of a paperweight his grandfather had given him as a child. It was one of those glass globes that filled with powdery snow when you turned it over. He had been enthralled with it as a child waiting eagerly for the snow to fall away to reveal the tiny little farmhouse with its barns and fences. There were even tiny little animals who didn't seem to mind the freezing snow a bit. Though the scene never changed, he waited just as eagerly as if one of the little cows were going to bear a calf during the snowstorm.

He wondered if any change would come from the storm that the investigating committee had created when they had turned the gloomy bowl of the Lockheed tunnel over. One thing was certain, it was going to take a lot longer for that snow to settle.

However, when Ralph Brisette—the only survivor—was called to testify, there was an almost-welcome relief from such snowy confusion.

His story was simple and stark. He told them of his first forebodings: the smell of gas in the tunnel and the strange pressure on his ears just before the blast occurred. His voice thickened with misery as he recalled the screaming that he'd heard seconds before the tunnel had turned into a sheet of flaming gas.

Hardly able to breathe, he had tried not to panic and crawled to the fanline. He did not know how long he'd lain there until Wallace and Rathbun had found him. In the hospital the realization that he alone had survived came as a painful and frightening reality to him.

As they had with everyone else, the committee asked Brisette for any statement he might want to make. But of them all only Brisette seemed lost to the many ramifications of the Lockheed tragedy. For him reality was what was buried in the tunnel.

He had no further statement to make, he said, "I was just thankful to be here and I thank the fellows who came in and everyone involved. It's been a very bad experience for me."

There was silence as Brisette left the witness stand, but the poignancy of his testimony seemed to have infected the committee with a sense of urgency. There would be no lunch break. Arvid Rasmussen was called quickly to the stand. He was to be followed by Ree.

Zavattero wished that he'd been smart enough to leave. First he was hungry, and lately he'd been having pains in his stomach every time he got hungry. Like a kid, he thought, but most of all he just didn't feel like hearing much more, especially not Rasmussen's recount of how many times that damned meter had gone up.

Rasmussen's testimony seemed to be as hesitant as Savage's, as if he too were feeling his way through a strange tunnel. His statement to the press on June 26 had been angry and specific. Alerts had been reached on several occasions, and ignored. Time had perhaps made the difference. After all everything on June 25 had been as vivid as a movie lit by the blast fire from the tunnel, but it was now September 3, and Rasmussen's testimony seemed to be heavy with earnestness, even uncertainty. Zavattero knew that Rasmussen had been the one to go into the tunnel with Ree and Biro when the meter was discovered, and he knew that the two men were friendly. Rasmussen was not being defensive for himself. Zavattero suspected that Rasmussen's testimony was influenced by his association with Ree, but it was difficult to tell. It would be interesting to hear Ree, who was scheduled to appear next.

Rasmussen, like everyone else, looked exhausted and

drawn as he finished testifying. There had been so many deaths and he had seen the gas readings. It had all become so confused now that no one knew what all the readings had meant. But Rasmussen had known that the tunnel should be closed, and he knew that Savage knew it, and that most of the men, especially Richardson, had known it. Richardson was not a Lockheed employee, but an employee of the Metropolitan Water District, and had been told that he could not close the tunnel without a written order from the MWD. Richardson, looking at the men working, had shrugged hopelessly and said "It doesn't matter; by the time I get the order it'll have blown up anyway." It had.

None of this was part of his testimony before the assembly, but he knew it all the same, and that was painful knowledge to him.

At last the assemblymen seemed to be overcome by the same pangs of hunger that had been burning Zavattero. A lunch break was called by Chairman Keysor. Ree would testify when they returned. Zavattero had planned to leave, but changed his mind when he heard that Ree would testify next.

As everyone prepared to leave for lunch, Bane nodded at him from his seat at the side, and Zavattero nodded in return to indicate that he would join Bane outside the hearing room for lunch.

On his way to join Bane, he avoided the crowd of reporters and TV men surrounding Fenton. For a moment he thought he saw Gina in the throng, pressing in around the tall figure of the assemblyman who had done so much to provide the element of drama to the morning's sessions. He could not see Mercy, who would have been highly visible with her leg in a cast up to the hip, and dismissed the thought that it might be Gina. Probably some young journalism student from the local junior college eager to try her journalistic wings. Whomever it was, she was making quite a ruckus, he thought.

He and Bane slipped out the side door and headed for a place where they could have a quiet lunch. It was a welcome relief from the noise of the hearing room. Zavattero was anxious and a little worried about what Bane's reaction to the morning sessions would be.

It was a relief to him that Bane was undismayed by Fenton's abrasive tactics. Bane understood Zavattero's anger at what he considered a betrayal by the committee whose investigators he had tried so hard to cooperate with, but it had not worried Bane.

Bane was reassuring. That was, after all, only par for the political course. And besides that, it was good training. It was nothing compared to what would happen to him when Lockheed was brought to trial. What had happened to him today didn't even begin to smell of blood. Zavattero liked the way Bane said *when* not *if*, though he knew there were still a lot of *ifs*. As for the rest, he was ready.

Bane, in his talks with Zavattero and in the morning's sessions, had been assessing him carefully. Before the case for the prosecution of Lockheed had been dropped in his slot in the beehive of the city attorney's office, Bane had known little of Zavattero.

Later he had heard that he was a highly committed safety engineer, honest, with a sound and thorough knowledge of the labor code and the tunnel safety laws. The orders he had written showed that. He did not write random orders or request frivolous prosecutions. But was he going to be tough enough? It would take toughness to withstand the kind of interrogation Lockheed's powerful lawyers would throw at him. Did Zavattero know what he was getting himself into?

After the morning sessions he was pretty sure he did know. He felt that Zavattero's toughness was not born of immediate random anger, but of a deep determination to protect the rights of all the hard, rough men like Brisette who earned their living underground. That was the kind of toughness that was needed, not the feisty touchiness of an easily angered man.

As they finished their lunch, both men felt more sure of the other. The prosecution would go on. When they returned to the hearing room with all the others, Zavattero could not see either Gina or Mercy though Bucky Micelli was there. Bucky had agreed to watch out for them, and Zavattero assumed that he must have seen that they had gotten home safely. He hoped they'd gone home. He didn't want Gina to be witness to another morning like this one.

After the pyrotechnics of the morning session, the afternoon session, which could provide little more copy for the late news, was anticlimactic.

Not only had Savage, Finkle, and McNary disappeared, but so had Ree. Whatever testimony he had been going to give, wouldn't be given this afternoon.

In addition both Fenton and Russell had gone, leaving the indefatigable McFettridge and Johnson to fill in for them during the afternoon sessions. Chairman Keysor apologized at length for the now decimated committee; he reassured everyone that their testimony would be taken and given the same weight as if the entire Congress were present. There was no mention of why Ree would not appear.

He also reassured everyone that "it is obvious to every member of this committee that more time is necessary to adequately investigate the circumstances surrounding the tunnel disaster and the adequacy of orders in the State Labor Code with regard to protecting the lives of California workers. I wish to thank, at this time, the people who volunteered information at this hearing and to express the committee's appreciation for the fine coverage afforded this investigation by the media. It was and is the unanimous opinion of this select committee that nothing less than a full, open investigation into all aspects of the disaster can be expected by the legislature."

Zavattero was glad to hear that. In spite of the morning's hearings, maybe there was going to be some thinking about some new tunnel safety orders. If that were true, it would be worth any trip through the forest of Jack Fenton's rhetoric—and that was a lot of rhetoric.

Zavattero had been puzzled by Ree's absence. If Lockheed's attorneys had decided not to let the project engineer testify, the decision must have been made abruptly, since Keysor had announced that Ree's testimony would be taken just after the lunch recess. And after the lunch recess, Ree was nowhere around.

Zavattero didn't think the committee was aware of Ree's part in taking the meter. There had been no mention of the incident in the two days of hearings. Zavattero doubted that the committee knew anything of it. He had not told Johnson or McFettridge about the strange disappearance of the meter nor its return after his meeting with Westfield. He did not believe that Denton had either.

As Keysor tried to hurry the meeting along, Zavattero rose to leave quietly. He was worried by the disappearance of Mercy and Gina and he already knew pretty much what the rest of the testimony would be. He could hear it later on tapes, and besides he'd had just about as much as he could take for one day.

It was nearly four o'clock when he left the San Fernando Valley City Hall, and the heat outside was oppressive, the dead heat of the afternoon unrelieved by even a hint of evening breeze.

He sat in his car for a few moments with all the windows open, hoping that some air would trickle through it and cool it at least enough so that he could grasp the steering wheel without getting his palms fried.

Sitting there waiting for the car to cool, he went over the morning's hearings. Most of his anger at Fenton had faded and left in its wake curiosity as to where the committee hearings were actually going. He wondered if they knew.

He was annoyed with himself that he had said he agreed with Fenton about the red tag. He wished now that he had gone on to explain that the red tag had no legal significance but that his orders did.

He wondered what would have happened if he had explained that if he had red tagged the tunnel, the tag would

Part 1/Prosecution   125

have remained there just as long as it took Lockheed to get to the division and the division to get to Hatton.

The tag would be removed, Lockheed would have an indefinite time to comply with his orders and he, himself, could be reprimanded by his own office for irresponsibly red tagging a job that the employer had already shut down. And then the tunnel would surely have blown up. At least if they had complied with his orders they had a chance.

And as for warning the men, what did they expect him to do? Gather the men around him and read the orders to them like Moses ticking off the Ten Commandments?

The union men, Bucky Micelli and Jack Shands, were both there. Why didn't they read off the tablets of the law?

He knew that such irritating self-questioning did no good, and he had sense enough to know what Fenton was doing with the red tag.

Still the self-questioning persisted. Now with all the hindsight, he could curse himself for not hanging the red tag and let the division take it off. But on what basis could he have hung it? The tunnel was closed. There was not even a whiff of gas. It would be like denying a man access to his car or giving him a speeding ticket just because his car was potentially capable of going 150 miles an hour.

You *could* give him an order to put a governor on that jazzy little dreamboat he was revving up like the Hollywood Freeway was Indianapolis or Le Mans, but you couldn't give him a ticket while he was standing still tinkering with his overhead cams and dual carbs.

Zavattero's teenage daughters had lots of boyfriends with their first cars. He would like to have put a governor on them as effective as the orders he had given Lockheed. In fact, in some cases, he would have liked to make a citizen's arrest before his daughters got into the car.

A brief grin lit up his tired face. He knew that he had the potential to be one overprotective bastard with his daughters. Maybe Mercy should put a governor on him!

His daughters gave him a great deal of pleasure, especially

fourteen-year-old Gina with her fluid young body, shimmering hair, and her golden skin humming with eagerness. At Porter Junior High she had won several awards for youth services. They were very proud of her.

He was touched, too, that she had become so deeply interested and concerned with the Sylmar disaster. He smiled. She was a good kid.

Paula was not so interested. She was older than Gina, and love was making loud knocks at her heart. Loud, loud knocks, Zavattero suspected. And when in the history of the world has any catastrophe knocked louder at the hearts of the young than love? He smiled again. She was a good kid too.

The small flicker of pleasure left his face, and he winced slightly in pain. His stomach was hurting again. He hoped to God he didn't have anything wrong with him. What he probably needed was a good stiff drink. He put the car in gear and headed for the freeway. He'd be glad to get home.

Zavattero was totally unaware of what had happened with Mercy and Gina. They had arrived at the hearing room later than the others. Mercy had to hobble along on her crutches. She had told Gina that she did not mind the crutches, but her leg felt like it weighed more than her whole body. She was glad when Bucky Micelli saw them and found a seat in the hearing room.

They giggled like schoolgirls when Bucky brought a special chair for Mercy to rest her leg on.

"Do you think they charge extra for this?" she whispered.

Gina was pleased to see her mother so cheerful. On the way to the hearing Mercy had been so quiet, almost brooding.

Mercy had, in fact, been brooding. She was filled with foreboding. She had not wanted Gina to come to the hearings.

She knew that Gina was being questioned at school, and just a few nights before, Gina had returned early from a party, her smooth, young face stormy and her eyes brimming with tears. She had gone to her room and said nothing to anyone.

When Mercy looked in on her, she was sitting at her dresser dabbing furiously at her long, beautifully tapered nails with a wildly scarlet polish. To Mercy she looked as if she were about to stab someone with them. Mercy had often wondered how Gina could type so well with such long nails, but Gina was very proud of her nails. She had always admired her mother's slender graceful hands, always so beautifully manicured, and it had meant more to her than a debutante's cotillion when she had finally been allowed to wear nail polish. Mercy closed the door and smiled. Whatever it was it looked therapeutic, she thought. Mercy had been reading a great deal about therapies of one kind and another lately. She had a feeling that everyone was going to need them before this was all over.

Later Gina told her that she had left the party because one of her so-called friends had begun making remarks about her father.

There had, in fact, been many queries since the Sylmar tunnel had exploded in their lives.

These had varied from open questions about her father's situation to gentle concern for her plight.

Of the two she preferred the obviously excited and titillated curiosity of her peers who viewed the whole situation with the delighted intensity they might have accorded Billy Jack.

It was the teachers and especially one school counselor who bothered her the most. The questions they asked so solicitously seemed in some way cruel and sometimes downright nosy. The last time she had been called into the vice principal's office, she had become so angry that she had stormed "You're just being nosy. I don't have to tell you a thing, and I'm not going to." With that she had stalked out of the office, every defiant line in her fourteen-year-old body protesting her loyalty and affection for her father.

Now at the hearing, her nervous giggling covered considerable awe. The assembled miners were familiar to her. She had seen and talked to many of them when they visited her father. Even Johnson and McFettridge, whom she had met when they came to her house to visit, were not strangers to her. But the others were.

They were not teachers or vice-principals, but something else.

They were not even policemen.

Gina had known policemen. In her mind they appeared variously as the fuzz, to be eluded whenever possible with a certain amount of not-unpleasurable fear, sometimes as the frightening pigs, sightless in their covered helmets, standing arm and arm in student demonstrations she had seen on TV. But most of all to her, there was her father's friend, Art Hembree, an enormous man, a motorcycle cop who often towered over her in mock anger, and loved her very dearly.

No, these men were really strangers. Neat, well dressed, well pressed and starched. They were not real people, but more like abstractions to be studied in the ninth grade American social studies class. Orderly, requiring deep concentration and rote memory. They were not the unruly fuzz or enormous, powerful Art. They were the law and the law makers.

And they were calling her father a murderer!

In her fancies her fourteen-year-old mind spun giddily between the principled loneliness of an Eleanor Roosevelt—about whom she had read so avidly, determined to devote her own life to patient sacrifice—and the quick desires of the pom-pom girl wanting victory. And in her confusion all she knew was rage.

As the session broke up she stood there in the hearing room next to Bucky Micelli, the union man who had promised to look after them, his broken-nosed face a mask of compassionate concern for her angry confusion.

She sprang at Fenton as he passed her, grabbed him, digging her long nails into his arm.

"I hate you," she shrieked, "I hate you. How dare you call my father a murderer!"

The pressure of the long nails and the face of crumpled passion were less disturbing to the assemblyman than the flowing pens of the reporters and liquid lights of the TV cameras.

Not ungently he pushed her aside, patting her on the head. "Someday," he said, "You'll understand."

"What will I understand? I understand now—you're accusing my father of murder!"

The murmuring of voices like locusts closed over her head as she was pushed back into the crowd. Bucky Micelli's massive body folded itself around her, pushing her, sheltered by his own body, back further into the crowd.

There they looked for Mercy, still seated, her leg in its stone white cast stretched out before her. She was staring helplessly up at a tall, lean man in a rumpled suit, moist hair hanging over his forehead. He was asking her who she was. His glance fell furtively to her broken leg.

"Were you in the tunnel?" he asked hopefully.

Mercy looked up at him bewildered, and wondered what to say. What did he expect? "Oh sure, I was in there helping him to kill those men. Only I broke my leg before I could get it done."

Instead she just shoved aside her crutches, shaking her head and closing her eyes in an agony of incomprehension.

"No," she said, "I was not in the tunnel. Get out!"

Startled, the man wandered off into the crowd, his thin body in its black suit propelled forward, like a surfer in a wet suit waiting for the crest of the next wave.

Mercy sat there stolidly until Gina came over to her. Bucky had gone back into the crowd. She tried to put her arms comfortingly around her mother murmuring "Oh, Mother, it will be alright. I told them. I did, I told them."

Mercy pushed her away angrily, and leaning over, she dropped her forehead onto her balled-up fist. She nodded approvingly at her daughter, but all the time she was muttering "Oh hell."

Nothing had happened to forewarn Zavattero about the effect of the hearings on Mercy and Gina. Mercy had told him nothing of the unkind harassment of Gina at the party, nor of the questioning at school. She wanted simply to protect him from any more pressure.

That had been a mistake. When Zavattero walked in he was surprised to see Mercy seated at the breakfast-room table slowly sipping a drink, her leg stretched out on the chair. She looked like she had been crying. The afternoon paper was laying in front of her.

He leaned over to kiss her, and then took her by the shoulders. Yes, she had been crying. He pushed the paper aside. He'd seen the picture of Fenton, and the headline.

"Say, what gives?" he gave her shoulders a gentle shake. "Why the tears? I'm the one they're after, not you."

With that, Mercy pushed his hands away from her shoulders and glared at him as if she'd just been sentenced to death. She reached out to hit him, but as she started to swing her fist, her leg slipped from its support and fell with a thump to the floor.

Wincing with pain she ignored it and leaned toward him, her black eyes streaming with rage. "Listen," she said in a low voice, "you shut up—you understand me, you just *shut up*!"

Bewildered he stared at her, what could have happened? Helplessly he tried to pat her but she brushed his hand away angrily, sobbing wildly.

"*You're* on trial. *You, you, you.* Don't you ever think of anybody but yourself. What do you think we are? Don't you think we even *care*? What do you think we are? We have to sit there and listen to that bastard accuse you of killing those men, and we're not supposed to care!"

Then it all spilled out. The whole story of what had happened at the hearings with Gina and Fenton, and what had been happening at school and with her friends. It all came out until at last the sobbing subsided and she sat with her head on her balled-up fist, just as she had at the hearing.

That touched him more than all the sobbing had done. "Oh, my God," he breathed. "I didn't think, I just didn't think."

"I know," she murmured. "It wasn't your fault but . . ."

her voice drifted off in a trembling sigh.

He got up and lifting her gently from the chair, said, "Come on, lie down, you'll feel better." Pushing her crutches to one side he helped her into the other room, and laid her down on the couch.

Shaking her head irritably she whimpered, "It's this damn leg. I can't sit down, I can't stand up, and when I lay down all I can do is flop around like a—like a damn mermaid," she added with a giggle. "Boy, I'm glad I wasn't born a mermaid."

"Stay there," he said smiling. "I'll be right back."

He went into the other room to find some talcum to help soothe the itching of the cast on her leg.

As he reached into the medicine chest, he noticed that the bottle of sedatives the doctor had prescribed to her was half empty. He frowned as he looked at it. He had not realized that she had had to take them so often. It worried him. He'd rather she got mad at him.

He brought the talcum back to her. "There, that will help the itching at least, Mercy Mermaid," he grinned, and went to make himself a drink, and bring hers to her.

He set the drinks down on the coffee table and sat down beside her on the couch.

"OK," he said, "let's have it."

She stared thoughtfully at him and for a moment, a long silence hung there between them. She sighed and then looked down at her drink, slowly stirring the ice with the lacquered tip of her nail.

Without looking at him she said slowly, "Wally, I want you to quit the division."

He nodded. It had been worse for her than he had thought. She had needed those sedatives.

Quickly she reached out for his hand, "Listen, Wally please."

"It isn't just this Sylmar thing—" she was speaking very rapidly now. "Ever since you started working in the safety division, in those damned tunnels, you've done nothing but worry. Every time you go to a job—I don't care where it is—you never know what's going to happen. All you know is that whatever happens you can't do anything about it."

"But this—" he started.

She put her fingers over his mouth and shook her head impatiently.

"No, you listen! Ever since I've known you, it seems like you've been bringing dead bodies home."

He stared at her. It was true! When they had first met, he had just returned from Korea and had been assigned to the funeral detail. The detail met the ships carrying the coffins of dead soldiers. They routed them to all those places—near and far—that had been home for the soldiers.

The job had not seemed morbid or depressing to him. It was all part of the army. He had seen death up close once when he had been wounded, and he had been grateful to be alive.

Sometimes though, when the procession of oblong boxes being carried from the ship's hold seemed as long as the eternity they were carrying their young contents toward, the job had saddened him. He had told Mercy about it—especially on the really long days.

He had almost forgotten it. He had been young then and in love, and he had remembered that far more than the sorry errand assigned to him by the army.

But Mercy had never forgotten it, nor the strange aura of tragedy it cast around this man who seemed daily to look so casually at death. She had wanted to save him. She too was young and in love.

Sometimes after they were married and he began working with the safety division, she would recall those days.

They were especially vivid on the days when he'd come home to sit down wearily at the kitchen table and begin to write out the reports immediately, as if anxious to get them out of the way.

All these dreary recollections were in her mind as she talked earnestly on.

"Wally, you could get another job. If you go on, you're going to lose your job anyway. You're almost top on the list, and you know people now. People who could help you stop this awful trafficking with death."

He started at what she had put so badly and stared at her.

Before he could speak she went on, "Wally, please think about it before you say anything." Then with deep and final earnestness she ended. "You can't do anything more about those seventeen men than you could have done about those dead soldiers—nothing, nothing at all." Her voice was low, and in it there was the shadow of hopelessness. What she said, she knew, would do no good.

She was right. It did no good. It was something he could hardly explain to himself much less to her.

He couldn't even recall whether he had actively sought the safety engineer job in the Tunnels Division or had simply drifted into it. Or perhaps, he had been drawn into it by the urging of Carl Harberg, an old friend, a former tunnel engineer who had become almost a father to him.

The old man loved tunnels, especially highballing tunnels. He even collected books on them and he knew the story of every great tunnel ever built. Like an old seaman he loved to spin yarns about the tunnels he had worked on. It never bothered Wally if his friend repeated himself. It wasn't age that made him repeat himself. It was just that he loved tunnels and his memories of them, and he assumed automatically that Zavattero shared his fascination. Whether or not he did, one thing was certain—everything that Zavattero had learned about tunnels he had learned from old Carl, not from the meager instruction given in the Divison of Safety.

No, there was no way he could explain to Mercy except to stammer awkwardly. "I know all that Mercy. I know I can't do those seventeen men any good, but—" He paused and shook his head like a trapped animal, not hurt, but puzzled at what was paralyzing it. "There are seventeen other men in this state alive now, and if I do nothing, they could die. I can do something about them, and I've got to. You can see, I've got to. It has to stop someplace. If Lockheed gets away with what they've done, I'd really have something on my conscience." He looked at her. He didn't know what else to say. Finally he smiled and patted her affectionately. "OK?"

She sighed and nodded.

"Don't worry too much about the committee," he added. "All this noise might even lead to a new law—one that will make it possible for us to do something really responsible to stop outfits like Lockheed from highballing men into their graves." He paused and stared wistfully out the window. "Maybe," he shrugged.

"Where's Gina?" he asked. He knew Mercy would ask him to quit again, and he had to talk to his daughter.

Zavattero nodded approvingly at Mercy when she told him Gina had gone to work.

"That's good," he said, "I'll talk to her when she gets home." He didn't know what he'd say, but he needed to talk to her, just to be sure.

"It won't be till late."

"Doesn't matter," he said. "Now I'm going to get you something to eat and put you to bed. You get chef's special, OK?"

Mercy smiled at him, knowing that chef's choice would be thick slices of baked ham, potato salad, the last of the season's artichokes for him, and slices of beefsteak tomatoes for her.

She was right, and when he brought the food the two of them ate in companionable silence. Neither of them mentioned the TV or the evening news. They'd had enough for one day.

Later when Zavattero helped Mercy to bed, he glanced worriedly at the sleeping pills on the nightstand, "Want a sleeping pill?" he asked.

She shook her head, "No, I'm so tired I think I could sleep for a week."

"Good," he kissed her gently on the top of the head.

As he walked toward the door and put his hand on the

light switch, Mercy called sleepily.

"Wally."

"Yes," he said turning towards her.

"Wally, I love you."

"I know," he nodded. "And I love you."

Then he switched off the light and left, quietly closing the door.

He went first into the kitchen and took the bottle of bourbon from the liquor cabinet. He took it with him to the music room he had built for himself. He would wait for Gina there. Paula, he knew would be alright, but he was worried about Gina.

He would talk to her when she stopped in to say goodnight. She always did when she saw the light and knew he was puttering around with the recording equipment.

He would talk, try to explain to her about the assembly hearings, but right now he couldn't think anymore.

He felt as torn in half as the body he and Butterfield had so carefully placed on that muck car that day. He sank into the heavy, leather chair, a gift from Mercy and the girls. He poured himself a long drink and drank it down. Then he poured another. He leaned back, put the earphones over his head, and closed his eyes. It was something of Beethoven's. He couldn't remember what. Just something he'd liked and taped. The thunderous and powerful music sounded more loudly in his veins than the whiskey. He gave himself up to it. Tomorrow he'd make a decision. Tonight he had to escape.

PART TWO
THE TRIALS

> "John Henry
> he said
> to the Captain
> A man ain't nothin'
> but a man
> But before I let
> that steam drill get me down
> I'll die
> with a hammer in my hand,
> Lawd, Lawd,
> I'll die
> with a hammer in my hand."

CHAPTER EIGHT

The next morning he was up early. He brewed himself some bitter coffee and slipped out of the house before anyone else was awake. He had not slept except fitfully in the early morning, when his dreams had been a parade of masked politicians, corporations astride enormous cannons, burning bodies, and women weeping behind veils of dark hair. In spite of it all he had made his decision. There was no way back. All he could do was go on.

He hoped to get into the office on Wilshire Boulevard before anyone else. He didn't feel like a postmortem on the story of the assembly hearings. He thought if he could just avoid that for a while, he really wouldn't feel bad at all. In fact, he felt rather better than he had in a long time.

The night before when Gina had arrived home, as he had expected she'd stopped in to see him in the music room. With an impetuous gesture of youthful drama she had thrown her arms around him, dislodging his earphones and knocking over his glass.

"Oh, Dad," she breathed against his shoulder as he tried to take off his earphones and hug her to him at the same time, not too successfully.

She was not crying, but was trembling with outrage.

"There," he soothed her. "Sit down a minute."

Still trembling a little she sat down on the hassock at his feet clinging to his hand as if only she could save him.

He was so moved by her earnestness that he had to clear his throat several times before he could speak.

"Alright, tell me what happened. I hear you took off at Fenton today. I heard the ruckus, but I sure never thought it was you." His voice sounded a little amused and not a little proud.

She knew this, and quickly told him the whole story of her encounter with the unsuspecting assemblyman.

"And do you know what he did?" she asked indignantly. "He patted me on the head and said that someday I would understand." She tossed her head in an inspired imitation of the lofty adult placating the unenlightened child.

No wonder students feel like rioting, Zavattero thought, but he was genuinely worried.

He thought for a moment and then said slowly, "Well, look, honey, he may be right. . . ." He tried not to pat her on the head, though he longed to push back the tawny shower that fell over her stormy young face.

It was just as well he didn't. When she lifted her head she was glaring at him, "Now don't you start that! I understand perfectly well that he was calling you a murderer."

"Oh help," he thought and leaned towards her taking her by the shoulders giving them a little shake.

"Gina, you mustn't let them get to you." As she started to speak again he motioned her to silence and then unexpectedly grinned at her.

"But I know how you felt. I wouldn't like to tell you what I was thinking while that SOB was shooting his mouth off."

That mollified her a little and she gave him a small, wan smile.

Patiently he went on to explain to her the political significance of the committee hearings and the hope that a new safety act for tunnels could be passed as a result.

He waved her to silence again as he saw her stick her chin

out and prepare for another tirade, and continued.

"What happened today is only the beginning. It's going to get much worse—" he shook his head, "much, much worse. I don't want any of you to be hurt, I could talk to George Denton and we would not have to pursue the prosecution of Lockheed any further. In fact, everyone, even our own office would prefer that, but if we did we would be lying. Lockheed is guilty and no one would be able to do anything about it." As he ended, his voice was low as if he were talking more to himself than her.

As Gina listened she watched him closely. When he'd finished she straightened up, pushing her hair back from her face. He had not asked her a question, but with youthful dignity she was ready with an answer. "Dad, when I was little you used to tell me to tell the truth. Now it's my turn to tell you. Tell the truth. Don't worry about us. We'll be alright." She sounded very firm, and very pleased with herself.

Then as if she had earned the adult right to end the conversation she said, "I'm going to have a coke. Do you want me to fix you a drink?"

He smiled at her and handed her his glass. "Just some ice please. I have some bourbon here."

As he watched her walk briskly off to the kitchen, he shook his head slowly. He wondered what the Board of Directors of Lockheed would think if they knew that a fourteen-year-old graduate of Porter Junior High School was responsible for the criminal prosecution of Lockheed.

Zavattero's plan to arrive at the office before anyone else failed. That seemed to be the day everyone had gotten up early. Probably to catch the early morning news, Zavattero thought miserably.

He was wrong. Surprisingly, nobody mentioned the blistering article in the news or on the TV. It was true that since the first efforts to prosecute, there had been a pool of dead silence around Zavattero and Denton; and Zavattero had fully expected even more silence, if not downright hostility, after the beating he had taken at Fenton's hands.

Instead quite the reverse happened. Hope had begun to rustle like a faint breeze. As Zavattero thought about it, he realized that this was not really so strange, for there was hardly a man in the Division of Industrial Safety who didn't want Lockheed to be tried. Though the fact that seventeen men had been killed in the Sylmar blast stirred the public to pity and alarm, it did not take seventeen men to stir the emotions of the division's safety engineers.

Most of them, if asked about the tragedy, would remark bitterly on the fact that it had taken seventeen men. Many of them had seen one man die, and they could do nothing about it. To them that one man's death spelled out all the pain they would ever want to be witness to. If this prosecution could stop even one death, they would be glad.

For the miners who had been close to it, who had fought their way into the tunnel to save their buddies, slowly pulling out what was left of them to be piled on muck carts or laid out on the ground waiting for the coroner to identify them, it was as immediate as the sweep of the second hand on their watches.

To the men in the safety division it was as inexorable as history. Nearly half the history of civilization is written in its tunnels. Men had always worked underground, but the earth did not yield easily. The adage was that a man died for every mile of tunnel, but maybe if you were lucky, you could do something to stave off death.

Sometimes the men, including Zavattero, working in the Division of Industrial Safety thought bleakly that that was all it ever was—a matter of luck. If you were lucky, you got someone who would act. If not, there wasn't much you could do about it. Especially since Reagan had appointed Jack Hatton head of the division. Maybe it was a predilection for educating contractors instead of prosecuting them. Maybe it was a fondness for Reagan's spirited budget cutting, but for whatever reason, corporations had little to fear from the Division of Industrial Safety. Maybe if you were lucky you got someone on the job you could trust. Maybe. Zavattero had trusted

Savage. He regretted it now.

The Division of Industrial Safety was included in the Department of Industrial Relations. Its responsibilities, according to the prefatory note to the enabling legislation of the Division of Industrial Safety, were "supervising places of employment to see that they are safe."

Under Division 5, Section 6312 of the State Labor Code, the division has authority to:

"Enforce all laws and lawful orders requiring work and work places to be safe;

Investigate disabling or fatal industrial injuries;

Check whether work places are safe;

Prepare standards of industrial safety (Safety Orders), which if approved by the Industrial Safety Board have the effect of law; and

Establish special orders, or rules and regulations to cover a specific individual place of employment or process of work.

The Industrial Safety Board is the body responsible for reviewing and approving proposed Safety Orders."

The men working in the Division of Industrial Safety were expected to fulfill these responsibilities in seventeen specifically designated areas, all caught up more or less in one giant package of safety, ranging from aerial passenger tramways to window cleaning.

Tunnels were included under the construction department in this unwieldy, bureaucratic melange of safety instructions.

This had always seemed a little curious to Zavattero. Tunnels not only had special peculiarities like dangerous gases and running ground that had to be dealt with, but tunneling also had a different psychology, something redolent of history and ancient mystique. Though few of them were aware of this, the attitude of the men who called themselves tunnel stiffs reflected it. Most of them did not want to work in any other kind of construction except tunnels.

They often made Zavattero recall a passage from one of the books that Carl Hageburg had given him. Written by a

Scandinavian engineer named Gosta Sandstrom, and titled simply *Tunnels*, publisher, Holt, Rinehart, and Winston 1963, the book was a history of all the great tunnels of the world. In its preface the author left no doubt about his view of the importance of tunnels and the men who built them. His statement was a passionate one. Said he, "It is infuriating to be confronted with the imposing archaeological remains of ancient civilizations and have to listen to harpings on the doings of gods and heroes, the behavior of captains in silly little tribal wars, or the death of an apostle, while the basic questions bearing on the economy and real life of the ancient cities, the raison d'etre of their existence, is shrugged off as the concern of slaves."

Zavattero and Hageburg couldn't restrain their amusement at his vehement statement. They often wondered if the author would have felt better if Jesus of Nazareth had been a tunnel stiff instead of a carpenter.

Of all the tunnels in the world the Simplon Tunnel was the most interesting.

It is still the longest tunnel ever built, and probably the most glamorous. Everything from Agatha Christie's *Murder on the Orient Express* to Alfred Hitchcock's *Night Train* had hurtled through it.

In fact, it is possible that more fictional characters died in the Simplon Tunnel than were ever killed by the frightening antics of the earth during its construction. Those antics had been formidable indeed. They appeared in the shape of an unheard-of type of running rock. The rock turned to a doughy mess which simply enfolded the terrified miners. Engineers had never encountered anything like it before, and miners never wanted to see the earth avenge itself in such an ugly outrage again.

Yet the Simplon Tunnel was a model one, and marked the first expression of official concern for the welfare of underground workers.

It was built at the turn of the century shortly after the construction of another famous tunnel, the Saint Gotthard

Tunnel. This undertaking had been a ghastly affair of death and human suffering.

The horrors of the Saint Gotthard had proved so unsupportable that when the time came for the building of the Simplon, the project was not allowed to go underground unless there was adequate ventilation, cooled air, fresh drinking water, and electric light, if possible. Workers should be provided with free baths and drying facilities for their clothes. There was also to be a benefit fund for widows and children of miners, and injured workers were guaranteed medical attention.

Also, before the Simplon could go underground, a special technical committee had been appointed to give their opinion of the feasibility of the ambitious effort, to be bored through Mount Leone on the Swiss-Italian border. Not only had the committee evaluated the proposed project, but it had also added some significant provisions of its own regarding medical supervision, food, and inspection. They must have constituted the first assembly hearing. In any event the Simplon was probably the first expression in modern times of official concern for the welfare of underground workers.

The almost primitive provisions made at the turn of the century were still an important part of the Tunnel Safety Orders. It had taken the tragedy of the Saint Gotthard Tunnel to bring these changes about, and as Zavattero read that there would be more assembly hearings, he wondered if the deaths at Sylmar might also serve a purpose. The politicians claimed that was their objective, but they were politicians. Zavattero at that time was feeling almost as bad about politicians as he did about corporations. Anyway it was *something* to hope for.

Though there was sure to be an additional hearing, maybe more, the men in the Division of Industrial Safety were showing more interest in the possibility of prosecuting Lockheed. Lockheed was big and so firmly entrenched in the southern California economy that it could push a button and make the San Fernando Valley look like a burnt-out storefront. Lockheed's power was not diminished by the fact that on September 9, its loan guaranty was granted.

The growing interest was not a matter of coffee-break gossip, as in normal offices. The life of a safety engineer does not include many office coffee breaks or chatty lunches. They are not clannish. They have no time for it. Most of their time is spent on the road. The boundaries of the areas assigned to them, especially to those in the tunnels and mines divisions, can be wide or narrow, but they must be traveled constantly.

It was not always pleasant. Sometimes it was tedious and tiring to travel over baking-hot roads to check the excavations of a gravel pit. Sometimes it was lonely to travel at night to a remote mine where rotting timbers could breathe carbon dioxide and instant death. But it was certainly exciting to be part of the activity of a highballing operation like the Lockheed tunnel.

But whatever it was, it was constant moving and did not make for office coffee mornings. Except at the end of the month, when the budget had run out. Then the only thing to do was return to the office. Sit there and shuffle papers with brisk authority.

These lulls in the budget, when the entire state of California could be blowing up like Mount Fuji and no one could do anything about it, were a source of exasperation to nearly everyone, but most of all to George Bunker, Northern California Engineer for the division.

His statements about what should be done to the budget cutters in Sacramento would have sent all the congressmen scrambling up the Capitol dome like the squirrels in the Capitol park. In fact, he was looking forward with eagerness to the next assembly hearing. The southern division engineer Clifford Farmer chafed against the same frustrations, but he was not so eager to face the assembly.

Normally Zavattero and Denton also resented the enforced inactivity during the budget lulls, but for now they were glad of it. It gave them extra time for investigation. Though they were officially assigned to the investigation, most of the actual work had to be done on their own time. George Bane was getting so little support from the city attorney's office that he had to rely heavily on the efforts of the two engineers.

What the charges against Lockheed were to be had not been agreed upon by the city attorney's office, if indeed there would be any.

Such charges were not of major importance to Johnson and McFettridge, who were busily raking through the muck in preparation for the next assembly hearing scheduled for September 23.

Lockheed too was investigating the causes of the accident, as they called it. So too were the federal representatives of the Occupational Safety and Health Administration, and the Metropolitan Water District was in busy session with geologists investigating early conditions in the tunnel.

Zavattero was beginning to wonder when everyone would stop investigating and start prosecuting. Not that that seemed to be any kind of an issue to anybody but him, Denton, and George Bane.

By mutual agreement the whole crew of investigators claimed to be doing the same thing. Trying to determine the causes of the explosion in order to avoid further tragedies.

All were bent on complete cooperation, but somehow they made a strange combination. Taken together they were curiously like a musical combo. All playing on the same theme but somehow never managing to play the same tune at the same time.

Occasionally this unlikely combo would all manage to hit the same note in unison—the note was usually one of lament for the dead men—and that was a moment of ecstatic cooperation.

But no one ever made the mistake of thinking that they weren't each listening to a distinctly different drummer.

Zavattero and Denton wanted evidence for prosecution. Johnson and McFettridge wanted material on the deplorable state of the Division of Industrial Safety for the next assembly hearings. Metropolitan Water District was busily gathering geological data to prove that Lockheed's threatened $10 million breach of contract suit was an affront and an outrage to all civilized thinkers. And Lockheed was looking for evidence that God had brought the whole thing about in a fit of existential peevishness. But they all agreed lugubriously that it was a terrible tragedy for the men and their families. They hit this note of blissful cooperation most often in the presence of the news media. There, not an uncooperative word was heard ... yet.

Leading the investigative parade were the two men from the legislature who had been assigned full-time to the investigation of the events at Sylmar by Bob Moretti, who was Speaker of the House and vociferous foe of Ronald Reagan.

After the events of the first hearing they were pleasantly surprised to learn that Zavattero was perfectly willing to provide them with any information they might need. Denton had not been subpoenaed, and had no reason not to be cooperative, but Johnson and McFettridge felt Zavattero did have.

It was, in fact, with Zavattero that they were to hit pay dirt. They had spent a long four-hour lunch talking with Denton and Zavattero, and had not only been given complete access to their files but were promised the cooperation of other safety engineers in the Division of Industrial Safety. Events had now reached a point where mention of the investigation of Lockheed was no longer met with a dead pool of apprehensive silence in the offices on Wilshire Boulevard. Almost everyone had some grisly story to tell of his frustrated efforts to prosecute in Hatton's rainbow world of enlightened employers who only needed a gentle reminder that such things as the lack of roll bars on tractors meant the likelihood of some man being crushed to death. From the engineers who tried to work in this climate, Johnson and McFettridge were to get more than they'd hoped for.

It was, however, at Zavattero's house where they had begun to feel so comfortable that they could lounge around on the floor and drink beer in easy story-swapping camaraderie, they got the story of the stolen meter.

Now, that information had a touch of glamour to it! Especially to Johnson, whose old news sense immediately started putting the story into nice fat headlines for the day of the hearings, which was now not so far away.

He shifted his heavy body forward, taking a deep breath from his ever-present inhalator. "Where's Ree, now?" he wheezed. He was thinking of Ree's disappearance at the first hearing.

Zavattero shrugged. "I don't know. I can't go looking for him."

"Doesn't Savage know?"

Zavattero shook his head. "I asked him. All he said was that Ree quit."

"That's all?"

"That's it. Period."

Johnson leaned back and whistled softly, free for a moment of his plaguing asthma.

"Finkle?"

Again Zavattero shook his head. "He wouldn't tell you."

McFettridge, who had been watching them both quietly, grinned amiably and said, "Don't worry we'll find him!"

And Zavattero knew they would. He felt sorry for Ree. He'd always rather liked him. He was a good tunnel man and a good safety engineer. He had the feeling that whatever had happened, it wasn't really Ree's fault.

As the two men left, they seemed quite elated by the news and promised to keep in touch with them about Ree. When Zavattero nodded good-bye to them at the door, he smiled. He suspected they were headline hunting.

CHAPTER NINE

Whether they were hunting for headlines, or not, on the second day of the hearings they got them.

The headlines were sedately matter-of-fact: "Tunnel Gas Tester Taken, Inquiry Told" read one; "Reveal Gas Testing Device Taken After Sylmar Blast," read another. What the story really could have used was a bit of *Variety* show biz panache like: "Lockheed's Midnight Looksee No Go," considering the consequences of the revelation.

Though the news report stated only that the members of the committee appeared puzzled over the action, they had in fact been more than puzzled. They'd been bowled over. Not only at the incident, but at the fact the Division of Industrial Safety had failed to take any legal action against Lockheed.

They were very quickly going to start asking why not. First to the stand was Crabtree who had traced, in vague outlines, the route of the meter from the contractor's office to Lockheed's attorney to the Bureau of Mines.

He was followed by Clifford Farmer who would be forced to bear the brunt of the committee's outraged queries.

After Crabtree's testimony Newton Russell turned sternly to Farmer.

ASSEMBLYMAN RUSSELL: What did you do, Mr. Farmer?

MR. FARMER: In my experience with the yellow tags and on crossing yellow tags, we have never had anything like this before, so we're going to turn this over to the attorney general's office.

FENTON: You are going to?

FARMER: Yes. Excuse me?

CHAIRMAN KEYSOR: You have not yet?

FENTON: It's only a month, not bad.

KEYSOR: When did you decide—did you decide you are going to turn it over right now, or did—

FARMER: No, we discussed it without legal advisors.

RUSSELL: You are thinking of turning it over to the attorney general's office?

FENTON: I would suggest you do it. I suggest you stop thinking, Mr. Farmer, and do it. Let them make a determination if there is any criminal or civil action to be taken.

As Fenton said that, Zavattero almost cheered. Then he wondered why the hell Fenton hadn't done it in the first hearing? It had already been a month then. Instead he'd chased Zavattero all over the lot with a red tag.

Assemblyman Russell stepped in with a polite inquiry as to why there was so much "temporizing." He offered a host of explanations, and received the appropriate answers from the somewhat flustered Farmer.

Then Assemblyman Russell arrived at the rather lame conclusion that "the democratic wheels grind slowly."

After the hearing Bane had observed that if they could keep those wheels grinding slowly enough, the statute of limitations could run out. After all, the statute on a misdeamenor was only a year. In the bureaucracy that was the mere blink of an eye.

The hearings were proving more cheering to Zavattero than he had hoped. Fenton had even learned to pronounce his name right. But most important, the committee listened when Zavattero tersely described the existing safety laws as "antiquated" and listened attentively to his suggestions. They were the same suggestions he had been screaming about in the division since he had arrived on the job.

His requests seemed obvious to him, but the committee made careful note as he outlined them; beginning with the need for training crews in the operation of breathing devices; strict elimination of ignition sources; more explicit direction regarding ventilation; specific requirements regarding operation of new boring machines; and importantly, a stipulation that the contractor must shut down operation for seventy-two hours when gas is encountered. As he mentioned the last, he stared for a moment out the window. If only he could have shut down Lockheed for seventy-two hours. He shook his head imperceptibly and brought his attention back to the committee.

Fenton was asking if he meant any amount of gas.

ZAVATTERO: I don't care. Any amount, because no one can tell what's in front of the face of that tunnel. The contractor can't, we can't, we're just guessing and investigate the evaluation, maybe test for it, and this sort of thing. I believe this would lay it on the line for all the contractors. They'd know if they run into gas, they have to shut down. There would be no decision like me going in there testing for gas; I found none. Well, if we had a procedure, an order, outlining this, it would be straightforward. There would be a good investigation.

Zavattero went on to describe ventilation requirements. They were complicated and precise. But Assemblyman Russell still seemed more worried about what was happening administratively. "Are these administrative orders he asked?" Zavattero replied yes, and again Fenton stepped in.

FENTON: Who formulates these administrative orders?
ZAVATTERO: The division.
FENTON: Do they call you in and ask you your opinion of them before they formulate?

Zavattero almost laughed at that. These days no one was asking his opinion of anything. His reply was simple.

ZAVATTERO: I usually give my opinion, Mr. Fenton.

FENTON: I know you do. You are very—I know you do. But they call you in to do it, or do you just come voluntarily?

There was a note of admiration in Fenton's voice.

ZAVATTERO: I volunteer.

FENTON: Now, these administrative orders that you're recommending would cost more to the employer, of course, to operate the job, wouldn't it?

ZAVATTERO: I don't think there is any question about it.

And that, Zavattero thought bitterly, was one good reason why they were not likely to get such a law.

Nevertheless, things were a hell of a lot better than they had been after the first hearing. Maybe Keysor's closing statement that reforms were being planned was something more than a pretty wrapping on a political package. Well, time would tell. Zavattero was not an optimistic man. He'd seen too much.

Johnson and McFettridge though were optimistic. They had talked to enough men in the division and in the unions to realize that the next step was a full-scale investigation, what the news media would refer to ominously as a probe.

They were also anxious to assist Bane in his efforts to locate Bob Ree.

At the assembly hearings, Tom McNary, who was still acting as Savage's personal attorney, had advised him not to testify. As far as Zavattero could determine the admonition to remain silent had not disturbed Savage. Savage was not in any event a loquacious man. He could always keep his own counsel, unlike Ree who was more voluble and in fact more articulate. There was, indeed, a good deal of public speculation that Lockheed had removed Ree from the scene for this very reason.

David Finkle, Lockheed's now omnipresent lawyer, had been impressively unforthcoming on the subject of Lockheed engineer's whereabouts when pressed by Fenton to produce the glaringly absent Mr. Ree. The last hour of the entry into the banned tunnel looked deeply suspicious.

Actually the fact that Ree, Rasmussen and Biro had entered the tunnel at such an unlikely hour was not strange to Zavattero and Denton. The world of tunnels is one of perpetual darkness. No sun rises to illuminate it, no cock crows to announce that the time has come to be busy about the world's work. It is always dark, and, as Rasmussen had told the committee, the job they had to do was better done when there was no other activity in the tunnel.

What baffled them was the whole, bizarre antic. After the hearing, they sat in the evening by Zavattero's pool trying to unravel the mystery.

They both knew that there had been another meter that could be equally damaging, but they had told no one of its significance. Lockheed might try to get its hands on that one too.

"Anyway, I don't think that was Ree's idea," Denton said.

"Neither do I," Zavattero agreed. "I think someone planted that meter in there and then sent Bob and Arvy and the cop in there to find it. I know it wasn't the same meter, that's for sure. They found it right next to the place where they found Warner's body, and there was only forty pounds of him left. The meter I sent to the Bureau of Mines was hardly scorched."

"They must have been nuts," Denton muttered.

Zavattero nodded, "Yep, I told you. They're a bunch of maniacs, that's what they are. They never seem to learn."

"Who," asked Denton, lost in his own thoughts.

"You know—Lockheed," Zavattero replied irritably, "Seattle, Burbank—" then he thought a moment and added, "that plant up around Sunnyvale or Mount View or wherever it is. It's right near that nut house, Agnew or something." He paused again and after a long moment he added musingly, "Say, maybe that's where they're recruiting their executives."

Denton, who sometimes wondered about Zavattero, stared at him. "Wally, you sure say the damndest things."

Zavattero grinned, "Well you have to admit they sure made a boo-boo when they took that meter. It's no good for anything now."

That boo-boo was nevertheless the pebble that stopped Lockheed's flight from prosecution.

The assembly subcommittee had practically demanded that some action be taken against Lockheed, and the public was now so incensed that there was no way to avoid prosecution.

In the city attorney's office, the decision was finally made that Lockheed and Otha Ree should be charged, on certain violations of the labor code, of entering the tunnel over the yellow tag; and under Penal Code 135 of concealing evidence. They were all misdemeanors. Zavattero and Denton signed the complaints.

A continuing investigation for prosecution on counts of gross negligence, violations of the tunnel safety orders and labor code would be pursued, but the prosecution of Ree and Lockheed in the meter case would be tried as a separate issue.

Bane, with a wary eye on the statue of limitations, decided to file on the already-determined charges of concealing evidence. The first case was to be tried separately because it did not involve gross negligence and fewer defendants and courts were involved. It irritated the not always even-tempered Bane when it was suggested that he wanted to try the case first as a test case.

It irritated him even more that he could get no assistance from his own office, the attorney general's office, or the Division of Industrial Safety.

The lack of cooperation in the attorney general's office was not difficult to understand. Bakaly—O'Melvany &

Meyers' attorney for Lockheed—had been a campaign chairman for Evelle Younger's shot at the attorney general's office. In fact, O'Melvany & Meyers seemed to occupy a generally strange place in the picture. They were also the bonding attorneys for the city of Los Angeles and more than close to City Attorney Arnebergh, who was more interested in real estate development than he was in the department stepchild, criminal investigation.

The only tide pools of clarity in these murky waters were Zavattero and Denton, whom Hatton had been pressured into assigning to the investigation of evidence for prosecution of Lockheed on gross negligence counts as well as the charges against Ree and Lockheed.

In the *Los Angeles Times*, November 3, Hatton commenting on the news that Moretti had ordered the "job safety probe," asserted that he would welcome the impending investigation and would do all he could to assist. He added, "I am not in agreement with all of the charges." He said, "I think many of them will be disproved at the investigation."

"This," as Zavattero observed to Denton and Bane one evening as the three of them were sifting through reports made by division engineers, "was a lot of bull. I don't know what he's been smoking, but I'd sure like some of it." Pot was a word that was beginning to be heard frequently in his household, and he had sometimes wondered what it was really like.

George Bane had scoffed at the statement for different reasons. At the rate the investigations were going, nobody would be alive to file the charges. They hadn't even been able to locate Ree yet.

Zavattero, who had not been reassigned after the explosion as he had expected, was constantly at the Sylmar office with Savage, going over the requirements for opening the tunnel again. Whenever he asked him about Ree, Savage could say no more than Ree had quit.

It was up to Johnson and McFettridge to try to locate the elusive Ree. At that time Bane told them he would issue a fugitive warrant, putting bail at $100,000 if necessary to bring him back to be arraigned on the stipulated counts.

When Bane mentioned the amount of bail, Zavattero whistled, but Bane explained that he could see no alternative if they were to hang on to Ree. There had already been rumors that Ree was being sent to Alaska, and Alaska was an awfully easy place to get lost in.

At that Denton nodded vigorously. "Yeah, they could send him to Point Barrow. I had a friend who went there to teach the Eskimos, and they only sent in two ships a year. When the guy came back he was a wreck. If I were Ree, I'd rather stand trial."

"It isn't what Ree wants. It's what Lockheed wants," Bane pointed out. "But don't quote me. I don't think we can charge Lockheed for putting witnesses on ice."

All three of them burst out laughing at Bane's unexpected and witty sally. George Bane was an intense young man, and on the score or prosecution of Lockheed was just as determined as Zavattero.

He was not given to laughter over the case, and he had even less reason to be when Johnson and McFettridge informed him that they were sure that Ree was now working at Lockheed's Seattle plant. By then it was late November, and Thanksgiving was just around the corner.

Bane went immediately to a Los Angeles judge with his request for a fugitive warrant with $100,000 bail, explaining his fear that Ree would run. When this information reached Arnebergh, Bane was summoned to his office, and for the first time the thin, pale city attorney who liked to give lectures on morals at his church, dropped his austere manner along with his low profile and demanded in an outraged voice what the hell the young attorney thought he was doing. In a tight, angry voice he called the offense nothing more than "a stinking misdemeanor."

To Bane's utter dismay, he was being castigated by his superior while a brace of Lockheed attorneys watched it all as if they might have been watching a cockfight.

Bane had been told that Lockheed's legal team were

repeatedly discussing the case with his superiors, but he had never had such graphic evidence of it until he stood there listening to the outraged recriminations of Roger Arnebergh.

Almost relieved by what was now revealed as open animosity, Bane turned and left Arnebergh's office. A ripple of congratulatory laughter reached his ears. That was OK. Now he was calm and very, very angry. He picked up the phone.

It was Thanksgiving eve in Seattle and Otha (Bob) G. Ree was just returning home from the offices of Lockheed Shipbuilding and Construction Company.

He was glad to be in Seattle, where the air was crisp and cold and you could tell it was really winter. The clean smell of snow hung over the city though it was early for snow. But maybe tomorrow it would snow, and the holidays would begin with the fragrance of Thanksgiving and the fairy quality of snow that made children laugh.

Los Angeles he knew would lay locked in the monotony of endless suburbs, where the seasons slipped in and out along the freeways like sun-colored snakes on their way to some airless desert.

That, he supposed, wasn't fair. The view from Mullholland Drive on a clear night at Christmas could make Los Angeles look like a city of sequins streaming through the endless branches of an eternal Christmas tree. Anyway that was what young lovers saw, but he was now no young lover, and even as the thought crossed his mind, he recalled that in 1928 the dam that Mullholland had built had burst sweeping 385 people, 12,240 homes and 7,900 acres of farmland in front of it. The day before, the dam had been inspected and declared safe by Mullholland and his chief assistant. The Lockheed tunnel was built in the same earthquake fault country. He know all about that dam. It was part of his job to know. And he also had heard that when Mullholland was forced into retirement he had said, "I envy the dead."

Ree shuddered uncomfortably, as if the cold air had

touched his bones, and walked toward his house.

As he neared the house, there seemed to be a lot of action going on around it. He wondered if they were going to have a party and no one had told him about it. He hoped not. He was awfully tired.

It was no unexpected party. Before he reached the front step, a loud voice told him he was under arrest. Several people seemed to be talking at once. The lights were bright and there were cameras and people everywhere, and the loud voice told him to put his hands against the wall.

He did. He couldn't believe it. He was being arrested, and hands were being run over him to make sure he wasn't carrying a gun. He felt silly. This was like something on a stupid TV show.

It had all happened too fast for him to grasp what was actually happening. When he did, he began to be alarmed.

He was to be taken to King's County jail and held there on $100,000 bail. He had taken the meter from the San Fernando Valley tunnel on July 16 and on and on it went. He could see where the loud voice was coming from now, and the man with it looked much smaller than his voice.

He nodded, and simply asked if he could call his lawyer as soon as they got to King's County jail. He looked around for his wife, but apparently she had not come home yet. He asked if they would tell her what had happened, and when reassured he climbed into the waiting car.

As the police car drove off, he started to ask what it was all about, but decided not to.

He was baffled. He couldn't understand what had happened. He had been expecting to hear from Lockheed that he should return to Los Angeles. He had been advised of his right not to testify at the assembly hearing and had thought no more about it. He had not, he felt, tried to cover his tracks. Why hadn't Lockheed, Finkle, or somebody told them where he was? He had talked to Rasmussen just a few weeks ago.

When he talked to Finkle on the phone he got no enlightenment on the subject, but Finkle assured him that he would take care of everything. Then Ree settled down to spend the night in the King's County jail.

The guard brought him some food and told him cheerfully that tomorrow they would have turkey. "It's Thanksgiving, you know," he said.

"Yeah, I know," Ree had replied.

The next day Finkle arrived and, with an immaculate dispatch that seemed to match his clothes, had the bail lowered to $1250. Bob Ree was free to go, but he would be booked in Los Angeles County the next day. Then Bob Ree went home to Thanksgiving dinner. They weren't going to have turkey though. They were going out for dinner. He didn't feel like turkey. The next day he was to be booked.

In Los Angeles, Zavattero and Denton, along with Laura and Mercy and occasional fleeting glimpses of their children, were spending the evening. They knew that something was pending, and they kept the TV going quietly as they tried to chat about other things—other times and more pleasant preoccupations—but they all kept looking back at the TV. They all felt that the TV should be used for more innocent diversions than finding out what might happen to you the next day.

When the news did arrive, it was almost anticlimactic. The news of Ree's arrest in Seattle had been usurped by a hijacking that had sent everyone hurtling to the other side of town.

They did learn though that Ree had been arrested, and that he would be spending the night in King's County jail. The news didn't cheer them much. What the hell, Ree was really just a tunnel stiff like them.

One of the young people got up to switch on something more to their liking, and Mercy and Laura went to fix fresh drinks for everyone.

"Well, that takes care of Ree, I guess," Denton said.

Zavattero nodded. He hoped the telephone wouldn't ring. He didn't want to hear anything from Savage, who now called him frequently at home, nor did he feel like talking even to Bane.

Mercy and Laura returned with the drinks, and Denton said, "Here's to Ree. He will probably be arraigned sometime early in December."

Again Zavattero nodded. He wondered if it would be on December 4. December 4 was Saint Barbara's Day, the patron saint of tunnel workers and artillery men. It was the only day except Christmas that the miners in the early tunnels had been allowed off. Even Lockheed, he thought, ought to take that day off.

CHAPTER TEN

Ree was not arraigned on Saint Barbara's Day, but on December 6, when Zavattero and Denton had duly signed the appropriate papers charging him with seven counts of violating the safety code. Following the arraignment, Ree had once again departed for Seattle to await notice of trial.

No trial date had been agreed on in the city attorney's office, and there still remained some question as to whether the meter caper, as it was now beginning to be called, would be just a part of a more serious trial involving not only Lockheed, but Savage, Ree, Eugene Pedigo (a walker in the tunnel) and Russell Van Guilder (a walker on the swing shift).

Bane was now being blocked from all sides. In the Division of Industrial Safety, Zavattero and Denton were permitted to help him only in their off-hours. Even though prosecution was now a certainty, they were not to be allowed time or funds for a thorough investigation. Moreover, they were in the difficult position of having to continue working on the reopening of the Lockheed tunnel.

With Johnson and McFettridge, though, the Division of Industrial Safety had finally been compelled to cooperate. The investigators had been given subpoena powers, by Moretti, and there was hardly a file that did not produce a dismal story of death and injuries left unprosecuted by the division since Hatton had taken over in 1968. What they had learned made them eager to assist Bane, but the evidence they amassed was to be made public at the final Assembly hearings in January. However, nothing that was pertinent to the prosecution of the Sylmar debacle would be allowed.

The hearing this time was to be chaired by Fenton, which came as no surprise to anyone, least of all Fenton. He had proved a redoubtable fighter on behalf of the working man and, Zavattero supposed, deserved the honor, if that's what it was. It amused and even pleased Zavattero that no effort on his part to explain the ins and outs of politics to Gina could alter her attitude toward the assemblyman. Fenton did not know it, but he had forever lost one vote for the Democratic party. Maybe all the votes in Porter Junior High. Gina could be very persuasive.

Two new men had been added to the committee. They were Dixon Arnett (R—Redwood City) and Larry Townsend (D—Torrance) who were to prove quite as testy as the flamboyant Fenton. After all, they'd learned, the man they were most anxious to interrogate was the head of the Division of Industrial Safety.

When Jack Hatton walked into the assembly hearing, he was a doomed man. To think of him now as "Fat Jack" would have been more cruel than amiable. He was indeed a heavy man. He wore heavy, black-rimmed glasses that made his eyes look large and rather kindly. His round cheeks were soft and jowly and looked as if they should be inflated to give him the appearance of the conventionally jolly fat man. It would have suited him.

Whatever he was, he had been braver than William C. Hern, Director of the Department of Industrial Relations, who had somehow managed to ignore subpoenas, telephone calls and letters for days before the hearings.

When Hern was finally located on the second day of the hearings, the committee chided him for an alleged statement that the hearings were nothing but a "witch hunt." He denied it, but if the hearings were a witch hunt, they had found their witches.

At the earlier hearings, Hatton had been easily confident and had not even prepared a written statement. At this one he took the proffered opportunity to make a statement. It was long, full of praise for the division, and absolutely meaningless.

After this, began the long procession of witnesses to the failure to prosecute.

Among the first witnesses was Gordon E. Bunker, engineer in the northern division. Over the years, Zavattero had met occasionally with Bunker and admired him. He seemed to have a thorough realization of the problems faced by the field man. Zavattero had often thought of the possibility of moving up north, and even talked about it with Bunker.

Bunker's testimony was straightforward and matter-of-fact. He did not falter over the budget cutting that had made a difficult job almost impossible, nor did he falter when assemblyman Townsend asked, "Let me see if I understood correctly. You mean that there are many times where men are killed when we do not prosecute because of safety violations?"

Bunker answered, "That is very true, yes."

His case in point was a typical one. A story that was to be repeated many times before the hearings were over.

In a highway construction near Redding in northern California, he had used every means to force the Ray Kizer Construction Company to install roll bars on their scrapers and trackers. Nothing had been done, not even when one man had been crushed to death. It had been a bitter experience for Bunker.

Bunker's recital of his two-year effort to compel the contractor to provide roll bars, plus his effort to obtain a prosecution after the death of one man when one contractor refused to comply with safety orders, appalled the committee. But it was only the beginning of what was being brought to light by witnesses.

During Bunker's statements, Jack Hatton, seated back in the audience remained silent. The witnesses were doing some frightening arithmetic and he knew it.

Jepson's testimony about electrical hazards was even more damaging than it had been at the first hearings. In 1966, before Hatton had been appointed, there had been five prosecutions for violations of electrical safety. In 1967, after Hatton's appointment, there had been forty-three instances of hazardous contact with high-voltage wires. Result: sixteen fatalities. Prosecutions: one. In 1970 the number of such hazardous contacts was seventy-six. Fatalities: twenty. Prosecutions: none.

And so the evidence kept piling up, all that long day and into the next when Zavattero had been subpoenaed to testify about the Angelus Tunnel.

Zavattero had not known if the committee would ask about the Angelus Tunnel. Lockheed had been one of the contractors and Lockheed was being threatened with prosecution. The story of the Angelus Tunnel and Hatton's part in it could be so damaging that Lockheed could cry prejudicial publicity, scream for a dismissal, and probably get it. Hatton had apparently assumed this—or been assured of it—and told the committee that he was unprepared to answer questions about the Angelus Tunnel. He did not think they would ask about it because of the pending Lockheed litigation, Hatton told the committee.

Hatton was wrong and, prepared or unprepared, he was going to have to answer some questions. He was asked to take a seat at the witness table. He was seated next to Zavattero.

Zavattero felt uncomfortable seated next to Hatton. Hatton made no motion, just sat very quietly except when he would lean on the table, his head bowed. He would rub the bridge of his nose occasionally, like a very old man who had lost his spectacles and could no longer see.

As Zavattero told about the Angelus Tunnel, Hatton rubbed his eyes often. Zavattero did not look at him but straight ahead at the committee.

He had reason to hate this old man who had thwarted him and had made his life a shambles, but when someone sits breathing beside you it is not so easy to do.

The Angelus Tunnel had been a big operation, $100 million project. Besides Lockheed the contractors were Shea, Kaiser and Healy. It had first gone underground in November 1966. Almost from the beginning it had spelled nothing but trouble for Zavattero.

As early as July 24, 1967, Zavattero had received service requests from operation Engineers Local 12.

He was to test for noxious gases. When he found them he had ordered the contractor to correct the condition. The contractor had refused which had made the situation far different from the one at Sylmar.

At Sylmar he had seen them bring in breathing devices, had watched Ree and the Bureau of Mines man calibrate the meter, and most of all Savage had agreed to call him if there were any gas. He would close the job down altogether when the readings reached two percent by volume anywhere in the tunnel. At that point Lockheed seemed to have learned something from their experience with the Angelus Tunnel.

At the Angelus Tunnel there had been no pause for thoughtful debate. Zavattero's senior, Mueller, had flatly refused.

When queried by Fenton about the deaths and injuries in the tunnel, Zavattero had added his dreadful arithmetic to the statistic. Three men killed, two hundred lost-time injuries and ten completely disabling injuries. None of these had, however, been due to gas in the tunnel.

The question of ventilation and gas in the tunnel had finally become critical later in August.

ZAVATTERO: I should conclude that on August 30 the noxious gases were still in there, the ventilation was inadequate. I went to Mr. Mueller and I requested a tag order. I had already received a show cause order on August 23.

CHAIRMAN FENTON: What does that mean?

ZAVATTERO: That means a contractor has to comply or show cause why he does not.

FENTON: For what was this?

ZAVATTERO: This was for the noxious fumes. Now, on August 30 I requested the tag order from Mr. Mueller.

FENTON: When did you first notice this gas?

ZAVATTERO: It was July 26.

FENTON: So from July 26 to August 30 he still hadn't complied relative to the gas.

ZAVATTERO: Yes, sir. I should bring something out here. The noxious gas is what I was trying to correct but there was also the presence of methane gas.

FENTON: What's the problem with methane gas?

ZAVATTERO: It will blow up.

FENTON: Okay.

ZAVATTERO: So, had I got the noxious gas taken care of and corrected, it would have done away with the methane.

FENTON: Right.

ZAVATTERO: On August 30, I went to Mr. Mueller and I requested a tag order. He called Mr. Hatton in my presence and asked for the tag order. Mr. Hatton refused to give the tag order. August 31 at 3:00 A.M. the tunnel blew up.

To Zavattero that 3:00 A.M. call had been a rehearsal for Sylmar. Even the cast of characters was almost the same. Lockheed was one of the contractors. Savage was an engineer at the Angelus Tunnel. That was where he and Zavattero had first met. They had not met again until Sylmar, when Zavattero had been glad to learn that Savage would now be the project manager. It was a step up for him, and Zavattero thought he deserved it. He was good. Even now Zavattero did not believe that Savage could have been responsible for what had happened at Sylmar. He knew, though, that Savage was going to be named in the prosecution, *if* the prosecution did not end with the meter theft. It had better not. If it did, they would hear him screaming all the way north to Alaska, west to Hawaii, and east to Washinton D.C. where, Zavattero thought, it would probably be strangled when it reached the desk of Secretary of Labor, former Lockheed executive James D. Hodgeson. Zavattero was feeling very bitter about Lockheed.

So presumably was Assemblyman Townsend, who, if he wasn't being bitter, was being awfully damned curious.

After Hatton denied that he had any recollection of the call from Mueller about the Angelus Tunnel, Townsend spoke up.

ASSEMBLYMAN TOWNSEND: Refresh my memory again. Yesterday how long did you say you had been an employee of Lockheed?

MR.HATTON: For twenty-eight years.

TOWNSEND: And you were an engineer—an industrial engineer at that company?

HATTON: Yes, sir.

TOWNSEND: Let me ask this. Are you on leave of absence now or did you resign?

HATTON: Did I what?

TOWNSEND: Are you on leave of absence now or did you resign?

HATTON: I resigned.

TOWNSEND: And you never think about your old company ties when Lockheed has a problem, do you?

HATTON: Lockheed, in my opinion, is a very fine company, but I never allow the fact that I worked for that company to influence my decision in the job that I have.

TOWNSEND: Did you retire from that company or did you resign?

HATTON: I took an early retirement.

TOWNSEND: Then you are receiving retirement from Lockheed, is that correct?

HATTON: I am receiving an early retirement, yes.

TOWNSEND: Let me put it another way. You are getting

a check from them every month are you not?

HATTON: Yes, a retirement check. Yes, sir.

TOWNSEND: I have no further questions.

As Townsend sat taking notes, Fenton stepped in to take over again. Hatton had made a request to have his attorney sit with him, or so Fenton understood. But there was, in fact, no attorney to sit with Hatton.

As Fenton resumed the questioning Hatton listened thoughtfully. At the first interval he requested permission to leave the hearing for twenty minutes. He had pressing business elsewhere. He was granted permission by the chairman. His head was bent as he left the hearing room.

The testimony went on relentlessly with Vince White, Hatton's assistant. "How many deaths took place in industrial injuires last year, Mr.White?"

"Roughly 700."

"Roughly?"

"Yes, but if it's 700 or 699, the problem is the same is it not?"

Fenton made a note as if doing arithmetic: "Not to the 700th and the family of the 700th, Mr. White."

To all this Bane listened intently. He was just beginning to realize what Zavattero had risked in confronting Lockheed.

As the questioning turned to events involved in the prosecution, Bane proved happy to explain his own dilemma to the committee.

The request for prosecution to the city attorney's office had not only been held up for more than a month after Zavattero's and Denton's original written request for prosecution, but the division had complained at the amount of time the two engineers were taking from the job. It had not been until January 3, six long months after the explosion, that they had allowed Bane a full-time investigator.

He was also quick to point out that the division had insisted that Zavattero and Denton be kept on the Sylmar job.

The reason: Their knowledge of the Lockheed tunnel and their expertise required that they be the ones to oversee the division's responsibilities in the reopening of the tunnel.

After listening to the testimony of Farmer and Crabtree, so full of praise for the skills of the two engineers who could not possibly be dispensed with for purposes of investigation, Fenton leaned back in his chair, eyed them quizzically, and leaning forward, said with a barely perceptible smile, "Well, at least we've gotten something out of this, we've learned that Mr. Zavattero and Mr. Denton are experts in this field, and I assume in the future when they make recommendations they will not be turned down as often as they have been in the past. If this committee has done nothing else, it has made you gentlemen noted as great experts in the field. Mr. Bane, do you want to say something?"

"Yes, Mr. Chairman," replied Bane. "I think there is one other point I'd like to make here. In a situation such as this, where there is a continuing investigation, and Mr. Denton and Mr. Zavattero have to work with the contractor whom they may be prosecuting for very serious violations, it's an unhealthy situation at best. In the initial phases of this investigation, I requested the division to relieve both Mr. Denton and Mr. Zavattero from any duty at the Sylmar for those reasons."

Before they were able to settle the question, Hatton had returned to the hearing room. His round face was pale and his eyes seemed smaller without his glasses. He looked around. There appeared to be no place for him to sit, but almost immediately the sergeant placed a chair next to Vince White's.

Hatton did not sit down. "Can I make a statement?—" he started.

"Relative to what Mr. Hatton?" asked Fenton.

"I'd just like to make a statement relative to the hearings," he replied.

"Would you like to make it now or at the conclusion?"

"I would like to make it right now."

"Oh, sure, Mr.Hatton go right ahead."

Hatton began his statement: "Well, I would just like to

say I have been listening to this hearing during the last couple of days. I am cognizant of the concerns of the Select Committee about the Division of Industrial Safety. I am also cognizant of the feeling of some of the division employees that they have not been backed up in some of the decisions that they wanted to make. Since I have been with the division, I enjoyed very much working with the division. It is a fine division, I think it is the best in the United States. It has been doing a terrific job. It has within it many of the finest safety engineers in this line. This is one of the things that has certainly been impressed upon me in my work with the division. I worked hard to try to improve the division. I've worked hard to try to eliminate injuries to California workers. I've taken my responsibilities seriously and did the best job that I can. But in view of the concerns of the committee and in view of some of the concerns of some of the people in the division, I would like to make a statement that I am, of this day, offering to resign to Governor Reagan. I just wanted to make that statement."

His speech had been as sincere and just as meaningless as his opening statement had been, but when Fat Jack sat down, he was a sad and broken old man.

When the old man sat down, Zavattero felt a little sorry for him, and wondered how many other people were going to be crushed before this was over.

Hatton did not leave the hearing but stayed on for a few moments. Before he left, one of his last official acts was to refuse Bane's and the committees' request to pull Zavattero and Denton off the Lockheed tunnel job.

Townsend had agreed with Bane that keeping them on the job was unhealthy and had bluntly added that it could also be dangerous. At that time Zavattero thought this was perhaps a little melodramatic. But the situation was a puzzling one, and most puzzling was why Vince White, Hatton, and Farmer had all been so adamant about it.

Like Fenton, Zavattero doubted that his and George's expertness was all that indispensable, though if they hadn't been experts before, they sure as hell were now! Still it didn't seem right.

When he talked to Mercy about it later, she had suggested that they wanted to keep him close to Savage so Savage could pump him for information.

"No" he snapped at her. He did not like that idea. Not at all. In the first place, if Lockheed's attorneys were assuming that, they simply didn't understand the basis of his and Savage's friendship.

It was no different from the relationship between two attorneys who oppose each other in court and meet for dinner at night. In trying to solve the problems of pushing that black hole through the last twenty-five hundred feet of dangerous, gassy ground, they had more in common with each other then they did with their attorneys. Besides, both of them were beginning to resent having lawyers tell them how to run every minute of their lives.

As for either one of them pumping the other one, that seemed unlikely. None of them, Denton, Zavattero, Ree, or Savage, really knew any more about what was happening at the top than the miners, working 175 feet underground, knew about the daily comings and goings of the citizens of Sylmar so far above their heads. The footsteps echoing in the corridors of Lockheed's Burbank plant couldn't have been more remote.

CHAPTER ELEVEN

After Ree's capture and arraignment, the burden of the prosecution rested with George Bane. Lockheed, along with project engineer Otha G. Ree, was charged on seven violations of the labor code and one penal count of concealing evidence. The charges were all misdemeanors, involving violation of the yellow tag and failing to maintain a safe place of employment or the protection of the employees' lives and safety.

From the time he had been reprimanded in Arnebergh's office just prior to Ree's capture, every obstacle had been thrown in Bane's way.

He had been ready to go to trial on January 4, thirteen days before the last assembly hearings. He had not been informed who the judge would be until after the decision had been made. The judge was one who was known to be in open conflict with Bane.

The decision had been made quietly in the city attorney's office by Arnebergh and Charles Bakaly, O'Melvany & Meyers attorney for Lockheed. The others present had little to say about it. It had apparently been made with the same contemptuous indifference that had made Arnebaugh try to dismiss the whole prosecution as "a stinking misdemeanor."

This had outraged the young attorney, and he had written a bitter memo reminding his superiors that the word was going around that the "fix" was in on the Lockheed prosecution.

Following the memo a new judge was appointed, but the trial date of January 4 was cancelled, over Bane's protest that he was ready to go to trial. George Bane had made dangerous enemies of Lockheed's supporters in the city attorney's office.

Judge Robert C. Nye was the judge assigned to the case, and the trial started on January 26, 1972. Both Zavattero and Denton were to be called as witnesses.

The postponement of the trial until after the January assembly hearings placed the prosecuting attorney at a disadvantage. Though the hearings had cleared Zavattero of any hint of wrongdoing, the hearings had made a shambles of the Division of Industrial Safety unwillingness to prosecute Lockheed. But, George Bane was determined that they would not succeed.

Zavattero was the first witness to be called by Bane. As he took the stand Zavattero was not nervous. He had gone beyond that. He felt as if he had no nerves left to be nervous with. He had been ripped up, subpoenaed, interrogated, investigated, hollered at, placated, threatened, and even pleaded with to drop the prosecution. There was nothing left of him to shake or sweat.

The first days testimony had been brief. Routine. Had Zavattero asked about the gas testing device? Yes. How long had it been until the meter was recovered? August 26. Had he spoken to anyone about it? Yes. James Westfield at the Mission Hills Inn.

Then Bane had asked about another meter. Not the one that had been taken by Ree on July 16 and turned over to Lockheed. The ensuing disclosure had caused something of a sensation.

It had been quickly picked up by the news media. In the news it was summed simply, "Zavattero testified that when he asked for the gas tester, Lockheed officials had refused to give it to him, and told him to contact the firm's attorney. According to the testimony the attorney told Zavattero that if he confiscated the tester the attorney would have him arrested or coldcocked."

Though the news story had not mentioned the attorney's name, it had been Finkle who had made the threat.

Zavattero was reluctant to testify to the episode. It had bothered him, and he did not want Mercy to know of it. But there was no way to avoid it on the witness stand.

He only hoped that he would have a chance to tell Mercy about it himself before she heard it on the news.

He had not told Mercy of the incident when it happened. Neither had George Denton told his wife, Laura. The two had agreed that the two women were worried enough without having to spend their evenings wondering if Lockheed was about to send someone with a lead pipe to drop them 175 feet down the Gate shaft.

After all, anything could have happened to Ree and Biro while they were stumbling around in the hold that night. So anything could happen to him and George if they'd been doing a little midnight investigating on their own. Anyway, they weren't going to try it.

Zavattero and Denton had wondered about the meter, which master mechanic, McCleland, had brought into the office that day, and simply set it down without comment. It was called a universal tester, and unlike the meter taken from the tunnel by Ree, it was not automatic and had to be hand pumped. It could not test constantly, but only as long as it was being pumped.

It provided a special kind of evidence relevant to the prosecution of Lockheed for violation of Zavattero's orders, for Zavattero's orders had provided for continuous testing for gas.

It was evidence not calculated to make Lockheed's heart leap up as they beheld it. They wanted that meter.

Denton had picked it up and said, "Hey, Wally, look at this." Savage, who had been on the phone, looked at the meter in Denton's hand.

"It belongs here," he said hastily. "It's evidence," Zavattero had replied and told Denton to put it in his car.

As Denton picked up the tester, Savage spoke. His voice was polite, but his eyes weren't. "You can have it after I call my attorney."

Zavattero shrugged, "OK, call away."

Savage had gone into the adjoining office, and neither of them could hear what he was saying. It didn't matter to them. They had the meter in their hands.

After a moment Savage walked back in and sat down. He looked smug. He had lots of faith in Lockheed's big guns. When the phone rang he pointed his thumb in the direction of the other office. "I think that's for you guys."

Zavattero nodded to Denton to take the call in the other office. He himself wasn't going to let that tester out of his sight, but he picked up the extension. He wanted to know what was going on. He heard Finkle's voice.

For once the suave attorney overlooked the usual pleasantries and launched immediately into a vaguely ominous outline of assorted legal improprieties connected with any attempt to remove the instrument from Lockheed property.

Neither Zavattero or Denton replied, waiting for further comment.

When it came, it startled them both "If you try to take that damned meter, I'll see you're arrested or coldcocked." His voice was cold and hard. He sounded like he meant it.

Savage had walked out whistling when the telephone rang, and Zavattero and Denton were alone as Denton came in from the other office.

He stared at Zavattero, "What the hell can they do?"

"I don't know. Let's find out." He picked up the tester and the two of them headed for their cars.

As he put the meter in the car, Denton looked at Zavattero and laughed, "Say Wally, you don't happen to have any Mafia relatives, do you?

Zavattero shook his head grinning, "Nope!"

Denton sighed wistfully, "I think maybe we could use some."

They had laughed.

But both of them had agreed not to tell their wives about the incident.

He was irritated with himself for not telling Mercy, especially when she looked at him reproachfully, wanting to know why.

He could think of nothing reassuring to say except to grin sheepishly and mutter, "Don't worry about it. Finkle's just bucking for an 007 from O'Melvany & Meyers."

Mercy tried her best to smile, but she didn't think it was funny.

Zavattero had been on the witness stand for three more days, testifying primarily to the violation of the yellow tag order, one of the major charges against Lockheed and Ree.

The yellow tag did not belong in the same spongy administrative area as the red tag which had provided Fenton and the legislative committee with such a lot of copy.

It was an unequivivocal legal order forbidding entrance to the tunnel without permission of the Division of Industrial Safety, unlike the red tag which simply warned that the premises were dangerous.

Not that the difference deterred Charles Bakaly, one of Lockheed's attorneys from O'Melvany & Myers, from making the criticism of Zavattero—at the assembly hearings—grist for his own mill. He was, in fact, eager to share with the jury the assembly's view of Zavattero.

Bakaly was undismayed by the court's refusal to allow the assembly hearings to be used. He had made his point and perhaps refreshed the jurors' memory of the first hearings held in early September.

Zavattero had been equally undismayed. He had been prepared by Bane for the fact that the first assembly hearings were going to haunt him through all the present and future proceedings against Lockheed. It did not bother him. In fact, by now he was beginning to feel almost court savvy, and when his testimony was over he resumed his seat, and began to observe with interest the attorneys being brought in by Lockheed.

There were a lot of them. McNary was still there for Savage.

Some of them he knew slightly, and they were certainly no pea-shooters. There was Bakaly, whom he knew only as an O'Melvany & Myers light, a Stanford man, and Lockheed's attorney in the firm. Making occasional appearances with him was Robert C. Gusman, a Cornell graduate and attorney for Lockheed, of whom he knew nothing except that Savage had once informed him that Gusman was over selling airplanes to the Chinese. Which Chinese Savage was referring to, Zavattero never knew, but he gathered from this that Gusman was a man of some status in the Lockheed corporate structure—a big, big gun.

With them was David Finkle, whom Zavattero was beginning to look on as an old, though not always welcome, friend. Tall and dark, he was poised and tensely alert, as if he were about to skim through the proceedings like a surfer hanging ten.

Charles Hollopeter, who was to be Ree's attorney, he had never met. He was a thin, trim man with a long, thin inquisitive nose and an emphatic manner. He came from the outposts of Pasadena.

On the city attorney side was George Bane, who looked as if he had lost so much weight since the prosecution's beginning that he had to take in a notch in the belt of his vest. With him were occasional young deputies from the city attorney's office, and somewhere in the background there was Roosevelt Dorn, earnest and soft-spoken, who had a trick of looking thoughtfully out the window before jotting down a note or two on the trial proceedings. He was one of the city attorney's best men in the Criminal Division.

Zavattero had to admire Bane's refusal to be crushed by the weight of his opposition. The odds against him were overwhelming.

Lockheed had both the power and the money to buy anything it wanted, from immediate trial transcripts to a dazzling array of attorneys with specialized expertise in any field. Bane had trouble getting $200 for a test on the gas meter. Unable to get the transcripts so readily available to Lockheed, he even had trouble wrenching a secretary away from some remote typing pool to take notes.

Zavattero was followed to the stand by Westfield, who gave his account of their meeting at the Mission Hills Inn and the final retrieval of the disputed meter from the vaults of Lockheed.

Loren Savage's demeanor remained—as it had been at the assembly hearings—cool, careful, and his testimony given with deliberate slowness. He was appearing as a hostile witness with Tom McNary there to advise him not to answer self-incriminating questions which might be used in the new investigation. On McNary's advice he refused to answer, and when Bane objected, Charles Bakaly stepped into the breach. Lockheed's attorney argued that Savage's mere refusal to answer questions would, because he was a Lockheed employee, prejudice the current case against Lockheed in the minds of the jurors. He also charged the city attorney with filing two separate cases in order to use testimony from the second in prosecuting the first. Judge Nye ruled that Savage must testify, but that was the last testimony that Savage would give.

George Denton, though calm and self-possessed, had seemed to Zavattero nervous and tense before the trial.

This was not unreasonable. Denton after all had not been plastered all over the front page when Fenton had done his sprightly turn at the first assembly hearing. But Denton had given his account of the meter theft forthrightly and clearly.

Of all the witnesses called, only Arvid Rasmussen seemed to be struggling with the sad dilemma of friendships betrayed.

He had met with Bane the night before to talk about entering the tunnel with Ree and discovering the meter.

He had told his story awkwardly. The awkwardness was

Part 2/The Trials   *179*

heightened more by his feelings of loyalty and affection for Bob Ree than from any language difficulty.

In his discussion with Bane he had waived any immunity stating simply that if he were guilty of a crime he wanted to be prosecuted. Denton had testified to this.

Rasmussen had watered down his testimony both before the assembly hearings and later in his deposition in order to protect Ree, whom he felt should not be made to take the blame. He had not, he told the court, lied, but what he had said was not quite correct.

During Bane's examination, Rasmussen had answered slowly and hesitantly about events following his discovery of the meter:

BANE: Mr. Ree had the pump and the meter in his hand at this point?

RASMUSSEN: Yes.

BANE: What did he do?

RASMUSSEN: I think he made a sign to take it with him. And I said that—well—I told him that Denton had been asking about it, so we might as well leave it and tell Denton about it. Well, Bob told me, we'll, we take it with us then. And I think Bob Ree put in kind of a sack and carried it out with him.

BANE: Did you tell him more than once in the tunnel to leave it there?

FINKLE: Objected to as leading and suggestive.

JUDGE NYE: Overruled.

RASMUSSEN: Yes, I believe so.

BANE: Did you not say it would not be right to take it away?

FINKLE: Leading and suggestive.

NYE: Sustained.

Under Bane's continued questioning, Rasmussen went on to detail the events of that night. He thought he had told

Ree that it would not be right to take the meter. Later, on the way home, Ree had told him not to tell anybody about it or about being in the tunnel. In the following week Ree had told him that he would not be paid for the trip into the tunnel. But he might get paid later on. Ree then informed him that he had told Savage about it, and Savage had laughed. The meter could not be turned over to the state. It was in a vault in Burbank.

Under Hollopeter and Finkle's cross-examination he told again how he promised Ree not to say anything, and had tried to protect Ree at the assembly hearing. In his later testimony he recounted his efforts to contact Ree in Seattle and get released from his promise not to say anything about the trip into the tunnel. On his deposition taken before the trial, he admitted sadly that he had lied.

His final statement was equally sad and given in a low voice. "I was worried someone may feel I was lying. Nobody told me I may be guilty of a crime, but I knew it."

As Rasmussen spoke, Zavattero understood why his testimony at the hearing had been so different from his first statements immediately following the explosion. It had not been forgetfulness, but friendship. Zavattero felt sorry for him. Whatever he had done he had done from friendship, without criminal intent.

When several cross-examinations, directs, and redirects later, Charles Bakaly made the opening arguments for the defense, it was a model of simplicity. The yellow tag did, in fact, allow Lockheed to enter the tunnel and the questioned meter had not been turned over to the Division of Industrial Safety for that most simple and innocent reason usually given in such cases: "Nobody asked for it."

The jury seemed to agree with Ree's right to go into the tunnel in spite of the strangeness of the hour, and they listened attentively as Ree explained about the controversial meter.

Ree's testimony was that he did not leave it where they found it for fear it might be damaged in future trips.

"I removed it from the tunnel because it might have

Part 2/The Trials 181

some importance. I brought it out and gave it to my boss. I believe it was the property of Lockheed and I was custodian of it for Lockheed."

However, Rasmussen's testimony had been upsetting. Ostensibly it was true that the midnight trip into the tunnel had been to search once more for the missing body of Ronald Demo, and that was all Ree had to cling to when confronted with the question of the secrecy surrounding their mission. He did not, he claimed, want to make Mrs. Demo anxious or rouse her hopes only to have them dashed.

His testimony regarding his conversation about secrecy with Rasmussen after the discovery of the meter differed from Rasmussen's in style, but not in content.

"Possibly, I may have said, 'The less said about this, the better.'" And as a reason again gave Mrs. Demo's distress.

That concern for Mrs. Demo was echoed in his explanation of why Rasmussen was not to be paid for Lockheed for the overtime spent in the search. "No, I think the mission shouldn't call for pay. It wasn't work. It was a humanitarian journey."

When Ree finally left the stand, he did not look happy with himself.

The last witness to appear for the defense was Roger Williams, employed as Lockheed Aircraft Corporation Assistant Chief Counsel until October 1971, four months after the Sylmar disaster. He had been 11½ years with Lockheed and assigned to legal problems arising out of the explosion on June 24.

His testimony was as guileless as a shopkeeper's who was simply too distracted to keep track of his wares.

The reason he had never told Zavattero or Denton about the recovery of the meter was simply that the occasion had never arisen. He was too busy with the problems of getting back into the tunnel and the matter of consent by the Department of Labor and the state.

He was, however, careful to have it preserved and made sure it was marked, preserved for evidence just as any shopkeeper would mark his stock. Also, just as any shopkeeper would, he put the matter in the back of his mind. And then he said, "The meter slipped my mind."

As his testimony concluded, the jury looked unimpressed by his tale of innocent forgetfulness, and when they returned their verdict after two days of deliberation, the verdict against Lockheed on penal code 135—concealing evidence—was an undisputed "guilty."

Due to the obdurate belief of one juror, that Otha G. Ree was indeed a mere custodian of Lockheed in entering the tunnel and causing an employee to enter the tunnel over the division's yellow tag, taking the meter, and turning it over to Lockheed, Ree was acquitted.

The first trial was over. It was a limited victory to be sure, but it was a victory. They had won the first skirmish and Bane was busily planning the next moves. He was hopeful. He explained to Zavattero that Lockheed was to be given the maximum fine. The fine was only $500, but more importantly Judge Nye was going to make a public statement that in his opinion the case should have been tried as a felony. Zavattero liked that. Someday, maybe, it would be something more than a misdemeanor, whether men lived or died underground. Maybe someday.

The next day he phoned Bob Ree. He congratulated him on his acquittal. It seemed the right thing to do. He did not feel that men like Ree or Savage should bear the total burden of guilt for Lockheed's greedy dilemma.

Ree had seemed touched at Zavattero's call. "Thanks, Wally," he said and after a thoughtful pause added, "You always were an honest guy."

"Sure," Zavattero said, and hung up.

He wondered how Ree would be feeling after the second and bigger prosecution of Lockheed got under way. He and Denton had both been working with Bane on the necessary investigation for the gross negligence case.

He also wondered what effect the judge's ruling in the meter case would have on the second case. The story in the

Times did include Judge Nye's remark that in his personal opinion the crime should be listed as a felony. It also included Nye's rejection of motions for a new trial by Lockheed's attorneys who were arguing loudly that the corporation should not have been held guilty when its employee, safety engineer Ree, had been acquitted.

"Mr. Ree was found innocent on a matter involving the very act for which his employer was convicted," Charles Bakaly and Robert Fisher were crying on behalf of Lockheed. This apparently carried little weight with Nye who "expressed the belief that the verdicts were not inconsistent."

However heartening the story might have been, before it could appear, and Lockheed could holler "Appeal!" the prosecution took another step backward.

Zavattero had been preparing some investigation reports for an appointment with Bane the next day. He was quite cheerful and read some passages to Mercy from the investigation statements at the time of the explosion. By this time she knew almost as much about those reports as he did, but it pleased her to see him in a more relaxed mood. It didn't last long.

The telephone started its shrill hammering, and Mercy winced as Zavattero picked up the phone. Mercy didn't know who it was but whatever he was saying, Mercy's hopes for a relaxed evening disappeared.

As Zavattero listened, his face began to take on the flat, hard look of disgust that Mercy had grown to dread. She watched him closely, and when he finally shouted, "They can't get away with this crap!" she suddenly burst out in a high pitched laugh that sounded strange even to her, "Oh, Wally, please don't say that!"

He gave her a worried look as he hung up. She was really going to pieces over this whole thing. "Say what?" he asked.

"That, that—" Mercy gulped, wiping her eyes as she choked with laughter, "that they can't get away with it—Every time you say that," she gasped, "something awful happens!"

He stared at her as if she'd developed ESP. "It has," he said. "There may not be another trial. Arnebergh just fired Bane!"

CHAPTER TWELVE

He was wrong. There would be another trial. Bane would see to that. The young attorney was too intense, dedicated, and fresh out of law school to abandon his sense of justice and do a cynical roll with the punches.

With Bane out of the way, and the public's outrage assuaged (by Lockheed's conviction for concealing evidence—already being appealed) Lockheed's future should have looked brighter. It wasn't.

Not only had Bane refused to roll with the punches, but he punched back with a memo that was going to make a lot more headlines to upset the corporation and its cozy relationship with the city attorney's office.

The city attorney, completely unperturbed by the Lockheed scandal and fully expecting the young deputy to take the count and do the honorable thing, had immediately appointed one of his senior trial attorneys, Ronald Tische, as the prosecutor to replace Bane. (His father was a management employee at Lockheed's Sunnyvale Missiles and Space Division plant.) In an embarrassed flurry, Tische backed out. That didn't seem to deter Arnebergh, who told Tische to review the evidence for the pending prosecution anyway.

When news of Bane's parting memo and his instant firing broke, City Attorney Arnebergh was in for more public exposure than he had achieved in his twenty years in office, and more than any man could afford in a campaign year, or any other year for that matter.

Too many questions were being asked, not only about the Lockheed prosecution but other interesting questions about real estate dealings and failure to prosecute those towards whom Arnebaugh was kindly disposed.

The media latched on to the story of the city attorney's misdoings with considerable gusto, but none of them with more fervor than Kenneth Gosting, the young reporter who had been the first to uncover the orders that Lockheed had so strenuously tried to bury.

His story in the *The Signal*, a Newhall paper in the San Fernando Valley, was simple and blunt in its lead: "The prosecutor in the Lockheed tunnel disaster case has been fired because he wrote a memorandum alleging the Los Angeles city attorney's office is not interested in prosecution of the culpable parties.

"George D. Bane was dismssed March 10 as a deputy city attorney only thirteen days after he won a conviction against Lockheed Shipbuilding and Construction for its concealment of a gas meter that purportedly was in the explosion.

"The hassle that resulted in Bane's dismissal involves further prosecution pending against Lockheed directly over the blast and fire which killed seventeen men last June 24 in the 5½-mile tunnel under Sylmar."

The story went on to detail some unpleasant allegations to the effect that Roger Arnebergh, of the low profile and sanctimonious ways, was "opposed to prosecuting Lockheed, and that Lockheed's defense attorney, Charles Bakaly, Jr., employed by the legal firm of O'Melvany & Meyers, received favors from the city attorney's office because the firm handles many municipal bonding cases for the city of Los Angeles."

The *Times* too had taken due notice of Bane's memo, stating: "John Daly, chief assistant to City Attorney Roger

Arnebergh, said Bane was fired because he wrote a memorandum to Arnebergh in which he suggested that the city attorney had caved in to pressures from Lockheed." And they, too, had remarked on the fact that Arnebergh had chosen the son of a Lockheed employee to replace Bane in the second, more serious prosecution for gross negligence.

The story continued, "Tische said he was removed from the case after Bane sent his memorandum. However, the memo proved to be Bane's parting shot.

"In the final paragraph of his memo, Bane accused Perez, Daly, and Arnebergh of failing to push hard enough on the Lockheed case, and he implied that they had abandoned the responsibilities of their posts.

"He was fired immediately."

(In fact, he hadn't implied anything. He'd simply made a point-blank statement: "In light of the imminent running out of the statute of limitations and various acts and statements on the part of yourself, Mr. Daly, and Mr. Arnebergh, I must reluctantly conclude that this office is not interested in a vigorous prosecution of the culpable parties in the Sylmar tunnel disaster. If true, this does a tragic disservice to workers throughout this state, to the families of the seventeen men killed, and to the cause of justice and equal enforcement of the law.")

Roger Arnebergh was out of town and could not be reached for comment.

In the headquarters of Burt Pines, leading opponent to Arnebergh for the upcoming city attorney elections, everyone was trying not to look like they were counting their chickens before they were hatched.

At Lockheed's Burbank offices everyone was still casting wistful glances in the direction of the statute of limitations while busily preparing motions to dismiss because their constitutional right to a speedy trial had been violated.

Both Zavattero and Denton had been shocked at Bane's firing, but when the three of them met the next day, Bane had been the most cheerful of the three.

In his interviews with the press Bane had castigated the Division of Industrial Safety for its lack of cooperation, but he had added firmly that safety engineers Wallace Zavattero and George Denton had given him valuable assistance.

Though both Zavattero and Denton had been flattered at the heroic implications of the statement, they weren't at all sure that the ensuing notoriety wouldn't make adverse waves through the halls of Industrial Safety that would eventually silently sink them without trace. It was possible. But at that point neither one of them cared anymore. They were too mad about what had happened to Bane's head to worry about their own.

However, Bane wasn't worrying. Whatever else might come of the noisy confusion over the Lockheed matter, there was no longer any doubt about the second and more serious prosecution.

The heat generated by all the publicity had compelled Arnebergh to assign Roosevelt Dorn, one of his best trial attorneys, to the case. Working with Dorn would be Richard Helgeson, fresh from law school, sharp, and eager for the fray. With them would also be Larry Moss.

As Bane explained it to Zavattero and Denton over lunch, the new attorneys had their work cut out for them, and they would be hampered by the fact that Arnebergh and Perez, Arnebergh's assistant, refused to let Bane work with them. They would not have the advantage of his experience in opposing Lockheed's powerful attorneys. And they could use all the help they could get.

The case was so legally complicated that the pretrial motions and jury selection alone could take months.

"Sick!" Zavattero moaned. "This thing's already dragged on for a year. One more year of this and my wife will divorce me."

"Mine," Denton announced morosely, "won't divorce me. She'll kill me."

"Well, it can and probably will drag on for another year," Bane told them. "This thing's so full of legal nit picking that

Part 2/The Trials

it's going to take a nit picker's nit picker to make sense out of it." Then he waved his hand impatiently, "But you already know all that. Section 6315 hasn't even been prosecuted since they put it in the labor code in 1913. Think what they can do with that one!"

"You think about it. I'd rather not." Zavattero muttered.

"How about a conviction?" Denton asked.

Bane nodded. "Dorn's good. He'll get a conviction. It won't be easy, but he'll get it. He'll get the conviction, but they'll probably appeal it. They are already appealing the concealing evidence decision."

"Yeah? How come?" Denton asked.

Bane looked at him rather pityingly, "Because they have the money," he said, "You know, money, that stuff you're going to buy my lunch with now that I'm an out-of-work attorney—money, m-o-n-e-y. And taxpayers' money at that."

The two men smiled and nodded.

Bane didn't smile but looked at Zavattero searchingly, "Wally, you hang in there. Everything depends on those orders. They'll try to impeach you as everything from a slobbering idiot to a power-mad maniac."

Zavattero grinned at him, "Yeah, I know. I also eat my young and don't know a tunnel from an asshole." Then he asked, "How about you, George, what are you gonna do now?"

As he got up to leave, it was Bane's turn to grin, "I'm going into private practice. I'm nervous, but my wife hasn't been so happy since the day we got married. She thinks I just escaped from a lunatic asylum."

"Amen!" Zavattero and Denton lifted their glasses in a cheerful farewell as Bane walked away.

Before they could meet with Dorn, Zavattero and Denton had been called to Sacramento for a special, statewide meeting.

The meeting was not just one of these busy, exploratory affairs so dear to the hearts of paper shufflers who consider an "in depth" study of a problem its solution.

The convergence of safety engineers, union leaders, and construction workers was no study. It was a hard, direct thrust at the industrial safety laws in California.

No study but a proposed bill was in the offing. It was to be introduced by the Assembly Select Committee on Industrial Safety, chairman, Assemblyman Jack Fenton. It was aimed specifically at tunnels and mines.

Busily drawing up the map to lead tunnelers and miners through the dark maze of the underworld, were Johnson and McFettridge, and they needed help from the men who knew what that underworld was all about.

There had been little publicity on the subject and Zavattero and Denton were consulted privately before the actual meeting took place. Their statements would be important in the shaping of the new bill. Denton, though bright and knowledgeable, was too inexperienced in tunnels to be as familiar with all the convulsive tantrums the earth was capable of as Zavattero. But both men were needed to put together something to replace the laws that Zavattero had so candidly told the committee were antiquated.

For the first time Zavattero had an audience for the protests he had made to nearly every senior engineer in the division. They were listened to attentively when he made them in the hearings. They were being even more attentively listened to now.

On the flight back to Los Angeles, he and Denton didn't talk much. It seemed to them they had been talking steadily for twenty-four hours. But for the first time in the long ordeal, Zavattero began to hope that the end of that tunnel that everybody talked about these days might be in sight.

They had finally gotten a prosecution. Lockheed had been found guilty on the concealing evidence charge. The door was now open for the prosecution for gross negligence, and if what he had just heard was true, they were finally going to get a tunnel safety bill with some teeth in it. Maybe there really was a light at the end of that damned tunnel. He'd see.

Right now he felt so good that he was even looking forward to the meeting with Dorn. Cheerfully he ordered a martini from the stewardess. It tasted great!

Roosevelt Dorn was black and a deeply serious man. His neat, salt-and-pepper beard located his age conveniently beyond youth, but the smooth texture of his skin was the skin of a young man. A back injury made a cane sometimes necessary. He used it with imposing dignity.

His voice was soft and reassuring. Consideration was its deepest vibration, except in the courtroom where it took on quite a different tone.

He was a thoughtful man who would often look out the window, as if he were looking for an answer—a philosophical answer—or reaching out for an intuition of reality.

It may have been in one of these long moments that he first perceived that eventually he would have to take over the Lockheed case. He had known that, even before Bane had fired off the memo that would end in tying the legal noose around Lockheed's neck.

He admired Bane even as he said to him that day, "George, you just fired yourself."

He had known Bane as young, conservative, strictly law and order, not burning with suspect radical passions, but the young attorney had just made a radical gesture in defying the very powers he believed in. To him the law was more important than how he stamped his ballot, he had assured Dorn. He might be a long time regretting what he'd done, but if he hadn't done it, he would be a lifetime regretting it.

Zavattero had met Dorn a number of times and admired him. Dorn knew Zavattero as bright, intense and committed. He had also seen him before the assembly and in court and he knew that he was a good, tough witness, hard to shake. But he also knew that he could be unpredictable, not easily programmed.

Now the two of them were meeting for a relationship that

would be a friendly one, but long, often wearying, and sometimes stormy.

Their talk was of the trial and the pending arraignment of Lockheed, Loren Savage, Otha G. Ree, Eugene Pedigo and Russell Van Guilder. Russell Van Guilder would turn state's evidence, according to Dorn.

As the conversation turned to Lockheed's probable attempts to plead an act of God, Zavattero snorted "Bull!"

"As far as I'm concerned," he said, "the only act of God that occurred was on the night before. That flash fire was one hell of a warning, and now Lockheed's acting like Noah complaining because God didn't give him the right specifications for the ark."

Dorn smiled. He was going to like Zavattero. "If we could just convince the jury that God gave you those orders we could close the book right now," he said ruefully.

Dorn waved his hand to interrupt any further dissertations on "acts of God." The important matter at hand were the charges to be brought against Lockheed and its employees.

They were to be charged on multiple violations of the State Labor Code, including sections 6400, 6401, 6402, 6404, 6315 and 6416. Dorn called the numbers off like an auctioneer at a cattle sale.

He did not have to explain the barrage of numbers to Zavattero. He probably knew the labor code better than the attorneys. It and the tunnel safety orders were the tools of his trade.

6400 through 6404 set standards and placed the responsibility for safeguarding employees on the employer. They included: furnishing a safe place of employment; furnishing and using safety devices, safeguards and practices; not requiring or permitting any employee to go in, be in, or maintain, any place that was not safe. Violations of any of these sections were misdemeanors.

6416 starkly stated in *West's Annotated Code*, Death From Employer's Gross Negligence: Every employer, who through his gross negligence in failing to provide a safe employment and place of employment causes the death of his employee, is punishable by imprisonment in the county jail for not more than one year or by a fine of not less than one thousand dollars or more than five thousand dollars.

"That too was a misdemeanor," Dorn said caustically.

Only Lockheed, Savage, and Ree were to be charged on 6416. Eugene Pedigo, a walker or foreman on the shift during the first flash fire was to be charged on four counts only, regarding a safe place of employment.

The last charge, 6315, was also a misdemeanor and it was the statute that most concerned the attorneys and Zavattero. Like Bane had said, there had never been a prosecution under this statute since its inception in 1913.

It read: "Any person who violates any order or recommendation made by authority of Sections 6313 or 6314 or who in any way obstructs or hampers any person conducting any investigation authorized by the division is guilty of a misdemeanor."

The 6313 and 6314 referred to were the two sections of the labor code that empowered the division to investigate all industrial injuries resulting in disability or death; and 6314 empowered anyone designated by the division to enter any place of employment, subpoena witnesses, administer oaths, and take testimony.

What is all amounted to was that Lockheed Shipbuilding and Construction Company and its employees had either been the first corporation to exhibit such astonishing indifference to safety precautions and orders, or they were the first to be prosecuted on it since 1913.

As they talked of the critical issue of the orders Zavattero wondered vaguely if there had been some poor safety engineers so many years before he was even born, trying to search out some justice for a pitiful heap of men lost underground. It would be interesting to know. But he would never find out. There had never been a prosecution. That was too bad. He would have liked to have known such men.

After Zavattero left Dorn's office, Dorn sat staring

thoughtfully out the window. He was pleased. There had been some worry that the men would be resentful of the black prosecutor because of Bane's firing. Dorn had talked to some of the men who would be witnesses and had found them to be very willing to help in any way they could. They were good men. Individualistic, independent and tough. They had no false allegiences to any corporation. The nomadic nature of their jobs—they were called boomers—precluded their ever becoming organization men. Their only organization was the tunnels where they were the bosses of the hard earth. Any other allegiences they owed were to their buddies and their unions.

Dorn was pleased that Zavattero too was so willing to help. He sat and thought about it for a long time. Lockheed was to be arraigned the next day. He needed to think.

The case of *People* v. *Lockheed Shipbuilding and Construction Company*, a corporation doing business in California, and Loren G. Savage, Otha G. Ree, Jr., and Eugene Pedigo, was not the normal fare to come before the bench of George W. Trammell III. It was not the normal fare to come before any municipal court.

Judge Trammell was an earnest and intensely thorough man. He had spent long hours in preliminary study of the case that was about to come before him.

On April 28, 1972, Lockheed and its codefendants would be charged with eighty state safety code violations. It was the largest single action ever taken under the State Labor Code. The complaints were filed by the State Department of Industrial Relations and signed by Wallace Zavattero and George Denton.

The case was big and Judge Trammel reviewed it carefully. He knew that Lockheed would be represented by the best legal talent in the city.

He was right about that. For the prosecution there would be only the city attorney's office representatives Roosevelt Dorn, Richard Mr. Helgeson and Larry B. Moss. A good team, but were they a match for Lockheed?

Part 2/The Trials   195

When Dorn briefed Zavattero on the first sessions, the lawyer was startled at the staggering array of talent and power assembled on Lockheed's behalf. They didn't need to shoot him. All they had to do was fall on him and crush him!

Dorn told him that they would all have a go at him when the trial started, if it started. Dorn explained that Lockheed had filed a motion for dismissal on the grounds that their clients had been denied their constitutional right to a speedy trial.

At that Zavattero spluttered with laughter, "Hell, that takes nerve—after all they did to gum up the works until the statute of limitations ran out!" He stared at Dorn in disbelief.

He was more concerned when Dorn told him that Lockheed was protesting the constitutionality of 6315, the hitherto untested statute that made it a misdemeanor to violate special safety orders. They were objecting on the grounds that the statute denied Lockheed's right to the due process of law. That is, the contractor was not allowed a hearing on Zavattero's safety orders.

Zavattero again shook his head in disbelief, "What the hell are they talking about? That tunnel was gonna blow up in matter of hours if they didn't do what I said. They didn't have time to hold a damned board meeting." To him that was like giving someone with a gun a chance to shoot it off to prove it wasn't loaded. It didn't make sense and was downright dangerous.

Dorn's further explanation didn't help much. The law was not particularly well written, and by testing it they were opening the door to a better, stronger law if necessary.

"Yeah, sure," Zavattero said glumly, "and there's also a Santa Claus."

All in all, to Zavattero the legal picture looked bleak. What irritated him most was the sluggishness of the process. He was, underneath, not a patient man. Patience was a virtue he had to work hard at, and now he was getting plenty of practice.

He had been in many courts to testify all kinds of safety

procedure litigations. They were nothing like this.

All this had a maddening remoteness to it, as if the army of attorneys were constructing an intricate geodesic dome that floated airily, far removed from the black, dirty hole in which so many men had died. If only it could all be anchored back down to that black hole—to the dead men. He wondered if anyone but him and Denton and the miners who had dragged the men out on the muck trains even remembered them.

Dorn had proved right. Twenty counts against Lockheed were dismissed when Trammel ruled 6315 unconstitutional. True, they were still stuck with sixty counts including the gross negligence count, but it was disheartening to Zavattero to read the *Times* story on it, boldly headlined: "Tunnel Safety Requirements Were Not Orders, Judge Rules."

According to the story "the ruling was a major legal victory for Lockheed Shipbuilding and Construction Company." It went on to report Dorn's protests that the ruling had "taken the heart out of the people's case."

Zavattero didn't know about the heart of the people's case, but it took some of the heart out of him. They were off to a great start with a smashing defeat.

The story went on to read: "The judge specifically ruled that the requirements were not 'orders' as defined in the State Labor Code. He said that when orders are issued, notice must be given so that the contractor can seek a hearing on them.

" 'No such notice or hearing was granted in these instances,' Trammel said."

The story concluded: "According to the judge, 'There is a legal significance in the terminology because orders are conclusively presumed to set reasonable safety standards.' "

The legal significance, Zavattero knew, was that now Lockheed would not have to bear the burden of proving that they had indeed fulfilled his requirements. The burden of proof would now rest with the prosecution.

In addition it also meant that Lockheed's attorneys could question the validity of the safety requirements. In other words, they could use all those fancy attorneys to inform the jury that Zavattero had written a really dumb set of requirements! That hurt his professional pride.

When he read the story Zavattero had been sitting in Dorn's office. As he finished it he threw it down on the desk and made a rude noise.

Dorn grinned at him, "OK, Wally, take it easy."

Dorn had not been unprepared for this and the ruling was already being set up for appeal.

What was more important to him was what effect this would have on their court tactics.

He leaned forward and picked up the paper, "Now, listen Wally, when we go to court what I want you to do—" his urgent statement was cut short by Zavattero.

"Whadya mean when we go to court! I don't think this thing's ever going to court," he snapped. "And what's more I'm sick of it, and I'm getting the hell out of here." With that he turned and walked out the door as if he weren't going to stop until he reached the place where the world fell off.

Dorn watched him go. He looked thoughtful and a little worried. Zavattero was a volatile man. And this was only the beginning.

For Zavattero, of course, it wasn't only the beginning. He had been fighting this thing for a year, and now they wanted him to go on fighting it against all the odds. To hell with it!

After he left Dorn, Zavattero didn't know where he was going. He headed out towards Malibu; he knew a quiet, lonely sea-swept bar out there where he could think. He wasn't sure. He'd just drive for a while. He didn't want to go home. He didn't want to talk to anyone, not even Mercy. And most of all he didn't want to talk on the telephone. He knew the minute he got in the door Denton would phone and so would Savage. Savage would begin all over again about the "big guns." It was all very jovial, and usually he enjoyed Savage's badly humorous account of the doings of Lockheed; but not now. He wanted to be by himself. Totally alone.

He kept on driving. As he threaded his way along the freeway, now almost free of its endless, restless burden, he smiled slightly to himself. He had reached that point of gloominess where it was almost a pleasurable feeling. That's what he wanted to do. He wanted to go some place, not to think, but just to feel good and gloomy.

He found it in one of those small tattered places that hang along the cliffs of the Pacific shoreline. It was still spring and the brisk liveliness of the season had not yet started. In its dark depths there were only a few old cronies, muttering in cheerless undertones between the pounding of dice cups on the bar. The only thing that lit the darkness occasionally was the flashing of the waitress, who sped with a tray of drinks from booth to booth like a hopeful comet. The music from the jukebox was low and melancholy, and outside the sea stirred with the soothing monotony of eternity.

When the pretty young waitress brought his drink, Zavattero did not smile at her. She set the drink down in front of him and he stared gloomily at it for a long time. He drank it, then ordered another one, then another, and at last decided that his tour of despair was over. He began to think of other things.

Dorn had said that they would appeal Judge Trammell's ruling on 6315. That was probably what Helgeson had been waiting to talk to Dorn about when Zavattero had left Dorn's office so abruptly.

Poor Helgeson, Zavattero shook his head. They had handed him quite a job on his first assignment. Helgeson had just passed the bar at the time of the meter trial, and Dorn had chosen him as part of the team to beat Lockheed. As he thought of Helgeson's first big assignment, Zavattero smiled. It reminded him of a story he had heard about a young intern. The intern was working in a huge middle western hospital. The day he entered the consulting room to make his first independent diagnosis, he emerged from it a shaken man. So much so that his colleagues began to fear that the young intern had caved in under the pressures of medical school. He had returned to the consulting room and again emerged dazed and mumbling. Finally they got it out of him. He looked at them bewildered, and announced that the only diagnosis he could make was that the guy had leprosy!

Zavattero grinned. Helgeson must feel like that intern, a bit dazed by the requirements of one of his first assignments. He had to write a brief on a law for which there was no precedent. When Helgeson had finished it, the brief was a long one, and one he was proud of. He had had to research back to 1885 to find a precedent, and to his own eloquence he had added the voice of that inspired old firebrand, Upton Sinclair, who in *The Jungle* wrote angrily about the "lack of thought given to the welfare of the laborers, when tunneling cost a life a day and several manglings." The brief was a good one, but he must have felt a little like that intern.

Thinking of Helgeson's problems, Zavattero began to feel better. He didn't have all the problems. Zavattero walked out into the night air. He had left the waitress a good tip and even smiled at her as if in apology for his earlier surliness. Outside the fog had begun to roll silently in, tasting faintly of salt. Zavattero took a deep breath and got into his car. His gloomy session had done him good. Tomorrow he would phone Dorn and apologize for walking out on him. He drove slowly home, went to bed, and for the first time in months fell immediately into a deep sleep.

The pretrial motions dragged on, but finally in late July, it all moved to the courtroom, and jury selection began.

That too was a long process. Zavattero and Denton by this time were beginning to wonder if there were some way they could suggest the possibility of highballing a trial. There wasn't a chance. There was no such thing as a highballing attorney.

The jurors came and went like beauty contestants being subjected to the evaluatively cocked eye of a host of judges.

When the attorneys weren't busy scrutinizing the jurors, they were in the judge's chambers. Lockheed and the city attorney's office were talking of settlements and plea bargains.

After careful consideration Lockheed would agree to plead no contest to the sixteen counts of gross negligence, with all other counts to be dismissed.

Charges against Ree, Savage and Pedigo would be dismissed.

The sentencing of Lockheed would be left open to the courts with Lockheed having the right to offer mitigating factors.

Lockheed's maximum sentence would be $80,000 with the payment of the fine to be stayed for further legal actions.

Had the decision on the plea bargain been in the hands of Zavattero and Denton, they felt that they would probably have accepted it. For one thing they were totally exhausted, and by now Zavattero's health had been seriously affected. At Mercy's insistence Zavattero had finally gone to a doctor. The verdict there had been nervous exhaustion resulting in ulcers. The doctor's advice: Try to forget the whole thing, get some rest, and if you needed something to keep your nerves from unraveling, stick to whiskey and water, no martinis or wine allowed. Unless the Lockheed offer of a deal went through, the only advice he'd be able to follow would be sticking to whiskey and water, and he'd probably need a hell of a lot of that.

Then, too, neither Zavattero nor Denton was particularly anxious to see Savage and Ree or Pedigo prosecuted. Pedigo especially seemed to have been caught in a too-wide net of culpability, though Denton had been the one who urged the inclusion of Pedigo on the four counts of labor code violations. Still their guns had been aimed at the corporation, not Lockheed's project manager and engineer.

Besides Zavattero had been drawn again into a beleaguered relationship with Savage and Ree. The families of the dead men were bringing a civil action for several million dollars. The first steps in the action had begun a few months after the explosion. That had been expected, and Zavattero had hoped the prosecution would help the civil litigation.

But because of the laws governing employer-employee

relations, the civil action put Zavattero in the anomolous position of being both a complainant and a defendant.

Under the California laws, the employer's (Lockheed) financial responsibility for injury or death was limited to the amount allowed under the Workman's Compensation Act. An insured employer could not normally be sued for more than that amount no matter what the causes of injury or death were. That meant that the families of the dead miners could not normally sue Lockheed civilly to recover damages for the deaths of their husbands; neither could Brisette and the miners injured in the first flash fire.

However, under the law, a third party, another employer such as the Metropolitan Water District, or other possible culpable agencies such as the Division of Industrial Safety and Mine Safety Appliances, could be charged and made liable for damages to the survivors of the deceased.

This, indeed, was what had happened. The attorneys representing these families had brought suit first against the Metropolitan Water District. The MWD had not been unprepared for such a possibility and had included in the original contract with Lockheed a "hold harmless" clause. This meant simply that in the event of a catastrophe, such as the one that had actually happened at Sylmar, the MWD would be held harmless by Lockheed and could recover whatever amount they were compelled to pay in damages to the survivors from the corporation. The powerful Metropolitan Water District had protected itself well.

Unfortunately for Zavattero the contractual, legal niceties involved in the suit against the MWD extended to the Division of Industrial Safety, and with it Zavattero was caught in the legal net. Suit had been brought against the Division of Industrial Safety and a suit for $35 million against him. The charges as he understood them at that early point were that the Division of Industrial Safety inspection had been a negligent one. If that were true, he hoped the case would go to trial and the jury be compelled to go through that tunnel with the inch by inch thoroughness that he had gone through it testing for gas.

The civil suit against Savage personally had been for the equally stupefying sum of $100 million. On the day the action was filed Savage had phoned Zavattero at his office in Panorama City. Since Dorn had taken over the case, Zavattero had been transferred.

"I hear they got you, too," was his gleeful assertion.

"Yeah," Zavattero said, "for a pittance of thirty-five million."

"Nothing to it," Savage replied, "they got me for a hundred million. Tell you what. I'll write them a check for it now if you'll buy lunch."

"Sure," said Zavattero and so they had met again at the Fin & Feathers. This time not separated by the gulf between prosecutor and defendant, but as allies, defendants in the case of *Luane Walker, et al.* v. *Metropolitan Water District* (et al).

When they met Zavattero was surprised. Savage looked tired and much older than just the year and a half since the night the Lockheed tunnel had exploded and his life had gone up in flames with it. Savage's cheery flippance had made Zavattero forget momentarily what a long and grueling time it had been.

As they sat down, a dark-haired waitress with a smile like a bright scythe shining in the darkness approached them. She had served them many times before when they had both been working at Sylmar.

"Martinis, right?" she asked.

Zavattero shook his had. "Jim Beam and water for me."

"Martini, double," Savage said.

When she left, Savage asked, "What gives, Wally? You off martinis?"

"No, I just got ulcers."

Savage raised his eyebrows, "Yeah, I thought you weren't supposed to drink."

Zavattero nodded. "I'm not. But after I told the doc my story, he said better I should drink than lose all my nuts and

Part 2/The Trials

bolts. I'm just about to, too. I hope some damn Lockheed executive's getting ulcers over this thing."

Savage glanced at him curiously, "Hix has already got his. He's dead."

"Man, when did that happen?" Zavattero's mouth dropped open and he just barely kept himself from adding, I hope that bastard died in an explosion!

Zavattero did not like Hix any more than Savage did. He had been doing a disappearing act into the distant manila folders of Lockheed's Seattle plant ever since the first investigation.

Zavattero knew there had been some kind of an exchange between Hix and Savage the day Zavattero had written his order, but he knew Savage would not talk about it. Maybe Savage didn't want to, but whether he refused to talk for his own reasons or because Lockheed's attorneys had ordered him to silence, he was saying nothing.

The whole thing was all wrong, Zavattero thought. Bob Ree had claimed to be present at the time Savage called Hix, but maintained loudly that Hix had not ordered Savage to "get his ass back in that tunnel." Ree's disclaimer had been a shade too quick and too loud. He had apparently realized that himself, and added lamely, "But you know when you first pick up that shovel what your job is." He was right about that. It was practically the tunnel stiffs' code.

"What did he die of?" Zavattero asked.

"Big C. Cancer," Savage replied dramatically. Then he went on musingly, "He died seventeen days after he found out he had it. Seventeen days, seventeen men..." his voice trailed off. He raised his hand for another drink.

Neither one of them had spoken of the suit being brought by the families of the seventeen men in the tunnel. It wasn't necessary. They both wanted the survivors to be paid. But neither one of them felt like being expendable pawns on that legal chessboard.

Still, in an unexpectedly quiet mood Savage looked at Zavattero. His look was grave and searching. "Do you suppose any good will come of all this?"

Again Zavattero was surprised at the way Savage had aged in the last year. "It's got to," Zavattero said. "We've already been consulted on a new tunnel safety act. It's a good law, but I hear it's already in trouble in the legislature."

"Aw, they'll never get that damn bill through," Savage said disgustedly. Then he added vehemently, "This whole thing's a farce anyway. I don't see why they don't pay everybody off and forget the whole crazy thing!"

"Maybe they will if Lockheed gets off with its no contest plea."

Savage refused to be reassured. "Don't worry, that judge won't let them, but—" he added sharply, "you can bet this. They'll never get me to plead no contest. We'll either go free or we'll pull so much garbage out of the sky they'll think it's flak heaven. Right?" He grinned at Zavattero like a co-conspirator.

Zavattero nodded and laughed. He was relieved to see Savage return to his normal cheerful belligerence.

"Who the hell knows what those lawyers will do? The other day Dorn was even threatening to have me prosecuted for withholding evidence," Zavattero laughed.

"No fooling!" Savage exclaimed.

"You're damn right. He got the idea I was going to back out because I told Denton I was so fed up with the prosecution that I wished I could have a lapse of memory."

"What would they charge you with, gross amnesia?"

"Nope. Penal code 135 just like Lockheed. I'd be big time."

While the two were still laughing, Douglas Dalton, Dave Finkle and Karl Ransom walked by their table. They stopped and after a few pleasantries about coincidences, they wanted to know what all the laughter was about.

Savage and Zavattero told them, and everyone cheerfully agreed that it wouldn't be necessary for Savage to plead no contest or Zavattero to suffer amnesia. The plea bargaining would take care of everything. It was all very friendly.

Then the lawyers left and Zavattero and Savage turned to

talk of more immediate things. The two men rarely spoke of their families, but today they talked about them and the shattering effect the Sylmar calamity was having on their lives. Savage had five children and normally enjoyed being a father, but not now. Zavattero nodded agreement. It was so hard to explain.

Zavattero knew Gwen, Savage's wife, and both he and Mercy had liked her when the four of them had met for dinner. Gwen had met Paula and Gina briefly and appeared to like them. It seemed natural to ask Savage and his wife to Paula's wedding. Savage had accepted readily. They had both forgotten for the moment that they were on opposite sides in the criminal suit. Neither one of them thought how such friendliness would look in a courtroom.

After his lunch with Savage, Zavattero was even more inclined to hope that the plea bargaining by Lockheed would be successful. The decision against Lockheed in the meter case had made the public so aware of corporate responsibility—or arrogant irresponsibility—that the new tunnel safety law would have to pass. Either that or face a public outcry that would rattle the hell out of their ballot boxes.

The decision, however, was not up to him or the Division of Industrial Safety, or Arnebergh's city attorney's office, or Dorn, but to Judge George W. Trammell III.

After long deliberation Judge Trammell rejected the plea bargain stating that "it would be a gross miscarriage of justice" to dismiss the charges against Savage, Ree and Pedigo.

And so the selection of the jury went on, and at 9:30 A.M. on September 5, 1972, all jurors having been seated, the second trial of Lockheed began.

CHAPTER THIRTEEN

With an almost audible sigh, Judge Trammell welcomed the jury. "Good morning, ladies and gentlemen. Well, we finally come to that day—"

In spite of the solemnity of the occasion, that first day had the air of guests meeting for a house party where the arrangements were particularly difficult.

The trial was being held in the new criminal court building and Judge Trammell's was the first municipal court in it. This posed special problems as the judge explained to the patiently attentive jury.

There were no eating facilities, no snack bar, no place with amenities for a coffee break. Would the jury care to pool their resources and bring a coffeepot? If everyone pulled together, the jury could have a sort of coffee club and make coffee in the jury room prior to each day's proceedings, the judge explained.

The jurors all nodded not quite sure who was going to find the cooperative coffeepot so cheerfully suggested by the court.

In addition, someone had been remiss, and notebooks for the jury had to be procured hastily at the last minute. There were apparently no more pads available, but would the jury be sure to keep notes. They would. The court had left no doubt in their minds that this would be a long trial.

The jurors having been dispensed with, there had remained the problem of what to do with all those attorneys. There would never be fewer than seven of them, and often more.

Before the judge's bench, the counsel table stretched almost half the width of the courtroom. At its end other tables could be added to form an L-shaped table. The extension would provide room for unexpected, expert lawyers.

Seated at the table in a row, fingering their pens and pencils, and adjusting their stacks of papers, as a dinner guest might place a napkin neatly to one side as he chatted easily with his neighbor, sat the attorneys and the defendants. There would never be fewer than ten of them at this long table.

So far, so good, but before the first course—the opening statements—had been completed, problems erupted.

The moment one of the attorneys asked to approach the bench on business that should not be disclosed to the jury, all seven attorneys waddled like a procession of ducklings after the first attorney. No one was going to say anything to the judge that the others weren't going to hear!

Dalton had made the first trip to the bench, followed by Finkle. Then Dorn had leaped up to protest that the court's ruling was that only one city attorney could participate in conference at the bench. Hollopeter countered with a plea for someone to describe the congested area in which they all stood.

And congested it was. The court agreed and ruled that one prosecution attorney would be deemed sufficient. Cries from Dorn that the people had as much right to a fair trial as the defendants moved the judge to change the ruling.

All the skirmishing about who was to be allowed to confer with the judge seemed to Zavattero to have a slightly theatrical air to it.

He would not have been surprised if Judge Trammell had leaped to his feet and started caroling, "My object all sublime.

I shall achieve in time. That's to make the punishment fit the crime."

And yet all the business they were about was deeply, desperately serious—a matter of life and death. What is the legal significance if a man should die through another's negligence?

But it was not the law's place to grieve for the dead. That would make the law a wild anarchy of emotions—not that it wasn't usual, Zavattero knew, for attorneys to rouse the wild anarchy of emotions if it suited their legal purposes.

As the trial progressed Zavattero grew to feel more and more that it was as if time had removed them all from the reality of that black hole 175 feet under the small community of Sylmar.

Now, neat well-groomed men with briefcases and thousands of pieces of paper, exhibits, enormous skeletal diagrams of the tunnel, and long lists of laws all given by number, had taken the dark, gargoyle shapes of the tunnel and transformed them into a jungle gym or geodesic dome floating far above the dark reverberations of the earth. They were building a lawsuit.

The opening statements were the first blocks in that construction.

Dorn had prepared well for this moment and from a dismaying array of technical data, had developed a compelling scenario.

That scenario was summed up in the *Los Angeles Times* by Myrna Oliver. Said the story in part: "Deputy City Attorney Roosevelt Dorn said both Savage and Ree were made aware of gas in the tunnel several times preceeding the fatal blast.

"Lockheed, Mr. Savage, and Mr. Ree stood to make a tremendous amount of money if this tunnel continued to progress at the rate it was going. Dorn said, 'There certainly were reasons why they didn't want the job stopped.'

"The Metropolitan Water District project was two years ahead of schedule when the blast occurred. The company, Savage, and Ree each had completion contracts which Dorn defined as 'the sooner you finish the job, the more money you'll make.'

"Savage refused to close the tunnel even after a gas testing meter showed a 100 percent reading in a crevice about 7 P.M., six hours prior to the blast.

" 'That 100 percent means a spark would explode it,' Dorn said. The tester called Mr. Savage and Mr. Savage got a reading of 80 to 100 percent. But he said, 'Don't worry about it; that is in the dirt.'

"Dorn's statement continued, 'Arvid Rasmussen operating the gas testing meter, continued to worry about the readings and believed they had been testing for lighter than air methane gas, and heavy gas was indicated.'

"Shortly before the fatal blast Ree was asked to examine four-inch-high 'gas geysers' in dirt being dumped five miles from the tunnel.

"Mr. Ree looked at it and indicated, 'Yes, it's gas,' and took no action, Dorn told the jury.

"The prosecutor said he would produce evidence showing Savage completely disregarded the safety of his men and completely disregarded safety precautions ordered June 23 by Division of Industrial Safety Inspector Wallace Zavattero. The inspector visited the site after a flash fire occurred in the tunnel at 1:55 A.M. about twenty-four fours before the fatal blast.

"David G. Finkle, attorney representing Lockheed, told jurors the Metropolitan Water District, the state of California and the Division of Industrial Safety all stand to gain financially by convictions in this case. A series of civil suits have been filed by relatives of the dead workmen.

Finkle termed the trial a 'political persecution' and said the defendants were being used as 'scapegoats' by the state Division of Industrial Safety.

The Division of Industrial Safety had the charges filed, Finkle said, to cover up and protect itself by placing the blame on these defendants."

The *Times* story had outlined the plot. The prosecution

and defense would not depart far from it, and the legal machinery would grind out thousands of pages of transcripts recording it.

It had been true that Finkle's opening statement had leaned heavily on the pathos of Lockheed's situation. "This," he had indeed declaimed, "is no prosecution, but a political persecution." According to his version, the Division of Industrial Safety had brooded unhappily in its tent after the assembly hearings before deciding to emerge and drag Lockheed twice around the walls of the Los Angeles courthouse, first for concealing evidence and now for negligence.

Dalton, Hollopeter and Ransom had bowed to Finkle's eloquence and postponed their opening statements until the ringing cry of persecution had time to sink into the consciousness of the seven men and five women jurors. They were expected to render a verdict on fifty-six counts in a litigation so complicated and technical that one attorney, Karl Ransom, had stated in the privacy of the judge's chambers that the case shouldn't be tried by a jury at all.

Dorn had watched the jury carefully during Finkle's opening statement. Perhaps, they were not yet ready for an assault on their emotions. At least, to him, they did not seem visibly stirred by Finkle's cry of pity for persecuted Lockheed. They had seemed rather to be fascinated by the alarming array of details that he had given them. It was as if they viewed it as a mystery he had invited them to help him solve—the mystery of the meaning of all this strange data.

Anyway, he hoped what he saw on their faces was interest. At least they didn't seem to be looking at some imaginary clock hoping this whole thing would be over in a few hours. They were apparently reconciled to the fact that it would be a long trial. Dorn was satisfied.

As Zavattero watched the jurors, he wondered if everything would hinge on one person as it had in the earlier trial.

Zavattero had little chance to observe anything after the jury selection. The first motion made by Douglas Dalton was that all witnesses be excluded. The motion was joined in by

Charles Hollopeter for Ree and David Finkle on behalf of Lockheed. Karl Ransom just muttered, "I join, Your Honor."

This was customary and Dorn acceded except to ask that George Denton be permitted to remain in the courtroom as the people's investigating officer. Zavattero was glad of that. George Denton knew the right questions to ask, and could be relied on to relay them to Dorn. But Zavattero did not relish the idea of sitting long hours in what the judge had referred to as the "hallway immediately adjacent to the court." It was a hallway, alright, and that was all. At 9:40 on that morning of September 5, it was hard, narrow, and long, and very, very lonely. There wasn't even, as the judge had so solicitously pointed out to the jury, a snack bar where he could get a cup of coffee.

He had to stay there waiting to be called in and out of the courtroom. Just sitting there wondering what was going on inside the courtroom was the most exasperating part of the trial.

After a while though, as the activities in the criminal court building began to mount up, there arrived for him a sort of company.

They were witnesses in other trials also excluded from their various courtrooms. They would sit on the wooden chairs along the hallway, smoking and chattering like starlings. "Well, I told him, I said—" "I know that's what she said too—" "Well, I don't know why that stupid jerk of a lawyer didn't ask—" "But don't you see, the laws of evidence don't allow—" "Ha-ha, what do you know about the laws of evidence—" "Well, I told him anyway—" On and on they chattered, no matter how minor the case, as they waited the terrible judgments of the law. Sometimes Zavattero wished he had someone to chatter with. But he didn't dare. If someone had seen him talking to anyone who could be associated with the Sylmar trial, Lockheed would have called an immediate mistrial.

No, his conversations had to come at night when Denton would phone him, or Savage would phone and tell him what had happened that day in court. Or Dorn would brief him on what to expect from the day's proceedings. The rest he read in the newspaper or watched on TV, which added little to his store of information.

Denton had been the first witness to be called by the prosecution on the second day of the trial. He had gone over the order he had given Lockheed, about gas inspecting in the tunnel, prior to the time when the tunnel had been returned to Zavattero's jurisdiction. According to Denton's account of that first day he had not been in any serious trouble, and felt that he had impressed on the jury the seriousness of his early concern about the efficiency of the gas inspections.

Almost as soon as Denton had hung up, Savage called, and according to his account, Denton had been driven to the wall by Douglas Dalton on cross-examination. Denton had been compelled to admit that Lockheed had always complied with his safety requirements and was most safety conscious and cooperative. Whatever else he wasn't getting Zavattero was getting both sides. The news media confirmed both stories. They were all not unlike the chattering witnesses in the hall.

That first day had not, however, been wholly taken up with Denton's testimony, but with the weighty problems of whether or not the judge and jurors were to actually see the tunnel. Dorn had urged that "it would be quite beneficial to members of the jury. They can observe the magnitude of this whole operation. It would be most useful for them to go out to and into the tunnel."

To this Hollopeter protested that taking jurors to the scene would be "emotionally prejudicial because of the tomb-like atmosphere where they can't help but be reminded of the seventeen brave men who lost their lives."

When Denton told Zavattero of this, Zavattero snorted, "What the hell are they supposed to be thinking about, Tri-Star jets?"

Actually the jury needed little reminding of the seventeen men. One juror, Harry C. Crockett, jury foreman, later said that the one point all the jurors were agreed on was that those seventeen men represented the highest hurdle Lockheed had to take. There was no way of going around them or leaping over them. They were irrevocably there.

Over Lockheed's attorney's objections, including Finkle's smiling assertion that he was not going to say that it would blow up, but he wasn't going to guarantee anything, Judge Trammell scheduled the visit to the tunnel for the second day of the trial.

Followed by all seven of the attorneys, Judge Trammell found the man trip which would take them all into the tunnel even more congested than the area before his bench; but nobody intended to be excluded. Nobody.

And so with the black earth curled around, Judge Trammell convened court in the dark heart of the Sylmar tunnel. It made good news copy, one of the more sensational headlines being "Judge to Travel Tunnel of Death." That dramatic event was photographed and televised with gusto, and it marked the first time that the jury was sequestered to protect them from publicity about the trial.

Denton had been with Dorn as investigator at the time of the trip, and his account to Zavattero was concise. They had spent two hours and sixteen minutes getting nowhere until someone had noticed oil seeping from a crevice. Then some of the attorneys had thrown agitated fits saying that they would refuse to go into the tunnel again with or without the jury. It was Denton's opinion that the jury would not be allowed in the tunnel.

He was right, though Judge Trammell, who had found the trip deeply impressive, at first ruled that the jury would be allowed. But memory of the oil seepage and ominous talk of pockets of underground gas held back "simply by a membrane that could give out at any time" made caution prevail. Instead they would see a movie of it prepared by Lockheed. It was a good film, and the tunnel was a notable achievement. Of that there could be no doubt. It was a startling contrast to the damaged and twisted wreckage that Savage and Zavattero had photographed on some of their first trips into the tunnel. Even so it was far from the tomblike reality so feared by Lockheed's attorneys.

However, even without trips into the tunnel of death, the drama of what had happened at Sylmar was not lost to the jury.

Dorn had brought Dolph Robbins, a Metropolitan Water District inspector, to the witness stand.

His story of the flash fire that had occurred the night before the fatal blast had been vividly graphic, and was given with intense emotion. According to the *Times* story written by William Farr, the inspector's voice had quavered and appeared on the verge of tears as he told of "flesh hanging from the arm" of one of the miners injured, and of his own terrified state when he was injured.

There was no doubt that Lockheed had been amply warned of the danger of gas. Dolph Robbins also had received a note from Louis Richardson, Metropolitan Water District construction inspector killed the following night. The note had warned "Robbie, there is a strong odor in the face that smells like diesel."

The mention of the note had brought cries of hearsay evidence and many trips to the bench from the defense attorneys. It was they who protested an out-of-court statement and Richardson could not be questioned about it because he was dead.

Dorn was orchestrating his prosecution well. The jury had heard not only of the note, but from other miners they heard of the men who had headaches and became nauseated by the pervasive smell of unidentifiable gas. They heard how chaotic the gas testing had been. They heard from Robin Romeo why he had refused to go into the tunnel on the fatal night. He had been the only man who had not needed safety orders to tell him what was happening in that tunnel. And most damaging, they had learned that Savage had refused to let Louis Richardson, the Metropolitan Water District Inspector, stop the work. Savage had told him he would have to get a written order from a Metropolitan Water District superior. They heard how Richardson had replied that by the time he could reach outside to call his boss "the damn thing would blow up anyway."

The mounting evidence was damaging. Lockheed had ignored all the warnings, and gone right on highballing it. Most damaging was the fact that they had ignored the safety orders written that very afternoon by Zavattero. The orders read: first to test constantly for gas, and if the readings reached one percent by volume, work was to be stopped and Zavattero notified; second, if two percent by volume were reached, the men were to be removed from the tunnel. If those orders had been complied with, the fatal blast would not have killed seventeen men. It was as simple as that.

Dorn had decided not to put Zavattero on the stand until the trial was well under way. His orders were the final link in the chain of foreknowledge of what lay in that tunnel.

During those early weeks, Dorn and Zavattero had met almost daily. They had grown to know each other well, and the relationship was an easy, relaxed one most of the time.

Dorn had been angry that Zavattero had continued to maintain amicable relations with Savage, but Zavattero had steadfastly refused to view his friendly relations with Savage as compromising in any way. He and Savage had worked together and shared the experience of the Sylmar holocaust and its aftermath.

Mercy tended to share Dorn's mistrust, but when Savage and his wife were to be invited to Paula's wedding, her mild objections to their being there were made for other reasons.

"Look," she had explained earnestly to Zavattero, "this is a wedding. It is supposed to be happy. Paula and Larry have a right to be happy with their friends. If Loren is here, you and Loren and George Denton will turn the whole thing into a wake for those seventeen men."

Zavattero shook his head impatiently. He attributed her objections to her increasing nervousness. The trials and the constant worry about it all; the effect it was having on the family and his health seemed to fill her with constant dread.

It had become so serious, that just the night before she had told him that she had made an appointment to see a psychiatrist.

When he looked at her in hurt surprise, she had told him in a low, determined voice, "I've got to, Wally. I can't go on any more. I haven't slept in a month, and the days are worse than the nights. If I didn't have Paula's wedding to keep me busy, I think I'd really go crazy. I've got to, don't you see?" she pleaded.

He nodded and put his arms around her. Her body shook with silent, hopeless sobbing. At that moment he hated Lockheed and the tunnel and everybody connected with it.

But Savage and Gwen had come to Paula's wedding reception, and Mercy's prediction almost proved true. After the cake had been cut, and all the toasts made, Zavattero, Savage and Denton had gone into the kitchen where they could only dimly hear the bright laughter and teasing of the wedding party.

At first they had all laughed at the strangeness of not having somebody's attorney hanging around to check up on everything, and inevitably the conversation turned to the night of the explosion.

At length, Zavattero looked searchingly at Savage, and once again he asked, "Loren, I still don't know what happened. Why did you do it?"

Savage didn't look up, but stared into his glass. He shook his head. "I can't tell you now, Wally. Someday when this is all over I'll tell you."

At that moment Mercy walked in. She shook her head angrily at him, but she was smiling and looked beautiful. The wedding reception was a success and she was all hostess. He did not want to spoil it for her, and the three men returned to the bright sounds and cheerful laughter.

No, he saw no reason for giving up his friendship with

Savage. Dorn did not press him further, but hoped it might in some way be turned to the prosecution's advantage.

As the time approached for Zavattero to take the stand, Dorn explained carefully what he could expect from Lockheed's battery of lawyers.

They would try to impeach him with everything he had ever said, no matter how insignificant it might seem, and everything he'd ever done. They were brilliant attorneys and they made no wasted moves. Whatever they asked, there would be a reason for it.

The most important thing would be the attack on the orders Zavattero had given. They had won their point that the orders were to be considered requirements or recommendations, not orders. But Helgeson had appealed that ruling, and while the appeal was pending, the status of the orders was still in a legal limbo. Dorn explained carefully that he was always to refer to them as orders no matter how the defense referred to them.

As Zavattero listened to Dorn, the picture of the alternatives for Lockheed began to emerge. They would try to convince the jury that (a) they had complied with Zavattero's safety orders; (b) the safety orders weren't orders, but mere recommendations not binding on Lockheed; (c) Zavattero was a damn liar about everything including whether or not Lockheed had complied with the safety orders which weren't orders anyway, but mere suggestions. Simple, Zavattero thought, very simple.

Aside from Zavattero's orders, the whole case was shaping up to have as many arms as an octopus, and also the attorneys in their trips to the bench looked as if each of them had eight arms and eight pockets. With lightning speed they would begin flashing into their pockets pulling out sheafs of paper covering previous testimony, depositions, documents, photographs, exhibits, precedents to be cited, and who knows what other lists and sublists.

One juror, at least, found all these trips to the bench bewildering and not a little frustrating. How could the jury be expected to render a verdict? They were forced to spend so much of their time staring noncommittaly at five or six shifting behinds and flailing arms, their agitations only interrupted by occasional whispered injunctions not to let the jury hear them. It was indeed bewildering.

To Zavattero there was nothing ludicrous about that forest of attorneys so often gathered at the court's bench. He knew that all those documents they produced so magically were brought forth to impeach him; to question his credibility.

The questions always seemed the same, but always were subtly different. "When had he written them? Who was there? Did he change them in any way? Had he insisted on drilling a hole at the face?"

The assembly hearings had been nothing. At this point he would have welcomed Fenton as a kindly old uncle who just wanted to get the truth.

During his testimony, the TV artists had sketched his picture a number of times. When he saw one of them he was surprised at how haggard he looked. He wondered if that was the way he looked to the jury. Nobody could trust anyone who looked that beat!

He was mistaken. One day as the court was adjourned, he had been so tired that he had not even had enough energy to get up from the witness stand. He just sat there wondering where his arms and legs were, and if they would be able to propel him to his car. At last he stood up and walked towards the door. The jurors were filing out, looking very tired themselves, and suddenly he heard a low growl next to him. "Hang in there." Startled, he almost turned to see who had spoken, but he wasn't so tired that his mind didn't flash "mistrial" if he so much as breathed a smile in that friendly direction. He wanted to, oh, how he wanted to! But instead he just propelled himself forward. He never knew who the juror was, but he was always grateful to him for that small growl of encouragement.

It was encouragement that he needed because the next day Dalton took off on a track that proved a turning point in the trial for Zavattero.

It had come after long questioning on burning and welding operations in the tunnel. The interrogation had shifted to the question of drilling a hole if gas were encountered.

In itself the question was innocuous and had been gone over a number of times, but Dalton seemed to be leaning particularly hard on Zavattero's memory of it. And in fact his memory seemed to be the most important issue. He was only a little puzzled at this because all during the interrogation Dalton had harped on his memory. He was doing so again, and this time he seemed to be doing so with a distinct purpose.

DALTON: And isn't it true that you testified that you remembered your exact statement?

ZAVATTERO: Yes, sir.

DALTON: And isn't it true that you said that you remembered this exact statement to you—you recalled it when you were on the stand outside the presence of the jury three or four weeks ago?

ZAVATTERO: That is correct.

DALTON: And that is when you first remembered it; isn't that right?

ZAVATTERO: Yes, sir.

DALTON: And didn't you also testify, Mr. Zavattero under oath, that your memory is no better than average?

ZAVATTERO: That's what I said.

Zavattero was still puzzled at all this talk of memory, but then it had always puzzled him why Dalton always seemed to hang up on it.

Dalton continued, "And isn't it also true that for you it is difficult to recall exact conversations and exact details and observations of something that happened about eighteen months ago? Is that difficult?"

Zavattero looked at him for a moment. He wished Dalton would get that air of smug insinuation out of his voice. He couldn't understand it. Nevertheless he answered easily enough:

> ZAVATTERO: Well, what I recall has to have significance.
> DALTON: But it is difficult to recall great detail and to recall exact words of conversations, is it not? Would you agree with me on that?
> ZAVATTERO: Yes, sir.
> DALTON: Now, Mr. Zavattero, you have had many conversations with the city attorney's office, have you not, regarding the events of June 23 and June 24, and so forth, since they occurred?
> ZAVATTERO: Yes, sir.

As he said that, a faint smile flickered across Zavattero's face. He held it back, and waited attentively for the next question. He knew now precisely what had brought on Dalton's continued concern for the state of his memory. Dalton was remembering the day at the Mill.

Dalton went on: "About how many times would you say you have been interviewed by them and they have gone over with you your memory of these events?

> DORN: Objection. Irrelevant.
> JUDGE TRAMMELL: Overruled.
> ZAVATTERO: Numerous times.
> DALTON: Well, give us some idea. How many? Would you say a hundred?
> ZAVATTERO: I just—they were numerous. That's all I could state.
> DALTON: Over what period of time would you say they started going over these things with you? When did it first start?
> ZAVATTERO: September 2, 1971.

DALTON: And it has continued up until today, has it not?

ZAVATTERO: Yes, on and off.

DALTON: And isn't it true, Mr. Zavattero, that they expressed displeasure at you and accused you of not remembering certain things about the case earlier in this case when they interviewed you?

DORN: Objection. Vague. When we interviewed—

TRAMMELL: Sustained.

DALTON: All right, let me ask you this: Isn't it true that you, yourself, were threatened with prosecution if you did not come up with more recollection and more testimony and more evidence about the events that occurred in June of 1971? Is that true or false?

Before he answered, Zavattero looked away from Dalton first at Finkle, then at Ransom.

"That is true," he replied flatly.

As he spoke there was a faint rustling along the counsel table, a mere shuffling of papers like a small sign. Dorn had not stirred.

Dalton looked steadily at Zavattero. "Thank you. I have nothing further."

He didn't need anything further. Zavattero had just admitted that he had been coerced into testifying, and possibly manufacturing evidence.

The court asked Dorn, "How long do you anticipate your redirect?"

Dorn replied stolidly, "Oh, approximately an hour, an hour and a half."

Then court was adjourned for that day.

As they left the courtroom Dorn leaned heavily on his cane, and as they walked back to the city attorney's office his expression remained as stolid as it had been when the judge had questioned him about his redirect. Zavattero walked beside him equally stolid.

When they had entered the office, Dorn threw his cane down on the desk and sank into his chair.

"And what the hell do you think you're doing?" he asked coldly.

"Telling the truth," Zavattero said amiably. He knew that would infuriate Dorn, but he was so sick of what was going on in that courtroom that he didn't care.

He was right. Dorn was livid. "Do you realize you've put me in a spot where I've got to impeach my own witness?" Dorn stared at him and then went on. "I've had to pull every bit of truth out of you like you were deaf and dumb, and now you start spreading the truth around like you were Billy Graham."

Zavattero felt sorry that he had seemed so indifferent to the position they were in, but he really was sick of lawyer games.

"I didn't pull anything," he said. "I told you you'd hear about that damn conversation."

Dorn looked at him for a long moment. "I'll bet Savage manipulated that."

Zavattero stared back at him, then shook his head, "How could he? I was only telling him what I'd told Denton, that I was tired of the whole prosecution and I'd just like to have a lapse of memory before they could get me on the witness stand."

"And why the hell shouldn't I?" Zavattero was mad, too, now. "My wife's a nervous wreck, my kid's getting bugged by all her friends and teachers, my own office treats me like I got leprosy, and for what?"

Zavattero waved his hand at the city attorney's offices, "To try to get the lousy city attorney's office to make one stinking little prosecution for the death of seventeen men nobody cares about anyway."

Dorn raised his hand to interrupt, but Zavattero went on savagely. "What makes you think I should trust you? They shafted Bane and who knows what they paid Arnebergh—why should I trust you?" As Zavattero said that he was sorry. He did trust Dorn, and more than that admired his integrity. "Sorry," he muttered.

There was a long silence as Dorn looked at Zavattero. "Yes," he said slowly, "I guess you don't have much reason to trust us, but Wally, Arnebergh is out now. They clobbered him in the election. And what you said was just plain stupid. Do you realize what they can do with that statement?"

Zavattero nodded, "Sure, I do, but there was nothing else I could do today. When Dalton sprang that on me, I looked at Finkle and remembered they were there during that conversation. You couldn't see them, but I could. They were just waiting to start hollering lie, or impeach or whatever the hell you lawyers call it; besides I'd already told you all about it."

Dorn stared at him for a moment, and then a wicked, lawyer's gleam came into his eye, "Yes you did, didn't you," he chortled. "I just wasn't listening then. I never thought your friendship with Savage could be this dangerous."

"Neither did I," Zavattero said worriedly. "Neither did I. What are you laughing at?" he asked abruptly.

"Nothing," Dorn said still smiling, "Come on, let's go have dinner. We're going to write a script, and Zavattero, you are about to become the most honest man since ol' Abe Lincoln."

The next day when the two men entered the courtroom, their attitude toward each other was a cold and hostile one. Lockheed's attorneys observed them carefully.

It was December 6, 1972, and the court, after making the usual welcome to the jurors, began the day's work.

"Mr. Dorn, you may commence redirect," the judge intoned.

Mr. Dorn rose and without a glance in the direction of the jury, the judge, or the other attorneys, looked at Zavattero and asked:

DORN: Mr. Zavattero, you indicated on cross-examination yesterday that you had known Mr. Savage since 1967; is that correct?"

ZAVATTERO: Yes, sir.

DORN: And you have been very close friends with Mr. Savage; is that correct?

ZAVATTERO: Yes.

DORN: You and Mr. Savage, you had lunch together; is that correct?

ZAVATTERO: Yes, sir.

DORN: In fact, you and Mr. Savage have gone out drinking together?

ZAVATTERO: Yes, sir.

DALTON: I object to this. May we approach the bench?

Once again the attorneys assembled at the bench. This time to discuss the propriety of the term "drinking together."

Mr. Dalton did not think it was serious enough for a mistrial, but certainly thought it an improper question. The connotations were bad.

Mr. Finkle also thought it was leading and suggestive.

The court did not agree that it was leading or suggestive. However, the court agreed that "to the ordinary individual it may connote that Mr. Savage is a lush, engages in a practice of continually drinking to excess." The term would not be used but the more sedate term "having cocktails together" could be substituted.

Having expunged this hint of rowdiness on the part of miners and tunnel stiffs, the court allowed the hearing to proceed.

(The following proceedings were had in open court, within the presence of the jury:)

DORN: May I proceed, your Honor?

TRAMMEL: You may.

DORN: Mr. Zavattero, you and Mr. Savage had gone out and had cocktails together; is that correct?

ZAVATTERO: Yes, sir.

DORN: On numerous occasions?

DORN: Yes, sir.

DORN: In fact, Mr. Zavattero, since this trial has been in progress, you and Mr. Savage have gone out and had cocktails together; is that correct?

ZAVATTERO: Yes, sir.

DORN: Also, Mr. Savage, his wife, and you and your wife had dinner together?

ZAVATTERO: That is correct.

DORN: Mr. Savage and his wife were invited to your daughter's wedding; is that correct?

ZAVATTERO: That is correct.

DORN: And throughout these proceedings you and Mr. Savage have remained very close friends; is that correct?

ZAVATTERO: That is correct.

DORN: Now, prior to the time that this case started you had a conversation with Mr. Denton in regard to your testimony in this case; is that correct?

ZAVATTERO: Yes, sir.

DORN: Would you relate that conversation.

The conversation was immediately objected to by Mr. Finkle as hearsay.

Mr. Dorn protested that the statement was not being offered for the truth of the matter stated; merely that Mr. Zavattero made the statement.

The court claimed understanding, but wanted an offer of proof. So back they all went to the bench.

There Mr. Dorn went to the offer of proof saying that Mr. Zavattero had indeed complained to Mr. Denton that the case was going very slowly and that he might conveniently not remember what had occurred in June.

Mr. Dalton objected to a conversation between Denton

and Zavattero as rank hearsay tending to show that Savage had influenced Zavattero to say this.

Mr. Dorn again protested that it was being offered to show what occurred as far as the prosecution was concerned.

The court cast an inquiring eye at Mr. Dorn and asked, "Is this something that leads up to?—" and broke off waiting.

Mr. Dorn nodded significantly, "That is correct."

Sternly the court continued its thought, ". . . Mr. Dalton's parting shot yesterday?"

Again Mr. Dorn nodded significantly, "That is correct."

Then Mr. Ransom and Mr. Finkle stepped in with more protests while Mr. Dalton fell back for a polite exchange with Mr. Dorn.

DALTON: Well, also, by way of offer of proof for your benefit, my understanding was that the threats to Zavattero did not come from Denton. They came from Mr. Dorn.

DORN: That is correct.

Mr. Dalton then was most deprecating, "And I felt it would be better not to mention Mr. Dorn by name at that time—"

Mr. Dorn caught Mr. Dalton up, "Mr. Dorn is going to mention Mr. Dorn," he said.

Dalton continued politely, "as a professional courtesy."

The court did not seem extraordinarily impressed with Mr. Dalton's professional courtesy and pointed out that Mr. Dalton had carefully avoided mentioning Mr. Dorn, for what did not appear to be matters of professional courtesy, and since Mr. Dalton had been the first to bring up the threat of prosecution of Zavattero, the court was going to allow Mr. Dorn to pursue the matter.

After this Dorn continued to steer a course, through the shoals of objections and trips to the bench, to arrive at the shore of some simple questions.

Had Zavattero been questioned about his conversations with Savage? Yes. Had he been asked to discuss the facts of the explosion with Savage? Yes. Had he subsequently called into the city attorney's offices? Yes. Would he relate the conversation?

ZAVATTERO: Well, I sat down and you stated to me, "I understand you're not happy with the progress of this case." I said, "Yes." Then you said, "I understand you are going to have an intentional lapse of memory." And I said, "No." And you continued, and you said that the city attorney's office and your office were going to prosecute the case vigorously; one. Two, that if I concealed any of the facts in this case when on the witness stand you would prosecute me under penal code 135 for concealing evidence.

DORN: Mr. Zavattero, at any time and in any of the conversations that I have had with you have I ever requested that you manufacture evidence?

Objections of incompetent, immaterial and irrelevant flew out of Dalton's mouth like a flock of birds.
(Overruled.)

ZAVATTERO: No, you told me to tell the truth.

Then Dorn asked Zavattero if he had told anyone else of their conversation.

Yes, the witness had told Mr. Savage and Mr. Dalton.
(More objections and another trip to the bench.)

To all the questioning Zavattero's answers had been given matter-of-factly, with no inflection whatever. When the storms around the bench continued to rage, Zavattero would sit quietly. He did not look at the jury, and he did not want to look in Savage's direction. He was forced to just sit there and try to look at nothing at all.

Occasionally lowering his eyes and rubbing them wearily, he would wonder to himself what this was really all about. Why wasn't it possible for a man to come into court and blurt out a simple, honest statement without choking to death on this rigamarole of dust-covered words. What he had to say was perfectly simple, why couldn't he just say it?

He finally got his chance. After the last, long trip to the bench, Dorn asked him:

At the time you indicated, Mr. Zavattero, that you would be cross-examined in this regard, what did I tell you?

ZAVATTERO: You said, "Let them go ahead."

DORN: And what did I tell you in regard to what you should do?

ZAVATTERO: Answer the questions truthfully.

DORN: And, Mr. Zavattero, has it been difficult for you to testify in this case?

To this Ransom took exception as being incomprehensible, and the court sustained it.

Then Dorn asked Zavattero again did he want to testify the case.

To this Finkle objected. Immaterial. Overruled.

Before answering, Zavattero looked at them all for a long moment. Then he said clearly: "No, but it is my duty to do it."

DORN: Why didn't you want to testify in this case?

This time Zavattero's pause was even longer. It was so simple he wondered if anyone would understand it.

ZAVATTERO: It's difficult to stand up in front of a friend and be his accuser. That's my responsibility and my duty as the regulations in the state service and the oath I took on becoming a state employee. I don't think there is anything in the state regulations that says I have to like it!

There, the simple truth was out. He had never wanted to testify against Savage, but now Savage had left him no alternative. As he spoke he thought he heard a faint, sympathetic gasp from the jury, but he couldn't be sure.

Dalton had risen to his feet, followed by Ransom, and both were being admonished by Judge Trammell to be seated.

Only Hollopeter had remained quietly seated. As Dalton and Ransom continued their protests, Judge Trammell ordered the jury to be dismissed and threatened to cite Dalton for misconduct. Zavattero never knew what they had been saying. He really didn't care. Zavattero left the courtroom along with the jury. He glanced at Savage. Savage did not look at him, but doodled idly on a blank sheet of paper.

After Zavattero's dramatic assertion of his reluctance to testify against Savage, Dorn was pleased. What Zavattero had said had the ring of absolute truth to it, and in this complex case that was an achievement.

When the examination resumed, everyone turned again to the dense thicket of technical data. Did Zavattero's order read testing should take place in the mainstream of return air? Had he considered the possibility of an unexpected in-rush of gas? What was the velocity of air being pushed through the special fans or blow joes ordered to clear the face of tunnel? Were the men to be evacuated when the atmosphere tested two percent or when gas was detected in probe holes or fissures? Was the gas methane or some other, heavier gas? Zavattero sometimes wondered what the jury could make of all his trips to the tunnel diagrams to draw some new technical point for one of the assembled attorneys.

When Dalton began his recross-examination, the case *People v. Lockheed, et al* again emerged from the technical underbrush.

As Dalton began his recross Zavattero braced himself. He was tired. It was the end of the day and he knew that Douglas Dalton was not going to let the sun set on that morning's testimony about Savage. He was right.

DALTON: Mr. Zavattero, you testified this morning about a conversation you had with me at one time. Do you recall that?

ZAVATTERO: Yes, sir.

DALTON: And you also testified about your friendship with Mr. Savage. Is that true?

ZAVATTERO: That's correct.

DALTON: You would come into contact with Mr. Savage almost daily out at the jobsite, do you not?

ZAVATTERO: It was so after the accident, yes.

At that moment Zavattero recalled Bane and Townsend's assertion at the assembly hearing. They'd both agreed that keeping him assigned to the Lockheed tunnel was an unhealthy if not dangerous situation. Maybe they'd been right.

Dalton's questioning continued going painstakingly over the occasion when they had met at the Fin & Feathers.

DALTON: And sometimes he would pay and sometimes you would pay; isn't that right?

ZAVATTERO: Yes, sir.

DORN: And isn't it true that Mr. Savage never at any time tried to influence you in your testimony or tried to get you to say things that weren't true?

ZAVATTERO: He did not try to influence me.

Then Dalton continued relating the innocent events of that day. How they had all talked of just happening to run into each other. Mr. Finkle and Mr. Ransom even happened to be there, and how they'd talked of being in the tunnel. And Dalton was sure that he, Mr. Finkle, and Mr. Ransom had not come there looking for him. To all of which guileless questions Zavattero answered appropriately.

He had answered affirmatively when Dalton asked if it was in that conversation that Zavattero had told him about the threat of prosecution. Then Dalton had inquired:

And it was in that conversation that you told me about your opinion of Mr. Savage as far as safety consciousness; isn't that true?

ZAVATTERO: I don't remember the safety, but I talked well of him. I know I talked well of him.

DALTON: Did you state to me, Mr. Zavattero, that you felt that Mr. Savage was not criminally responsible in this case?

During all this Dorn had made only one objection, but he had been watching it all intently. So had Judge Trammell.

When Dorn protested loudly, the objection was immediately sustained by Judge Trammell.

Shocked, Judge Trammell stated, "I can't help you but think, Mr. Dalton, as a lawyer of your experience you should have known that a question and the innuendo before a jury is improper."

Now it was Zavattero's turn to listen intently as the arguments flew back and forth. Whatever feelings he may have about Savage's part in the disaster, they were being given a whole new life in the hands of the attorneys.

Dalton insisted that the whole thing be argued right now, and so Judge Trammell dismissed the jury. As the jury drifted patiently into the jury room, Finkle spoke up that it would not be appropriate for this to be done in the presence of the witness. The court agreed and once again Zavattero was consigned to the hallway adjacent.

But this time Zavattero was genuinely exasperated. On previous occasions he had simply shrugged and accepted it all as part of courtroom antics. It had even amused him in one dispute when someone had remarked portentously, "We all know where we're going, but Zavattero doesn't. He should be sent out of the courtroom." He had duly been dismisssed, and in the hallway chafed with irritated amusement. It sounded so much like a kid's game. He wondered if, when it was over, the bailiff would come and holler "All free!" to indicate he was now free to return for another game of hide-and-seek.

However, the moments when Zavattero could muster up a sense of humor at all were becoming rare. He had been on the stand now for fourteen days. He was tired, and besides, what was happening now made him feel as if he were being stripped of any human feelings he might have. Those feelings could be dangerous. If he had them he'd better damned well keep his mouth shut.

It would be quite a while this time before the call came, "Mr. Zavattero to Division 45, please. Mr. Zavattero to 45."

Inside Dalton was determined to get Zavattero's opinion of Savage before the jury. He wasn't having much luck. Judge Trammell was saying that Dalton's effort to bring the witness's opinion as to the defendant's criminal responsibility before the jury was an unbelievably unprofessional action.

Dalton was protesting that he had never heard of a court allowing the kind of testimony Zavattero had given about his motives that morning on the witness stand.

The court reminded Dalton that he had been the one who had opened that "Pandora's box" on the previous day with his questioning. The court told Mr. Dalton that he would not allow the attorney to tell the jury that he had been witness to statements by Zavattero that could be regarded as approving of Savage.

Finkle and Ransom interjected that they had both been witnesses to such statements, and Hollopeter announced that

Part 2/The Trials   233

he had concurred with his colleagues that there was no impropriety in bringing such testimony before the jury. With this Finkle agreed and concluded that Zavattero's statement "definitely went to impeachment."

With some acerbity the court denied this, stating that if the situation were turned around and Mr. Dorn had asked Zavattero if he had ever felt that the defendant Savage should be "convicted and sent to jail for a long time, the defendant's attorneys would be screaming for a mistrial and probably get it."

The matter thus being settled, the jury and the witness were recalled. Dalton concluded his recross-examination with a few perfunctory questions, and at last, after nearly three weeks on the witness stand, Zavattero was told that he could go. He would be recalled if needed. Court was adjourned for that day.

Later at Dorn's office, the prosecuting attorneys were jubilant. It was a major victory. Lockheed's sensational efforts to use Zavattero's friendship with Savage to impeach him, discredit the prosecution and demand a mistrial had been routed. Dorn, though he did not say so, was relieved. Zavattero's compromising relation with Savage was ended. Zavattero too was elated. He felt as if they had all been saved from some terrible, nameless catastrophe. Yet as he recalled Savage's refusal to look at him, he felt saddened. Something had happened that was no credit to any of them.

Zavattero was glad, though, that he would not be hearing the call "Mr. Zavattero to Division 45, please" for a while. He could spend Christmas far away from that endless corridor. Maybe, he wouldn't ever be recalled to the stand. The judge had said that the anticipated end of the trial would be January 26. The date was a tentative one, but he could always hope.

His hopes were unfounded. The trial went relentlessly on. But then in February, Lockheed moved for acquittal of all charges.

"What the hell is that all about?" Zavattero had asked Dorn.

Maybe Ronald Demo had returned and confessed to blowing the whole thing up because he was a terrorist and didn't like Lockheed's pay scale. What the hell had happened?

It had been nothing so dramatic Dorn explained. There had been some fancy footwork going on in the legislature, that was all.

In April 1972 some amendments had been added to a bill concerning leaves of absences that made it impossible to hold supervisory personnel such as Ree and Savage responsible for acts of negligence toward fellow employees. It had slipped quietly through the House and Senate and floated lightly on to Govenor Reagan's desk to be neatly signed, stamped, and passed into law.

There was only one thing wrong with it. The amendment had nothing to do with the title of the bill which merely said that the bill gave leaves of absences to state workers. It violated a section of the state constitution designed to prevent misleading titles of bills. Judge Trammell had therefore ruled it unconstitutional.

Lockheed's attorneys had disagreed and requested a hearing from the Supreme Court on motions to throw out all charges, on the ground that the municipal court lacked jurisdiction to continue the trial because the three defendants could no longer be considered "employers."

As Zavattero heard all this he just shook his head. "What the hell are they doing all this for?"

Dorn shook his head too, "They want to get out from under the whole thing, and they're using all their clout and money to do it."

"Can they get away with it?"

Dorn grinned cheerfully, "Don't worry, they can't get away with it."

Dorn was right. The Supreme Court dismissed Lockheed's petition summarily and the trial went on.

All these political maneuverings did nothing to cheer

Zavattero. He only wondered what was likely to happen with Fenton's proposed new safety bill. It had already failed to pass in the Senate once, and was now up for consideration again. And where did Savage stand in all this? Was it the legislative flimflamming that had made him so sure that the prosecution would come to nothing? Zavattero wondered, but he never had the chance to ask him.

Following the delay caused by the Supreme Court deliberations, the wheels of justice began again to grind slowly.

The witnesses had followed one after another, each with his story to tell. Each made some small contribution to the legal mosaic being constructed by all the attorneys.

There had been little room for drama in the long trial. The dead world of cold iron, metal, and machinery were its central figures until Dorn brought Ralph Brisette to the stand.

Brisette brought to the mindless world of machinery a drama of guilt and remorse. He had been the only one to survive. Why?

He was to testify to the conditions in the tunnel, the possible amount of gas present, the sources of ignition and the kind of testing being done. The technical questions he answered in a low, calm voice.

The rest of his story was more difficult. Before the explosion he had felt a pressure on his ears. Then the air had gone still. That was before it blew. He could hear someone yelling from the heading to turn off the belt. He himself had yelled to the motorman to move the train so the men could get out. The tunnel had gone completely dark and he had fallen. In the blackness someone had stumbled over him. It was Will Carter, Carter had not known who he was. Carter asked if he had a light. He did not. Carter urged him to get out with him. He had tried, but he couldn't. He was too weak and as Carter ran, he crawled through the water to the fanline. Behind him he could hear the screaming men. He could do nothing.

As he told his story, his simple, fumbling misery was an echo from the heart of every human being who had ever been within distance of a dying cry and could do nothing. The cry still haunted his mind, ringing with grief and anguish around the circle of what he did not do. It made no difference that there was nothing he could do. Death had cried out and seized another man. All that mattered was that he could not stop death. No one can.

That terrible and intimate reality had shattered this simple man and quietly, gently, all the lawyers dismissed him. There would be no further interrogation from either the prosecution or defense. All the loud, noisy traffic of the courtroom was stopped in deep, still silence. For that day the court was adjourned.

Listening to Brisette, Zavattero sat absolutely motionless. He did not even close his eyes, staring fixedly at Brisette. But across the screen of his memory swam the images of Will Carter's discarded body lying in a crumpled heap on the muck pile and the disarrayed bones that he and Denton had left lying in the slanting rays of the evening sun. That had been so long ago. Over two years. So long ago. He couldn't close his eyes and lose the vision. It was fixed forever. Quietly he left the courtroom, shutting the door behind him.

The trial continued and at last the closing arguments were in sight. But before they began, Zavattero was cheered by the fact that at last Fenton had pushed the Tom Carrell Tunnel Safety Act through the Senate. It was a good bill. He knew. He had helped to formulate it. And just as importantly the Assembly had passed Fenton's bill AB150 which repealed the 1963 act that had reduced the seriousness of gross negligence resulting in death to a misdemeanor. The crime could now be prosecuted as a felony. There was hope. The safety bill had passed in May. The closing arguments in the long and tangled trial had begun in the first week of June and would last until July 3.

During that time Zavattero would sit outside the courtroom in the hallway adjacent waiting for the call, "Mr. Zavattero, to Division 45 please."

Inside Division 45 things proceeded as usual. The jury was advised of the profound seriousness of the task they were about to undertake. They were to render judgement on the charges made against all defendants. Not all defendants were charged on the same counts. They alone must judge on the matter.

In their opening addresses to the jury, all of the attorneys, especially those of the powerful defendant Lockheed, employed what seemed to be one of the occupational tools of the lawyers trade—a deep humility.

Dalton, who Zavattero had heard was receiving fantastic sums for the defense of Savage from the impressive firm of Ball, Hunt, Brown & Baerwitz, was in reality nothing more than a small-town attorney from Long Beach, he assured the jury.

David Finkle, with outspread hands, pleaded that he had never before argued a case before a jury.

Hollopeter felt like a horse without a rider, and Ransom was afflicted with butterflies and weak knees.

Aside from their common efforts to convince the jury of their absolute humility and yearning for justice, each of the attorneys would argue on behalf of his own client. Each would try to turn the spotlight on his own client's innocence, except for Dorn, who would turn his spotlight on their total guilt.

The arguments took a long time, and, as the jurors had learned to expect, most of that time was spent at the bench. The prosecutor, Dorn, had begun covering almost every detail of gas meters and gas readings, and he had dwelt at length not only on the general safety orders which Lockheed had violated, but on the special orders written by Zavattero the very day of the catastrophe. It was long, technically detailed, and in his conclusion Dorn assured the jury that "the overwhelming facts showed that each and every defendant was guilty of each and every charge." He then thanked the jury and said that he was sure they would be just as attentive to defense counsel's arguments.

Hollopeter was the first to argue in defense of Ree. He protested in his emphatic manner that Ree could not be considered an employer and therefore could not be held responsible for the employer's responsibility to provide and maintain a safe place of employment. The responsibilities that he had assumed as a safety engineer had been thrust on him without providing him with the authority to discharge the responsibility. He concluded emphatically with the assertion that his client "was in this case for one reason only—because he was cursed with the title of safety engineer."

Karl Ransom then stood up on behalf of Eugene Pedigo. His defense was simple. Pedigo, a walker or foreman on the job had limited responsibilities and those responsibilities he had fulfilled to the utmost. The attorney then apologized for any displeasure he may have caused "any person or party" in the courtroom and sincerely hoped it would not reflect on his client, and with that unaccountable statement he sat down.

David Finkle had the most difficult job defending that remote, impersonal entity, the corporation. That nonhuman agency could only be defended on its corporate integrity. His argument in defense of Lockheed was the longest of the defense arguments, requiring seven days to give and covering 435 pages of transcript. During it there would not be a geological report missed, an order, a statement, a technical question of ventilation, or a single inch of the ripper claws on the excavating machine overlooked. His concluding argument turned to the human. He asked the jury to consider the fact that no one else had stayed at the tunnel, not Zavattero or Brown of the Metropolitan Water District. He did not mention Richardson of the Metropolitan Water District who had died in the tunnel, but protested instead that the defendants had stayed there, and that could not be gross negligence.

Whatever impact on the jury his plea might have had was lost. The court's solicitude was directed toward a juror who had become ill. Everyone's sympathetic attention had gone to poor juror Rivero, who everyone agreed would be better off at home. The court assured Mr. Rivero that he should not feel compelled to come the next day. The trial had gone on so long, another two or three days wouldn't matter.

To Zavattero they did. He had to sit out in the hall while all this was going on. Actually he had grown not to mind sitting in the corridor. In the year and a half of trials, he had come to recognize nearly every clerk, secretary, and lawyer who made up the traffic of the courthouse.

He always watched them with interest. The judges all seemed to cluster around the elevator at lunchtime. They were always unencumbered, but not the lawyers. The lawyers were always burdened down with briefcases as big as suitcases, bulging with who knows what points and authorities, briefs, depositions, subpoenas, citations, writs, and all the other paraphernalia of the law. It was literally a heavy profession.

Some of the young attorneys appeared to carry their burden lightly. They walked along, confident as athletes who were about to hurl their heavy briefcases into the courtroom like a shot put.

Others, most of them older, seemed bent with the weight as if the burden of the law had become so heavy they could hardly drag it into the courtroom.

Once in awhile the showman appeared. He always entered like a movie star surrounded by a coterie of noisily busy assistants carrying his paraphernalia of the law for him. They were rare but they were fun to watch.

Fun, also, were the new reporters. He liked them and had grown to know quite a few. They were usually a briskly cheerful lot, full of their own special news jargon. No, he didn't really mind it so much anymore, but he still wished he knew what the hell was going on today inside the courtroom. Well, he'd find out soon enough. Court must be adjourning for the day.

As Dorn came out Zavattero rose and looked at him inquiringly. Dorn looked tired. "What's up?" he asked.

Dorn shrugged, "Rivero's sick," he said.

"You don't say!" Zavattero blinked.

Dorn nodded. Then he said, "Look, Wally, I'm beat. I'll talk to you tomorrow, OK?"

"Sure, but who's Rivero?"

"One of the jurors," Dorn said. "He's got a stomach ache or something."

Again Zavattero blinked as Dorn walked away. It must have been one hell of a day. A juror got a bellyache.

The next day, Mr. Rivero having recovered his health, Douglas Dalton spoke on behalf of Savage. Again the same material was gone over, but with an added emphasis on Denton and Zavattero's part in the safety orders. Along with a natural eloquence Dalton had a flair for the homely simile and the picturesque phrase. He concluded with a simple plea to the jury to bear in mind that any indecision in their minds must be construed as a vote of not guilty because it meant the prosecution had not sustained the burden of proof. He went on to add, "I won't have a chance to talk to you again. I am going to listen to Mr. Dorn argue in rebuttal, and I am going to enjoy that about as much as having a nosebleed with a shark circling me." Another trip to the bench followed.

The following day Dorn began his career as a barracuda circling the bleeding defendants. And circle them he did. His rebuttal was long, exact, and thoughtful. At last he reminded the jury that the evidence in the case was overwhelming; that guidelines had been given to prevent what had happened and they were totally disregarded, the orders written specially for the Sylmar tunnel treated as though they had never been written. There was no way anyone could say the defendants had cared! It was now all up to a remarkable jury, and with that no one disagreed. The jury had been sitting there for over a year. They were indeed remarkable.

Before the jury could adjourn for its deliberations, Judge Trammell would instruct them in the law. The jury was dismissed for the Fourth of July holiday, and Judge Trammell prepared his instructions. It was a back-breaking job, harder than any physical labor performed by miners in their dark underworld. The trial had been the longest, most complicated, and involved more legal issues than any trial in the history of the municipal court. The instructions were an accumulation of all those issues from gross negligence to simple violation of the general safety orders. They took days to write and hours to deliver to the jury. But at last the jury would begin their deliberations.

Sitting in the corridor Zavattero realized from the sudden rush of reporters that something was happening. The reporters were always there. Zavattero wondered who was in the courtroom. He had seen no one going in. When he rose to leave, he was surprised to see Gwen Savage coming out of the courtroom. She was alone. An exceptionally pretty woman, her face now was gray with fatigue and worry. She looked almost plain. Zavattero was surprised when she came up to him and put her hand on his arm as if to stop him from leaving.

He felt helpless. He did not want to talk to her, and he did not want to see Savage or Ree. The jury was out and all he wanted to do was go home.

Savage's wife pressed his arm and then dropped her hand to her side. Her voice when she spoke was low, almost inaudible. "Wally, do you think any good will come of all this?" It was not a reproach, he realized, but a genuine question.

He did not know how to answer her. He wanted to tell her that just the month before the Tom Carrell Tunnel Safety Act had passed. That was good. But he knew that would be no comfort to her and instead he said gently, "Gwen, if the jury convicts, they may only find against Lockheed. They won't find—" he stammered for a moment. He could not bring himself to say the word guilty. Then he went on, "They may not find against Loren and Bob. Bob was acquitted, remember?"

Gwen Savage's beautiful eyes brimmed for a moment with grateful tears, but it was no use. She knew he was lying. If the jury found for conviction—she too could not say guilty—her husband would also be convicted. She pressed his arm again and turned to look for her husband who was still inside the courtroom with Lockheed's attorneys.

She was right. He was lying. If Lockheed went down, Savage would go with them. If only, he thought angrily,

Savage had spoken out. Told Lockheed's attorneys to go to hell and testified in his own defense. If only! If only! But he hadn't. He had kept silent.

As he watched Gwen leave, he shook his head. It had been so hard on them all.

Even Dorn looked tired as he came out of the courtroom. He leaned more heavily on his cane than usual and his smile was a professional one, thinly covering the strain of so many months.

"So what do you think?" Zavattero asked.

Dorn shrugged. "Who knows? They tell you all sorts of things, like notice where the jury's looking. If they look at your client, that's a good sign, etc., etc." said Dorn, "Bull, the only thing this jury looked like to me was that this was the year they wished they'd stayed in bed. So do I," he added tapping his cane against his shoe. Then he grinned, "One thing is certain, they'll be out for a long time. I'll call you as soon as it looks like they're coming back. For now, go home and get some rest. You look like you could use it." He paused. "You've done a good job, Wally."

"You, too," Zavattero said warmly. Then he left wondering what he was going to do with himself for the next few days. He guessed it would be a few days at least.

It was more than a few days. The jury was out for thirteen days. During that time Zavattero resumed an almost blessedly normal life. He had time to spend with Mercy, who seemed more at ease since her psychotherapy sessions. From them she had gotten what she most needed: reassurance that she wasn't becoming totally deranged by the ordeal. He had even had time to do some fishing. His work in Panorama City had necessarily been light to allow time for his constant attendance at court, so now it was no burden.

This blessed normalcy lasted for about forty-eight hours. After that, he wished his job were more demanding, because no matter how hard he tried to set it out of his mind, the trial haunted him. His head reverberated with the voices of attorney's shouting, "That goes to impeach, objection, sustained, overruled, this witness is lying, do you swear to tell the whole truth, Your Honor, my client has the right to remain silent, that's hearsay, Your Honor may we approach the bench, he said, she said, let the witness leave the courtroom, bring the witness in, move for mistrial, Mr. Zavattero will you step up to exhibits a, b, c, d, e, f, g, People's A, Defendants A., Mr. Zavattero will you point out, objection heresay, overruled, sustained, strike that last, the jury will ignore, good morning ladies and gentlemen, may we approach the bench, dismiss the jury, bring in the jury, Your Honor, can I take the witness on *voir dire*, mistrial, discover, offer of proof, good morning ladies and gentlemen, let the record show that the defendants Savage, Ree, Lockheed are present, mistrial, heresay, objection overruled, sustained, goes to impeach, will the witness leave the courtroom, bring the witness back . . . ."

Like a strange, ragged army of incomprehensible foreigners the phrases marched through his head in spite of himself. Had he made himself clear? Had they understood?

No, he had left so many things unsaid. He'd just sat there feeling like a battered animal, sticking doggedly to his assertion that a "man had a right to go to work in the morning and to expect to come home at night." Lockheed had refused to do the few simple things that were necessary to assure that right. Almost all those simple rules were now incorporated in that new law, but that brought him no more comfort than it could have brought Gwen Savage. The ragged army kept right on marching. He sometimes even wished to go back into court and explain all over again how simple it was. At that thought he would shudder—good God! Never again!

Then after thirteen days the jury came back from their own march. It was an awesome trip. Each day they were confronted with thousands of pages of testimony, documents and over fifty exhibits. The jury room wall was covered with diagrams of the tunnel and geological maps. The only pleasant note was struck when they learned that they would be lodged on the *Queen Mary* in Long Beach, many miles from downtown Los Angeles. None of them minded the daily trip.

The *Queen Mary* was a welcome relief from the strictures of the cluttered jury room.

When Dorn had called him at the office that day, he had been out in the field. The job had been an easy one, a simple inspection. The project, no highballing operation, was smoothly run and the contractor was pleased with himself and the efficiency and safety of his project. So was Zavattero. It was a good job.

For a few pleasant hours Zavattero had forgotten Lockheed, Sylmar, and the endless trial. The trial had gone on over a year now and it was over two years since the Lockheed holocaust had exploded in their lives.

As he stopped at the first intersection before hitting the freeway, Sylmar sprang back into his mind with a loud bang. On the newsstand was the late final of the *L.A. Times*—its headline shrieked: "Tunnel Verdict: Lockheed Convicted in 17 Deaths". With a swift maneuver that caused some squealing brakes and loud curses behind him, he crowded into the right lane. He tipped an apologetic nod at the driver behind him, leaped out of the car, grabbed the paper, and turned off at the nearest intersection just before the jammed-up freeway.

He pulled up beside an empty schoolyard and settled back to read the story. The July heat in the car didn't bother him. Not this time, it didn't.

The story had been written by Farr and had even crowded the Watergate scandals off the front page. He quickly picked out its highpoints. Lockheed Shipbuilding and Construction Company had been found guilty of gross negligence leading to the death of the seventeen workers in the Sylmar tunnel.

The jury had been required by Judge Trammell to publicly render the seventy-six verdicts they had reached after thirteen days deliberation.

Both Lockheed and Savage were found guilty on sixteen

counts of gross negligence. Lockheed was guilty on ten counts of violations of the state Industrial Safety Act. Savage was convicted on nine counts and Ree on three counts of Labor Code violations.

The jury had reached an impasse on the sixteen gross negligence charges against Ree, and the judge ordered them to resume deliberations on them. Pedigo had been acquitted on the four charges against him.

No date had yet been set for sentencing and Judge Trammell had set bail for Savage at $25,000 pending further proceedings. Ree was allowed to remain free on his own recognizance while the jury continued deliberations on the sixteen gross negligence counts involving him.

Zavattero set the paper down beside him, and gazed out at the empty, dusty schoolyard. Did anyone learn anything there? Had they learned anything at Sylmar??

He started the car and shook his head thoughtfully. So now it was over. Lockheed had been convicted.

As he maneuvered back on to the freeway, he suddenly began to grin and was surprised to find himself whistling John Henry. The lines "John Henry, he felt a roaring in his head" jingled in his mind like a TV commercial. For John Henry that roaring had been bad news, but not for Wallace Zavattero.

At last, speeding along the freeway he didn't notice the heat or smog for once. He just kept feeling better and better. Then he threw back his head and laughed aloud.

"And that," he announced firmly to no one in particular, "takes care of that misdemeanor."

EPILOGUE

That, of course, did not really take care of that misdemeanor, but it did end Zavattero's long and often despairing confrontation with the power of Lockheed.

Judge Trammell had set the sentencing of Lockheed and its employees for December 17, 1973. The sentence was a stiff one. Lockheed was fined $205,000 and Savage and Ree were given jail sentences.

The story in the *L.A. Times* was written by William Farr.

Said the *Times* story, "Municipal Judge George Trammell who imposed the sentences, described the actions that led to the June 24, 1971 explosion as a 'complete breakdown of corporate safety.'

"In sentencing tunnel project manager Loren Savage, the judge said, 'I can't imagine any other case where so many warnings of impending doom could so callously and coldly be ignored.'

"The judge initially sentenced Savage to twenty years and six months in jail on sixteen counts of gross negligence and nine labor code violations.

"He then reduced Savage's jail time to five years as a condition of being on probation for ten years.

"For safety engineer Otha G. Ree, the judge's original sentence called for eighteen months in jail for three safety code violations.

"Trammell reduced Ree's sentence to six months as a condition of ten years probation.

"The judge then delayed the time they would have to start serving the sentences until January 9, 1976, and indicated he might modify the punishment at that time.

"He would consider lessening the jail time commensurate with Ree and Savage's efforts to improve industrial safety in the interim two-year period.

"The judge told both defendants 'Mere compliance with the minimum standards of the law will not suffice. Each of you must demonstrate a high degree of concern for industrial safety and an equally high practical application.'

"Trammell had been harsh on Savage in his earlier sentencing remarks, saying: 'In fixing primary responsibility for the killing of seventeen men and seriously injuring another, it is abundantly clear to the court that such responsibility rests singularly with the defendant Savage.' "

As Zavattero read that, he shook his head. He still had the feeling that something else had happened. Something that Savage wouldn't talk about. Now he would never know. Savage's silence was sealed. He wondered if Savage recalled his own statement that someday, when this was all over he would tell Zavattero why he had done it. He didn't think so.

According to the story "The fine for Lockheed was more than double that which was expected as a maximum. Trammell fined the company $5,000 on each of sixteen counts of gross negligence and an additional $500 for each ten safety code violations.

"Then the judge surprised the courtroom by ordering Lockheed to pay another $120,000 to a state indemnity fund created to reimburse the victims of 'crimes of violence.' "

Zavattero wondered if the severity of Trammell's sentence echoed a public sense of outrage at the abuses of industrial safety. He hoped so. It was true that the new Tunnel

Safety Act had once again made felony prosecutions in cases like Lockheed possible, but that was no guarantee that without public concern, prosecution, felony or otherwise, would be any easier to get.

Since the conviction of Lockheed, Zavattero had not seen either Ree or Savage. He did know, however, that even as the jurors were rendering their guilty verdicts, Lockheed was preparing an appeal on behalf of the corporation and Savage and Ree. Lockheed had lost its appeal on the first concealing evidence trial. They did not intend to lose this one.

Ever since the conviction the attorneys for the civil suit on behalf of the survivors had been making a brisk path in and out of the courtroom of Superior Court Judge Bernard S. Jefferson in search of a settlement.

The settlement was finally reached and $9,315,000 was awarded, $9 million to the families of the men who had been killed, and $315,000 to the men injured in the first flash fire. The charges against Zavattero, Savage and Ree in this civil suit had been dismissed. There had been no question of the dismissal of the charges against Zavattero, but Mine Safety Appliances had questioned the dismissal of the charges against Ree and Savage.

The settlement of the civil suit had not come about for nearly a year, and the three men had met again for the first time since the conviction.

Their conversation was easy and casual, almost as if they had never been more than barely remembered acquaintances. Zavattero noticed that the conviction had not shaken Savage's imperturbability, though his attitude toward Zavattero was not as friendly as it had been. Ree seemed cheerful and more relaxed, as if he were just glad it was over. As for himself, Zavattero thought he probably looked exactly what he was, a man with a bad case of ulcers. That was too bad.

The day of the dismissal was March 29, 1975, and it was his twenty-fifth wedding anniversary. He wanted to celebrate.

The other two men congratulated him on his anniversary and one of them, Zavattero didn't know which, remarked that it would probably be nice not to worry for once that you were going to find a subpoena in your champagne bucket. They all laughed mildly at this and parted with no word of meeting again.

They did meet again, however. Five months later, in August, the conviction verdict was reversed. It had been reversed in the Appellate Court by Judges John W. Holmes, Arthur K. Marshall, and Arthur L. Alarcon.

The reversal was not based on sufficiency of evidence but on alleged technical errors, and instances when Judge Trammell had given improper instructions to the jury.

The decision of the appellate court had not upset Zavattero. He had almost expected it. His story had really ended the first day that Lockheed had been brought into court. After that it had been the lawyers' story.

No matter what happened now, there was not likely to be another contractor who would view lightly the possibility of prosecution. There were not many contractors who could afford the sums Lockheed had spent in its own defense. No contractor, no corporation would soon forget what had happened to Lockheed with all its power.

He knew that in the city attorney's office all the machinery for a new trial was shifting into gear. After talking to Dorn he knew that he would have to be taken off his job again. Letters and memos were going back and forth between his office and the city attorney's office. A new trial would require his entire time. He would have to review over an eleven thousand-page transcript, and spend who knows how many hours on the witness stand or sitting in that damned corridor.

Nevertheless when Dorn asked him, his answer was instant, "Hell, sure I'll go again." Then he grinned, "In fact, I'd like to see how much bigger the guns are going to get this time around."

It was sheer bravado and Dorn knew it. Zavattero's health had worried him all during the second half of the trial. Now it was no small worry. His face was ashen, and when he felt unnoticed, his body bent in pain.

Dorn watched him closely. After Zavattero left, Dorn had a lot to think about.

The day of decision came on Thursday, October 25, 1975. That was the last time that Zavattero, Savage, and Ree met.

Unlike the carnival scene of the earlier trials, the courtroom this time was empty except for the assortment of officials necessary to do the business of the court.

Dalton was there to represent Savage, Hollopeter with Ree, and Charles Bakaly instead of David Finkle was there on behalf of Lockheed. As they all passed by Zavattero there was only time for a cursory nod. Savage did not look well. Zavattero wondered what had happened.

He knew from Dorn that Lockheed expected to plead no contest, but this time they would be forced to plead to all twenty-six of the pending charges. How the rest of the pleading would go he was not sure.

It was all very brief. Ree and Savage faced the judge as he asked the routine questions; Did they understand that they waived all rights to a jury trial? Did they understand that the nolo contendere plea was the same as a guilty plea?

All the questions were asked tonelessly, and each one was answered tonelessly, with a barely audible yes.

To Zavattero in the rear of the almost empty courtroom, Savage seemed to look smaller, as if the winds of the past four years had worn away at him, reducing him physically. Even his slow, considered voice had changed as he barely whispered his plea of no contest on the charge of gross negligence, and one labor code violation.

He was fined a total of $6,875 and placed on three years probation.

Ree, too, had changed. He did not look smaller, but very much older. His no contest plea to one labor code violation was given in the same toneless voice as his answers to the judge's questions. He was fined $625 with one year probation.

Bakaly spoke for the corporation with brisk impersonality. Lockheed was then given the maximum fine of

$106,250, and Bakaly's abrupt nod seemed to say, "Yes, but we are already preparing an appeal, Your Honor." Lockheed's appeal was denied in March 1977, and Lockheed was compelled to pay the largest fine in the history of the municipal court.

Thus in a brief, unattended session ended the four-and-a-half-year nightmare that had engulfed so many people.

Ree had left immediately with Hollopeter. He did not speak to Zavattero.

But as Savage and Dalton turned to leave the hearing room, Savage paused in front of Zavattero. His face was very pale.

The two men looked at each other for a moment, and then Savage slowly held out his hand.

Zavattero took it and said, "I'm glad it's over."

Savage nodded, "So am I." Then he turned and left.

They would not meet again.

Zavattero followed them out. He did not stop to talk to Dorn, who along with Bakaly, Dalton and Hollopeter were giving their respective stories to the gathered reporters.

As Zavattero got into his car, he stretched as if casting off a great burden.

The October air was chill. In a few weeks it would be Thanksgiving. Five years ago Ree had been arrested in Seattle, and the first steps in the trial of Lockheed had been taken.

On his last trip away from the courthouse, Zavattero's mind was not on what Dorn, Dalton, Hollopeter, and Bakaly were telling the news media, but on a story that had appeared in the August, 1973 edition of *Western Construction*, a magazine of little interest except to engineers and contractors.

In its concluding paragraph of an article titled "Disaster and Aftermath" it stated "Much was lost in the San Fernando tunnel: lives, careers, money. One can only hope that much was gained as well: a better understanding of the hazards of working in gas-bearing ground and better techniques for coping with them. The higher standards of safety imposed at Sylmar have already radiated through the industry and are leading to safer conditions wherever men are working underground."

What had really been important? The lives, the careers or the money? It seemed to him that in reality the order was reversed. It was money, careers, and the lives.

In spite of the gains, his had been a story of disillusionment. It had begun with his simple belief that "a man had a right to go to work in the morning and expect to come home at night."

It had seemed to him self-evident, not a legal or civil right, or any of the assortment of rights subsumed under the many categories of the law and politics, but a simple human right.

To him it had seemed this right must certainly be the prime consideration of everyone involved, the Division of Industrial Safety, the employing corporations, the executive personnel and the law-makers.

He thought back over them all. He had felt that his own department had blinked too often at corporate violations of safety regulations. But the fact that his division seemed lost in a rainbow world of enlightened employers and benevolently chastising safety engineers, had been accepted by him as confusion rather than a betrayal of the miners. He recalled Hatton's fumbling efforts to rescue dignity from his relations to Lockheed.

Then the lawmakers, the legislative investigators, had come as a shock with their unabashed willingness to fish the political catch out of such troubled waters. He remembered Fenton and the savagery of his attack. He resented it even though now Fenton had changed completely toward him and had worked ceaselessly to pass the new safety act. He wished Fenton well, though he was glad he didn't have to vote in his district.

He recalled the attorneys, the legal instruments of the law. Strangely he liked most of them. They were no highballing tunnel stiffs, but more like high-rolling poker players, manipulating, maneuvering and bluffing in a high-stakes game.

As he rode along he recalled them all and he wished them all well. He even thought briefly of Ronald Demo, and wondered if he had escaped from the tunnel that night to run off to Canada in possession of some important secret. If that were true, he hoped he'd been well paid for it. Was it fraud?

He laughed. Looking back over that long, long journey through the dry and arid courtrooms, who knew what was fraud? He laughed again and wished Demo well.

No one would ever know what had really gone on in that tunnel. They were all dead except Savage, and Savage had remained silent. Maybe there was nothing. Maybe yes, maybe no. Whatever it was, Zavattero wished Savage well. That gaunt, cold silence would be with him a long time—maybe always.

As for himself, Zavattero thought, there was Santa Rosa, a quiet town where it was still a certainty that the sky was blue, not yellow.

There was a garden for Mercy, and a humming college campus for Gina. It was fall when the pink and juicy salmon start their run up the Russian River. And he'd heard they were planning a highballing tunnel in Los Banos. That was alright. He still liked a highballing tunnel.